Mary Francis Cusack

The Patriot's History of Ireland

Mary Francis Cusack

The Patriot's History of Ireland

ISBN/EAN: 9783337308193

Printed in Europe, USA, Canada, Australia, Japan

Cover: Foto ©ninafisch / pixelio.de

More available books at **www.hansebooks.com**

THE PATRIOT'S HISTORY OF IRELAND

by

M.F. CUSACK.

AUTHOR OF "THE ILLUSTRATED HISTORY OF IRELAND."

Erin chants a Song of Hope for the future of Irish Patriots.

IRELAND:
NATIONAL PUBLICATION OFFICE, KENMARE, CO. KERRY.
AMERICA:
L. KEHOE, CATHOLIC PUBLICATION HOUSE, 126, NASSAU-STREET,
NEW YORK.

[*The right of translation and reproduction is reserved.*]

1869.

DUBLIN:
Printed by J. M. O'Toole & Son,
6 & 7, Great Brunswick-street.

TO

My Countrymen and Countrywomen

IN IRELAND, IN ENGLAND, IN AMERICA, IN AUSTRALIA,

TO THE WARM-HEARTED CELT, WHEREVER

HIS ABODE MAY BE,

THE PATRIOT HISTORY OF IRELAND

IS

Dedicated.

M. F. CUSACK,
Kenmare, May 6th, 1869.

PREFACE.

I HAVE been asked to write a short, concise History of Ireland for the benefit of those who have not time to read a larger work, and for the use of schools, as an Introduction to Irish History. I have complied with this request; but the reader should remember that it requires some care and thought to understand a history written with care and thought, and that, while "stories" about Ireland may amuse, and rudely-written rhymes may excite, it requires something higher, something of which Irishmen are specially capable, to enable them to like and to profit by what requires some study. This History is intended for thoughtful men and women, as well as for thoughtful boys and girls. It contains the result of many years' careful and anxious study, given to the reader in the form in which, as I hope, it will be most easily understood and remembered. It is not intended to take the place of a larger History, nor is it intended for the senior classes in colleges; for such use a larger work, containing more general information, given in the form best suited for students, is now ready. Particulars of that work and of the National Illustrated History of Ireland, both of which may be read with advantage, after the careful perusal of the present volume, will be found at the end of this book.

The present volume is the cheapest history of Ireland ever offered to the public; no one now can have any excuse for not knowing the history of Ireland thoroughly. The price places it within the reach even of the poorest; I believe there are few indeed, who would make the sacrifice which we have done in offering Irishmen so cheap a book. But I believe we shall not regret it, and that Irishmen will show their nationality and their appreciation by circulating the Patriot History far and wide in Ireland, in England, and in America. Remember that we have no newspaper offices where we can print our books at a mere nominal cost; and no shop where we can sell them at full profit. When we have paid printers, for printing and paper; engravers for designs and engravings; postage, circulars, *and the large per centage that we allow our agents*, our profit is small indeed. But we are willing to make this sacrifice; our printers are Irish, the money is spent either in Ireland or on Irishmen in England, for even in England nearly all our agents are Irishmen; and I must add one word of thanks for the generous kindness of the editors of all the Irish national papers, and of several of the English liberal Protestant papers, in helping us in every way with advertisements and reviews of our publications. There has been only one exception to this rule, and that exception is, I am sorry to say, the proprietor of a so-called "national" Irish newspaper.

One word more. Let every Irishman and woman who reads this try to induce their friends to give orders to our agents for this work, or send orders direct to the address given below.* I hope such a generous response may be given to my request, as shall induce me to continue my labours for my countrymen; and to refuse the large profit which might be obtained for the poor for other literary engagements of a less national character. Every penny spent in the purchase of the Kenmare publications goes to charity. It goes to benefit trade in Ireland, and any profit that may accrue is devoted entirely to the poor.

* Orders may be sent and payments for copies enclosed to the Superioress, Convent of Poor Clares, Kenmare, County Kerry, Ireland. In America all orders should be sent to Mr. Kehoe, Catholic Publication House, 126 Nassau-street, New York. All our other publications may be ordered as above also. The "National Illustrated History of Ireland" is also one of the cheapest works ever published, some of the full page engravings are worth as much as would pay for a whole bookfull of inferior ones. We should be sorry to think that Irishmen of the middle and lower classes are incapable of appreciating a high style of art. The immense sale of this work has proved the contrary. Had this History been published by a London house, they would have charged two pounds for it; yet it can be had in parts at two shillings each, or bound handsomely in one volume.

THE PATRIOT'S
HISTORY OF IRELAND.

CHAPTER I.

INTRODUCTORY REMARKS—The first inhabitants of Ireland—The Valuable Old Manuscripts which record the Ancient History of Ireland—The Five Great Invasions of Ireland.

HISTORY is one of the most interesting subjects to which the human intellect can devote itself. A man who does not care to know the history of his own country, and to know it well, to know its every detail, and, as far as he can, to study it carefully, does not deserve to have a history. He might almost as well be a savage, with no further knowledge of the past than what his parents relate to him of their early lives. A man who does not care to know the history of other countries, and who cannot make a generous allowance for the failings even of his enemies, and take a generous interest in their triumphs, scarcely deserves the name of being a man. We should first learn the history of our own country, and then learn the history of those countries most immediately connected with ourselves. But a really well-written history of any country should give some general information about the condition of other nations, for each nation has some influence, however remote, on the history and politics of every cotemporary state.

The Bible is the oldest book of history in existence. There could not, of course, be any history of man, before man was created. The Bible gives an account of the creation of man, and the principal events in the history of man, from the creation to the flood. We know that this history is the most ancient in the world, because there is no history whatever which claims to tell what the Bible does; and we know it is a history, every word of which must be true, because Almighty God inspired those who wrote it; and the Church tells us that it is true. When we come to the period after the flood, we find that there were only a very few persons in the world. These few persons increased rapidly, and it is by them and their descendants that the earth was peopled by those who now inhabit it.

When Noah came out of the ark, he found himself on a mountain, called Ararat. This mountain is situated in Asia, but it is in that part of Asia nearest to Europe. According as the families of Noah's sons increased in numbers, they went further and further from this place, just as in America, the settlers go further and further into the distant forests, as new arrivals create a want for more space.

The Irish, according to the best established traditions are descended from Magog, the son of Japhet, the son of Noah. Keating, who wrote his history from some valuable old manuscripts, not in existence now, informs us that this was the opinion of the oldest Irish historians. Those people were called Scythians by the Greek historians. They settled on the borders of the Red Sea, and from thence came further and further towards the west, until, according to the general opinion, they colonized Ireland by coming thither, direct from Spain. After some time these Scythians were called Phœnicians. Thus the Irish are more generally said to be descended from the Phœnicians. The Phœnicians were very skilful as navigators, and hence they made their way across seas, which would have been impossible for others to traverse. They were also a very learned people. According to the accounts of the great Grecian historians, they were called Phœnicians, from Phœnix, one of their kings; he had a brother named Cadmus, who, it is said, invented the use of letters.

Now I must briefly record the authority for ancient Irish History. The love of literature, and as a necessary consequence, a great respect for all who devoted themselves to it, seems inherent in the Irish character. Hence, we find that centuries before the introduction of Christianity, there was in Ireland a certain class of persons called files or bards, whose sole occupation consisted in learning and teaching the history of the country. There were regular colleges where these bards received instruction, and where they afterwards instructed others. You will find a full account of these bards and these colleges in the *Illustrated History of Ireland*, page 40. It cannot now be ascertained whether the Irish had learned the art of writing before the introduction of Christianity, but it is probable that they had some method of recording their history on wood or stone, by inscriptions like those on pillars called the Ogham writing. It is at least certain that the bards transmitted the history of Ireland from one generation to another for centuries before the time of St. Patrick.

Soon after his arrival in Ireland, accounts of the ancient history and laws of Ireland were written down; and many of these histories are still in existence.

If the student reads this work carefully, he will find in it all the great facts of Irish history. Above all, he will learn the true character of the Irish Catholic patriot. He will find the Catholic patriot sacrificing his life again and again willingly and cheerfully for his holy faith. He will see what sacrifices and privations the priests endured to keep up the knowledge of religion in Ireland, and what sacrifices the people made to protect their devoted priests in the hour of danger. That this holy bond of union between Faith and Patriotism may never be broken, should be the most earnest prayer of every Irish Catholic patriot, of every Irish priest, and of all the faithful.

I must now briefly describe the five great invasions or "takings" of Ireland, as they are called in our ancient annals. This is the first historical fact to be remembered, and the next chapter should be read carefully by those who wish for more than a mere superficial knowledge of Irish history.

CHAPTER II.

The Landing of Partholan—History of the Five Great Invasions of Ireland—(1) The Nemedians—(2) The Fomorians—(3) The Firbolgs—(4) The Tuatha de Dananns—(5) The Milesians—The Famous Stone of Destiny—The Reign of Tighernmas.

THE five great invasions of Ireland may be thus classified :—(1) the taking by the Nemedians, (2) the taking by the Fomorians, (3) the taking by the Firbolgs, (4) the taking by the Tuatha de Dananns, (5) the last and final taking by the Milesians. But our annals go back still further, so far back indeed that our claims to great national antiquity are met with the taunts and laughter of those, who if they were wise would first inquire our authority for these claims to antiquity before they ridicule what they do not understand. There is not a single nation in Europe or in America which has such ancient and authentic manuscripts as we have, and in these the traditions and history of our country for centuries before the Christian era are recorded. Some of those records may be incorrect versions of real occurrences ; many of them, without doubt, are impartial records of facts. Now the most ancient manuscripts mention that Ireland was visited before the Flood by a maiden named Cesar and her companions. It is, however, very improbable

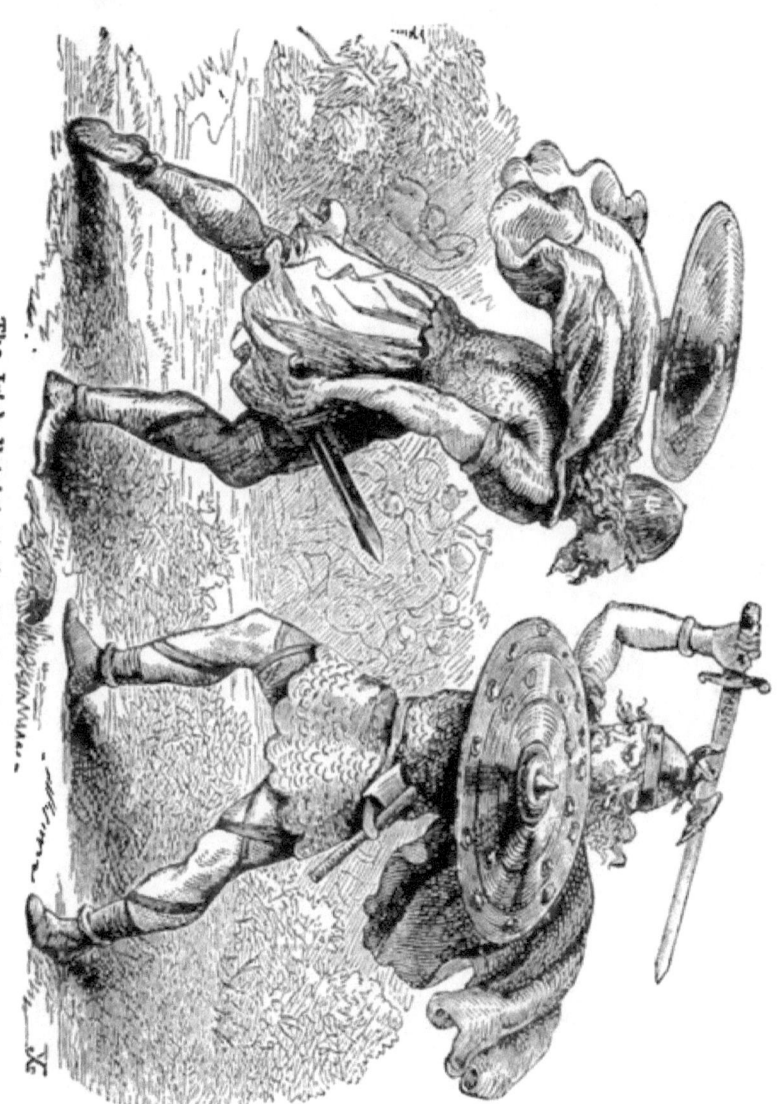

The Irish Patriot at the Battle of Clontarf.

that any record could have been preserved of such an event, even if it ever occurred. The next tradition relates that Ireland was visited soon after the Flood, and during the life time of the great patriarch Abraham, by Partholan. He landed at Inver Scene, now called the Kenmare river, in the County Kerry, on the 14th of May, in the year of the world 2520. This man was a parricide, and fled from his country in disgrace and shame. One must suppose that the few traitors who have disgraced the Irish name from time to time have descended from this outcast. But he brought the plague with him; and although he and his followers lived long enough to clear many forests, and plant many colonies, vengeance came at last. Eventually, nearly the whole colony perished by plague. The place is still shown where thousands were buried in a common tomb. It is called Tallaght, and is near Dublin, the name Tallaght meaning *Tam Lacht*, or the plague sepulchre.

The first of the five takings which I have mentioned, however, is that of the Nemedians. They came to Ireland, or Ierne, as it was then more poetically called, about the year 2859, and erected forts to protect themselves against invaders, clearing plains to support their flocks and herds. Those Nemedians also came from the high table-lands in Asia, travelling westward, and settling in various places. But Nemedh and his followers were not destined to have sole and undisputed possession of Ireland.

The Fomorians, a race of pirates, of whom little is known, attacked them by sea and land, but principally by sea. According to the Annals of Clonmacnois, "they were a sept descended from Cham, the sonne of Noeh, and lived by pyracie and spoile of other nations, and were, in those days, very troublesome to the whole world." The few Nemedians who escaped alive after their great battle with the Fomorians, fled into the interior of the island. Three bands are said to have emigrated with their respective captains. One party wandered into the north of Europe, and are believed to have been the progenitors of the Tuatha de Dananns; others made their way to Greece, where they were enslaved, and obtained the name of Firbolgs, or bagmen, from the leathern bags which they were compelled to carry; and the third section sought refuge in the north of England, which is said to have obtained its name of Briton from their leader, Briotan Maol.

The third immigration is that of the Firbolgs; and it is remarkable how early the love of country is manifested in the Irish race, since we find those who once inhabited its green plains still anxious to return, whether their emigration proved prosperous as to the Tuatha de Dananns, or painful, as to the Firbolgs.

The Firbolgs divided the island into five provinces, governed by five brothers, the sons of Dela Mac Loich:—"Slane, the eldest brother, had the province of Leynster for his part, which containeth from Inver Colpe, that is to say, where the river Boyne entereth into the sea, now called in Irish Drogheda, to the meeting of the three waters, by Waterford, where the three rivers, Suyre, Ffeoir, and Barrow, do meet and run together into the sea. Gann, the second brother's part, was South Munster, which is a province extending from that place to Bealagh-Conglaissey. Seangaun, the third brother's part, was from Bealagh-Conglaissey to Rossedahaileagh, now called Limbriche, which is in the province of North Munster. Geanaun, the fourth brother, had the province of Connaught, containing from Limerick to Easroe. Rorye, the fifth brother and youngest, had from Easroe aforesaid to Inver Colpe, which is in the province of Ulster."

The Firbolg chiefs had landed in different parts of the island, but they soon met at the once famous Tara, where they united their forces. To this place they gave the name of *Druim Cain*, or the Beautiful Eminence.

The fourth, or Tuatha de Danann "taking" of Ireland, occurred in the reign of Eochaidh, son of Erc, A.M. 3303. The Tuatha de Dananns were a brave, high-spirited race, and famous for their skill in what was then termed magic. But it is probable that all the magic of which they were guilty, was being able to exercise many mechanical arts of which those who had previously invaded Ireland were then ignorant.

Their leader was called Nuad of the Silver Hand. This chieftain had lost a hand in battle, and his artificer or smith, as such workmen were then called, made a silver hand for him with joints which he used. This artisan was called Credne Cert; but Nuad had also a very skilful physician, named Mioch, and he completed the convenience by infusing motion and feeling into every joint and finger of this wonderful hand. Of course this could not be literally true, as there could be no feeling without life, and God alone can give life. But it is probable that the smith and the doctor worked together, and turned out some clever substitute for a hand which the great Nuada found very useful.

The ancient laws of Ireland, called the Brehon Laws, were then in force, and these laws require that a king should be free from every personal defect. Nuada, therefore, was obliged to resign his sovereignty after the loss of his hand, until a substitute was made for the defective member. Nuada and Eochy, the Firbolg monarch, had a great battle, recorded in our annals as the battle of Moyturé. The Firbolgs were defeated, for they were no fair match for the famous Tuatha de Dananns. Their king was slain at Ballysadare, in Sligo. This battle is one of the most famous recorded in our ancient history. Full details are given of it by the bards or poet-historians of that age, and these details afford the most important illustrations of the habits, manners, and customs of the ancient Irish. Their dress and weapons are fully described, and those who doubt the truth of our traditional history would do well to remember that the traditions, as recorded in our ancient annals, are, day by day, more and more verified by the researches of those who devote their time to the study of antiquities, such as the ancient weapons, domestic utensils, &c., found in the great cairns, or tombs, of ancient Irish chieftains.

One of these ancient bardic accounts describes an interview between the two brave warriors, Breas, the Tuatha de Danann, and Sreng, the Fomorian. They conversed with each other, protected by their shields, fearing mutual treachery, as well they might in these wild times. Then gaining confidence, and finding that they both spoke the same language, the old Celtic tongue, they commenced an examination of each other's weapons. These were very different. Breas had "two beautifully shaped, thin, slender, long, sharp pointed spears," and Sreng was armed with "two heavy, thick, pointless, but sharpley rounded spears.' Now, it has always been the tradition of the Irish, that weapons of the former class were made by the Tuatha de Dananns, who were so highly skilled as artificers, and weapons of the latter class by the Firbolgs; and it is remarkable that weapons of these very different kinds have been found in the cairns, or grave mounds belonging to each tribe—

the inferior kind in Firbolg cairns, and the superior kind in these of the Tuatha de Dananns.

These wonderful people have also left records after them in the traditions of fairies, and "good people," so common in Ireland. The light, gay, joyous element of the Irish character may be traced to them also; and the special respect always shown to the possessors of superior intellectual power, as honourable to those who pay this respect as to those who receive it. The Tuatha de Dananns also brought the famous *Lia Fail*, or Stone of Destiny, to Ireland. The history of this stone is not easily verified. All kinds of wild tales have been told about it. Some traditions claim for it the honour of being the stone pillar on which Jacob reposed. It will be remembered that it was usual for the Jews to erect altars of stone or pillars of stone to commemorate any special event. As the Tuatha de Dananns undoubtedly came from the East, and as the Celtic tribes claim a descent from Japhet through the Phœnicians, it is quite possible that this stone was really one of those thus consecrated. It is at least certain that it is still in existence—a fact which shows the peculiar veneration with which it was regarded, which veneration secured its preservation from age to age.

According to one account, this stone is now under the coronation chair in Westminster Abbey.

It was brought thither from Scone in Scotland, where it was used in the same way. Those who believe this account say that it was brought from Tara, by Fergus king of Scotland, who wished to be crowned on the stone of destiny. According to another account, this pillar stone is still at Tara. A pillar stone was removed in 1798 to the centre of the mound of the Forradh; it formerly stood by the side of a small mound lying within the enclosure of Rath Riogh. The late Dr. Petrie believed this stone to be the identical *Lia Fail*, or stone of destiny.

The fifth invasion, or taking of Ireland, was that of the Milesians. This is, undoubtedly, one of the most important subjects of our ancient history. The four masters, the great authorities of Irish history, thus record the event. "The age of the world 3500. The fleet of the sons of Milidh came to Ireland at the end of this year, to take it from the Tuatha de Dananns, and they fought the battle of Sliabh Mis with them on the third day after landing. In this battle fell Scota, the daughter of Pharaoh, the wife of Milidh; and the grave of Scota is [to be seen] between Sliabh Mis and the sea. Therein also fell Fas, the wife of Un, son of Uige, from whom is [named] Gleann Faisi. After this the sons of Milidh fought a battle at Taillten against the three kings of the Tuatha de Dananns, MacCuill, MacCeacht, and MacGriéné. The battle lasted for a long time, until

MacCeacht fell by Eiremhon, MacCuill by Eimheur, and MacGriéné by Amhergen."

According to the ancient accounts, the Milesians landed at the mouth of the river Sláingé, or Slaney, in the present county of Wexford, unperceived by the Tuatha de Dananns. From thence they marched to Tara, the seat of government, and summoned the three kings to surrender. A curious legend is told of this summons and its results, which is probably true in the more important details. The Tuatha de Danann princes complained that they had been taken by surprise, and proposed to the invaders to re-embark, and to go out upon the sea "the distance of nine waves," stating that the country should be surrendered to them if they could then effect a landing by force. The Milesian chiefs assented; but when the original inhabitants found them fairly launched at sea, they raised a tempest by magical incantations, which entirely dispersed the fleet. One part of it was driven along the east coast of Erinn, to the north, under the command of Eremon, the youngest of the Milesian brothers; the remainder, under the command of Donn, the elder brother, was driven to the south-west of the island.

But the Milesians had druids also. As soon as they suspected the agency which had caused the storm, they sent a man to the topmast of the ship to know "if the wind was blowing at that height over the surface of the sea." The man reported that it was not. The druids then commence practising counter arts of magic, in which they soon succeeded, but not until five of the eight brothers were lost. Four, including Donn, were drowned in the wild Atlantic, off the coast of Kerry. Colpa met his fate at the mouth of the river Boyne, called from him Inbhear Colpa. Eber Finn and Amergin, the survivors of the southern party, landed in Kerry, and here the battle of Sliabh Mis was fought, which has been already mentioned.

The battle of Taillten followed; and the Milesians having become masters of the country, the brothers Eber Finn and Eremon divided it between them; the former taking all the southern part, from the Boyne and the Shannon to Cape Clear, the latter taking all the part lying to the north of these rivers.

This arrangement, however, was not of long continuance. Each was desirous of unlimited sovereignty; and they met to decide their claims by an appeal to arms at Géisill, a place near the present Tullamore, in the King's County. Eber and his chief leaders fell in this engagement, and Eremon assumed the sole government.

Our annals afford but brief details from the time of Eremon to that of *Ugainé Mór*. One hundred and eighteen sovereigns are enumerated from the Milesian conquest of Ireland (according to the Four Masters, B.C. 1700) to the time of St.

Patrick, A.D. 432. The principal events recorded are deeds of arms, the clearing of woods, the enactment of laws, and the erection of palaces.

Tiernmas was undoubtedly the most famous of these Milesian kings, and it is said that he introduced the custom of worshipping idols into ancient Erin; this statement requires some explanation.

After the fall of man, the knowledge of God, and consequently the knowledge of the way in which the Almighty should be worshipped by his creatures, was confined for many years to the Jewish race. They were God's chosen people, and to them He made known His will through special revelations to their prophets. The Jews worshipped the one true God, in the way in which He had Himself directed. But the heathen, and all who were not Jews were heathen, worshipped idols. Some of them actually offered worship to devils; some knelt before wooden or stone images, and prayed to them, imagining that they could hear them, or, perhaps, in some few cases looking on them as the image only of some great unknown deity. Some of the forms of worship used by the heathen were very terrible. They sometimes burned their children to death, thinking that this cruel act would please their false gods. They did not know that the true God was a God of love. They often performed the most immoral rites, not knowing that God was a God of purity as well as a God of love. But there were some few amongst the heathen nations who got some idea of a purer religious worship from the Jews; or who, perhaps, had preserved some traditions of true religion from the time of the dispersion of mankind after the building of the tower of Babel, and these men generally became Sun-worshippers. They saw that light and heat, and consequently vegetation, and countless other blessings, emanated from this great luminary, and they put it in the place of God; not knowing, or not reflecting, that, as a creature, it must have had a Creator, greater, incomparably greater, than itself. This worship, however, though idolatrous, was comparatively pure and simple. This was the worship of the *Magi*, or wise men of the East, of whom we are told in Scripture, and who were led by divine inspiration to Bethlehem, that they might there see and know the true Light of the World.

The early colonists of Ireland brought some such form of worship with them from distant lands, and undoubtedly there was some marked change in the pagan religion of Ireland during the reign of the Milesian king, Tiernmas. Where and how he learned idol worship is another question, and one which probably will never be known. He set up the famous idol called Crom Cruach on the plain of Moy Slaght, in the present county Cork. This hideous figure was surrounded by twelve smaller idols, and was worshipped by the Irish until it was destroyed by St. Patrick.

Tiernmas also has the credit of having introduced certain distinctions in rank amongst the Irish, which were indicated by the wearing of certain colours. This was probably the origin of the Scotch plaid.

Keating says that a slave was permitted only one colour, a peasant two, a soldier three, a public victualler five. The Ollamh or poet-historian ranked with royalty, and was permitted six—another of the many proofs of extraordinary veneration for learning in pre-Christian Erinn. The Four Masters, however, ascribe the origin of this distinction to Eochaidh Eadghadhach.

This monarch also employed a refiner of gold, and some of the very beautiful specimens of skilful workmanship in this metal, preserved in the Royal Irish Academy, may have been manufactured during this reign. Engravings of those works of art of which every Irishman is justly proud may be found in the Illustrated History of Ireland, the committee of that society having granted us the rare privilege of making them public. Our Illustrated History of Ireland, indeed, is the only Irish history ever published, which has made even an attempt at giving representations of these treasures.

Silver shields were now made (B.C. 1383) at Airget-Ros, by Enna Airgtheach, and four-horse chariots were first used in the time of Roitheachtaigh, who was killed by lightning near the Giant's Causeway. Ollamh Fodhla (the wise or learned man) distinguished himself still more by instituting triennial assemblies at Tara. Even should the date given by the Four Masters (1317 B.C.) be called in question, there is no doubt of the fact, which must have occurred some centuries before the Christian era; and this would appear to be the earliest instance of a national convocation or parliament in any country. Ollamh Fodhla also appointed chieftains over every cantred or hundred, he constructed a rath at Tara, and died there in the fortieth year of his reign.

Who does not desire to know something of Tara and its ancient glories? For centuries it was supposed that Irishmen who spoke of the glories of "Tara's Halls," indulged in sentimental romance about past imaginary greatness. But those who thought thus only displayed their ignorance of everything Irish, or their prejudice against everything Irish. Tara was, and is a reality, and may be said to be a reality even now. The remains of its "halls" may still be traced out, and have been traced out by the late Dr. Petrie; and, like every other research into Irish antiquity, all that was discovered tended to prove that our ancient records were ever literally correct in their accounts.

A national parliament was held here every three

years; and learned men were summoned to attend it, as well as men of rank. For six days the king entertained all his guests at his own expense, and did his utmost to promote social intercourse. Here the poet-historians brought each his record of the events which happened in his province or district during the time that had elapsed since the last assembly; here also the national records were examined with the greatest care. All that is on record concerning this subject leads one to believe that some method of conveying information by writing must have been known to the Pagan Irish. No people could have been, and no people, in point of fact, ever have been so jealously careful of their records. Family pedigrees were also examined and corrected in this assembly. This was a point of great importance.

A man's right of inheritance to property depended on his genealogy, except in the rare cases where might took the place of right, as will happen even in civilized nations. Hence, the care of the ancient Irish in transmitting the names of their ancestors was very great. When a man died possessed of property, it was divided equally among his sons. This custom had great disadvantages in many ways, but it was a noble recognition of the equal right of all to a share in the common stock of national goods. But when the principle came to be applied to royalty it eventually proved the destruction of Ireland. The successor to the throne of each little state was elected from amongst the members of the reigning family—thus it was both elective and hereditary. When a king was elected his successor was generally chosen at the same time. This successor might, or might not, be the eldest son of the monarch; and this plan of electing a person to a position which he might never fill, caused the most sanguinary divisions even in families, and led to the many violent deaths which disgrace the early annals of Ireland. Men who dared not assassinate the reigning monarch made little scruple of assassinating the heir apparent or Tanist, as such persons were called; and the plan of subdividing property weakened the kingly power more and more, and consequently lessened the national strength.

CHAPTER III.

Names of the Princes from whom the principal Irish families are descended—Ugany Mor—Story of the Tain bo Chuailgne—Reign of Tuathal—History and Origin of the Boromean Tribute—Conn of the Hundred Battles—Reign of Cormac—Laws of Ancient Erinn—Fin Mac Cuil—Division of Ancient Erinn—Niall of the nine Hostages—Death of King Dathi in France.

THE great Irish families all trace their descent from the Milesian chiefs, Ir, Eber, and Eremon, and their cousin Lugaid, the son of Ith. In the north the families of Magenis,

O'Hara, O'Flynn, &c., claim their pedigree from Ir. The O'Driscolls, O'Carrolls, O'Kennas, &c., from Lugaid. The M'Carthys and O'Briens from Eber. The O'Neils, O'Donnels, O'Connors, and MacMurroughs from Eremon.

Ugaine Mór, or the great, was one of the most famous of the Irish pagan kings. He was the foster son of Queen Macha, who founded the palace of Emania about 400 years before Christ. Three brothers, Hugh Roe, or the Red, Darthbre, and Kimbay claimed the throne. It was at last agreed that each should reign for seven years in turn, and the agreement was observed until each had reigned three times in turn. At last Hugh the Red was crowned at Assaroe, which still bears his name. His daughter, Macha, insisted on reigning when her father's turn came round; and when her two uncles refused to acknowledge her claim she had recourse to arms. She defeated her opponents, slew Darthbre, and banished his sons. In order to prevent further opposition from Kimbay, the only survivor, she married him. The exiled princes returned, and revolted against her once more, but they were again defeated, and the relentless queen compelled them to work as slaves, and erect a palace for her use.

It is said that she marked out the site of this palace with the pin of her golden brooch, and that it obtained thus the name of *Eo-Muin*, or Emania. It is now fully two thousand years since this fort was built, and its remains still exist near Armagh. This is one of the most interesting and important of our Irish antiquities. The fort covers upwards of eleven acres of land, and from the summit of one of the forts situated on the slope of a hill, there is a splendid view of the surrounding country. Here also the famous military college was erected, called the "House of the Red Branch." A neighbouring townland still preserves the tradition in the name of Creeve Roe.

Emania survived her husband seven years, and was at last slain herself, and succeeded, as I have said, by her foster son, Ugainé Mór. His reign was long and prosperous, and he was singularly devoted to learning. His sons also distinguished themselves in this way. Ugainé also exacted an oath from his subjects, by the elements, which, as Sun-worshippers, they would consider specially sacred, that they would never deprive his family of the sovereignty of Erin.

We must now reluctantly pass over the reigns of many Irish monarchs who succeeded Ugainé Mór, as the limits of this work will not permit further details; neither can I give here a description of the social life of the ancient Irish,—of their houses, their dress, their weapons, their mode of life, their food, their language, their games, their studies;—all this I must pass over; but those who have carefully studied the outlines of Irish history contained in this volume, and *every* event of importance is fully recorded herein, will find a double interest afterwards in reading larger works which will contain full details. In my Illustrated History of Ireland many entire chapters are devoted to these subjects.

We come now almost to Christian times, and to the reign of King Cormac Mac Nessa, and of the brave Queen Méav, or Mab. This lady's exploits are so wonderful that they have been recorded in a tale called the Tain bo Chuailgne, which is, perhaps, one of the most interesting bardic stories on record. Méav was married first to Conor, the celebrated provincial King of Ulster; but the marriage was not a happy one, and was dissolved, in modern parlance, on the ground of incompatibility. In the meanwhile, Méav's three brothers had rebelled against their father; and though his arms were victorious, the victory did not secure peace. The men of Connaught revolted against him, and to retain their allegiance he made his daughter Queen of Connaught, and gave her in marriage to Ailill, a powerful chief of that province. This prince, however, died soon after; and Méav, determined for once, at least, to choose a husband for herself, made a royal progress to Leinster, where Ross Ruadh held his court at Naas. She selected the younger son of this monarch, who bore the same name as her former husband, and they lived together happily as queen and king consort for many years. On one occasion, however, a dispute arose about their respective treasures, and this dispute led to a comparison of their property. The account of this, and the subsequent comparison, is given at length in the story of the *Táin*. They counted their vessels, metal and wooden; they counted their finger rings, their clasps, their thumb rings, their diadems, and their gorgets of gold. They examined their many-coloured garments of crimson and blue, of black and green, yellow and mottled, white and streaked. All were equal. They then inspected their flocks and herds, swine from the forests, sheep from the pasture lands, and cows—here the first difference arose. It was one to excite Méav's haughty temper. There was a young bull found in Ailill's herd, which had been calved by one of Méav's cows; but "not deeming it honourable to be under a woman's control," it had attached itself to Ailill's flocks. Méav was not a lady who could remain quiet under such provocation. She summoned her chief courier, and asked him could he find a match for Finnbheannach (the white-horned). The courier declared that he could find even a superior animal; and at once set forth on his mission, suitably attended. Méav had offered the most liberal rewards for the prize she so much coveted; and the courier soon arranged for the purchase of one from Daré, a noble of large estates, who possessed one of the valuable breed. A drunken quarrel, however, disarranged his plans. One of the men boasted that if Daré had not given the bull for payment, he should have been compelled to give it by force. Daré's steward heard the ill-timed and uncourteous boast. He flung down the meat and drink which he had brought for their entertainment, and went to tell his master the contemptuous speech. The result may be anticipated. Daré refused the much-coveted animal, and Méav proceeded to make good her claim by force of arms; at last the bulls ended the dispute by having a battle of their own, the "white-horn" was killed, and Donn Chuailgne the victor, dashed out his brains in a fit of mad fury.

The insurrection of the Attacotti, is the next event of importance in Irish history. Their plans were deeply and wisely laid, and promised the success they obtained. It is one of the lessons of history which rulers in all ages would do well to study. There is a degree of oppression which, even the most degraded will refuse to endure; there is a time when the injured will seek revenge, even should they know that this revenge may bring on themselves yet deeper wrongs. The leaders of the revolt were surely men of some judgment; and both they and those who acted under them possessed the two great qualities needed for such an enterprise. They were silent, for their plans were not even suspected until they were accomplished; they were patient, for these plans were three years in preparation. During three years the men saved their scanty earnings to prepare a sumptuous death-feast for their unsuspecting victims. This feast was held at a place since called *Mach Cru*, in Connaught. The monarch, Fiacha Finnolaidh, the provincial kings and chiefs, were all invited, and accepted the invitation. But while the enjoyment was at its height, when men had drank deeply, and were soothed by the sweet strains of the harp, the insurgents did their bloody work. Three ladies alone escaped. They fled to Britain, and there each gave birth to a son—heirs to their respective husbands, who had been slain.

After the massacre, the Attacotti elected their leader, Cairbré, the cat-headed, to the royal dignity. He died at the end of five years, and his son, the wise and prudent Morann, refused to succeed him, and advised the people to recall the rightful heirs.

Morann was the inventor of the famous collar of gold, which was said to have closed of itself round the necks of the guilty, and expanded to the ground when the wearer was innocent. Tuathal is the next monarch whose history demands special notice; he was the son of a former legitimate monarch, and had been invited to Ireland by a powerful party. He was perpetually at war with the Attacotti, but at last established himself firmly on the throne, by exacting an oath from the people, "by the sun, moon, and elements," that his posterity should not be deprived of the sovereignty. This oath was taken at Tara, where he had convened a general assembly, as had been customary with his predecessors at the commencement of each reign; but it was held by him with more than usual state. His next act was to take a small portion of land from each of the four provinces, forming what is now the present county of Meath, and retaining it as the mensal portion of the Ard-Righ, or supreme monarch. On each of these portions he erected a palace for the king of every province. Tuathal had at this time two beautiful and marriageable daughters, named Fithir and Dairiné. Eochaidh Aincheann, King of Leinster, sought and obtained the hand of the younger daughter, Dairiné, and after her nuptials carried her to his palace at Naas, in Leinster. Some time after, his people persuaded him that he had made a bad selection, and that the elder was the better of the two sisters; upon which Eochaidh determined by stratagem to obtain the other daughter also. For this purpose he shut the young queen up in a secret apartment of his palace, and gave out a report that she was dead. He then repaired, apparently in great grief, to Tara, informed the monarch that his daughter was dead, and demanded her sister in marriage. Tuathal gave his consent, and the false king returned home with his new bride. Soon after her arrival at Naas, her sister escaped from her prison, and suddenly and unexpectedly encountered the prince and Fithir In a moment she divined the truth, and had the additional anguish of seeing her sister, who was struck with horror and shame, fall dead before her face. The death of the unhappy princess, and the treachery of her husband, was too much for the young queen; she returned to her solitary chamber, and in a very short time died of a broken heart.

The insult offered to his daughters, and their untimely death, roused the indignation of the pagan monarch, and was soon bitterly avenged. At the head of a powerful force, he burned and ravaged Leinster to its utmost boundary, and then compelled its humbled and terror-stricken people to bind themselves and their descendants for ever to the payment of a triennial tribute to the monarch of Erinn, which, from the great number of cows exacted by it, obtained the name of the "Boromean Tribute"—*bo* being the Irish for a cow.

The tribute is thus described in the old annals:

"The men of Leinster were obliged to pay
To Tuathal, and all the monarchs after him,
Three-score hundred of the fairest cows,
And three-score hundred ounces of pure silver,
And three-score hundred mantles richly woven,
And three-score hundred of the fattest hogs,
And three-score hundred of the largest sheep,
And three-score hundred cauldrons strong and polished."

It is elsewhere described as consisting of five thousand ounces of silver, five thousand mantles, five thousand fat cows, five thousand fat hogs, five thousand wethers, and five thousand vessels of brass or bronze for the king's laving, with men and maidens for his service.

The levying of the tribute was the cause of periodical and sanguinary wars, from the time of Tuathal until the reign of Finnachta the Festive. About the year 680 it was abolished by him, at the entreaty of St. Moling, of Tigh Moling (now St. Mullen's, in the county Carlow). It is said by Keating, that he availed himself of a pious ruse for this purpose, asking the king to pledge himself not to exact the tribute until after Monday, and then, when his request was complied with, declaring that the Monday he intended was the Monday after Doomsday. The tribute was again revived and levied by Brian, the son of Cinneidigh, at the beginning of the eleventh century, as a punishment on the Leinster men for their adherence to the Danish cause. It was from this circumstance that Brian obtained the surname of *Boroimhé*.

Conn of the Hundred Battles, commenced his reign about the year 123. He was constantly at war with Eoghan, or Owen More, a prince of the race of Eber, who had passed most of his early youth in Spain. The cause of quarrel was the shipping arrangements in Dublin, which was even then a seaport of some importance. The northern, Howth side, was considered the best, reversing the opinion of the present day, and when each claimed the best, only a battle could terminate the dispute. Conn won the day, though his forces were far inferior to those of his rival, whom he slew.

Conn was succeeded by Conairé II., the father of the three Cairbrés, who were progenitors of important tribes. Cairbré Musc gave his name to six districts in Munster; the territory of Corcabaiscinn, in Clare, was named after Cairbré Bascain; and the Dalriada of Antrim were descended from Cairbré Riada. He is also mentioned by Bede under the name of Reuda, as the leader of the Scots who came from Hibernia to Alba. Three centuries later, a fresh colony of Dalriadans laid the foundation of the Scottish monarchy under Fergus, the son of Erc. Mac Con was the next Ard-Righ, or chief monarch of Ireland. He obtained the royal power after a battle at Magh Mucruimhé, near Athenry, where Art the Melancholy, son of Conn of the Hundred Battles, and the seven sons of Oilioll Oluim, were slain.

Cormac Mac Airt is unquestionably the most celebrated of all our pagan monarchs. During his early years he had been compelled to conceal himself among his mother's friends in Connaught; but the severe rule of the usurper Mac Con excited a desire for his removal, and the friends of the young prince were not slow to avail themselves of the popular feeling. He, therefore, appeared unexpectedly at Tara, and happened to arrive when the monarch was giving judgment in an important case, which is thus related:—Some sheep, the property of a widow, residing at Tara, had strayed into the queen's private lawn, and eaten the grass. They were captured, and the case was brought before the king. He decided that the trespassers should be forfeited; but Cormac exclaimed that his sentence was unjust, and declared that as the sheep had only eaten the fleece of the land, they should only forfeit their own fleece. The people applauded the decision. Mac Con started from his seat, and exclaimed: "That is the judgment of a king." At the same moment he recognized the prince, and commanded that he should be seized; but he had already escaped. The people now recognized their rightful king, and revolted against the usurper, who was driven into Munster. Cormac assumed the reins of government at Tara, and thus entered upon his brilliant and important career, A.D. 227.

His name is famous in Irish annals for the kingly state that he kept at Tara, and also for the laws which he made. These laws of the ancient Irish, are a code of which any nation might be justly proud. They were collected into one volume about the time of St. Patrick. The Irish in which they are written is so different from what is now spoken, that it can only be understood by those who have made it a special study. Even nine hundred years ago the language would scarcely be understood.

The great hall of Tara was also erected by Cormac. This was also the great house of the thousand soldiers, and the place where the Fes or triennial assemblies were held. It had fourteen doors—seven to the east and seven to the west. Its length, taken from the road, is 759 feet, and its breadth was probably about 90 feet. Kenneth O'Hartigan is the great, and indeed almost the only, authority for the magnificence and state with which the royal banquets were held therein. As his descriptions are written in a strain of eloquent and imaginative verse, his account has been too readily supposed to be purely fictitious. His account of the extent, if not of the exterior magnificence, of the building, has been fully verified; and there remains no reason to doubt that a "thousand soldiers" may have attended their lord at his feasts, or that "three times fifty stout cooks" may have supplied the viands. There was also the "House of the Women," a term savouring strangely of eastern customs and ideas; and the "House of the Fians," or common soldiers.

This reign was made more remarkable by the exploits of Cormac's son-in-law, the famous Finn Mac Cumhaill (pronounced "Coole"). Finn was famous both as a poet and warrior. Indeed, poetical qualifications were considered essential to obtain a place in the select militia of which he was the last commander. The courtship of the poet-warrior with the Princess Ailbhé, Cormac's daughter, is related in one of the ancient historic tales called *Tochmarca*, or Courtships. The lady is said to have been the wisest woman of her time, and the wooing is described in the form of conversations, which savour more of a trial of skill in ability and knowledge, than of the soft utterances which distinguish such narratives in modern days. It is supposed that the Fenian corps which he commanded was modelled after the fashion of the Roman legions; but its loyalty is more questionable, for it was eventually disbanded for insubordination, although the exploits of its heroes are a favourite topic with the bards. The Fenian poems, on which Macpherson founded his celebrated forgery, are ascribed to Finn's sons Oísin and Fergus the Eloquent, and to his kinsman Caeilté, as well as to himself. Five poems only are ascribed to him, but these are found in MSS. of considerable antiquity. The poems of Oísin were selected by the Scotch writer for his grand experiment. He gave a highly poetical translation of what purported to be some ancient and genuine composition, but, unfortunately for his veracity, he could not produce the original. Some of the real compositions of the Fenian hero are, however, still extant in the Book of Leinster, as well as other valuable Fenian poems. There are also some Fenian tales in prose, of which the most remarkable is that of the Pursuit of Diarmaid and Grainnè—a legend which has left its impress in every portion of the island to the present day. Finn, in his old age, asked the hand of Grainné, the daughter of Cormac Mac Airt; but the lady being young, preferred a younger lover. To effect her purpose, she drugged the guest-cup so effectually that Finn, and all the guests invited with him, were plunged into a profound slumber after they had partaken of it. Oísin and Diarmaid alone escaped, and to them the lady Grainné confided her grief. As true knights the were bound to rescue her from the dilemma. Oísin could scarcely dare to brave his father's vengeance, but Diarmaid at once fled with the lady. A pursuit followed, which extended all over Ireland, during which the young couple always escaped. So deeply is the tradition engraven in the popular mind, that the Cromlechs are still called the "Beds of Diarmaid and Grainné," and shown as the resting-places of the fugitive lovers.

There are many other tales of a purely imaginative character, which, for interest, might well rival the world-famous Arabian Nights' Entertainments; and, for importance of details, illustrative of manners, customs, dress, weapons, and localities, are, perhaps, unequalled.

Cormac died A.D. 266, at Cleiteach, near Stackallen Bridge, on the south bank of the Boyne. It is said that he was choked by a salmon bone, and that this happened through the contrivances of the druids, who wished to avenge themselves on him for his rejection of their superstitions.

Nial of the Nine Hostages and Dathi are the last pagan monarchs who demand special notice. In the year 322, Fiacha Sraibhtine was slain by the three Collas, and a few short-lived monarchs succeeded. In 378, Crimhthann was poisoned by his sister, who hoped that her eldest son, Brian, might obtain the royal power. Her attempt failed, although she sacrificed herself for its accomplishment, by taking the poisoned cup to remove her brothers' suspicions; and Nial of the Nine Hostages, the son of her husband by a former wife, succeeded to the coveted dignity. This monarch distinguished himself by predatory warfare against Albion and Gaul. The "groans" of the Britons testify to his success in that quarter, which eventually obliged them to become an Anglo-Saxon nation; and the Latin poet, Claudian, gives evidence that troops were sent by Stilicho, the general of Theodosius the Great, to repel his successful forays. His successor, Dathi, was killed by lightning at the foot of the Alps, and the possibility of this occurrence is also strangely verified from extrinsic sources.

CHAPTER IV.

Christianity first preached in Ireland—St. Patrick's Birth Place—His Captivity in Ireland—His Generosity in coming to preach to the Irish—The great success of his Mission—He meets the King at Tara—The Conversion of the whole Nation—St. Patrick's Death and Burial.

THE first Christian mission to Ireland was that of St. Palladius. St. Prosper, who held a high position in the Roman Church published a chronicle in the year 433, in which we find the following register: "Palladius was consecrated by Pope Celestine, and sent as the first Bishop to the Irish believing in Christ." This mission was unsuccessful. Palladius was repulsed by the inhabitants of Wicklow, where he landed. He then sailed northward, and was at last driven by stress of weather towards the Orkneys, finding harbour, eventually, on the shores of Kincardineshire. Several ancient tracts give the details of his mission, his failure, and his subsequent career. The first of those authorities is the Life of St. Patrick, in the Book of Armagh; and in this it is stated that he died in the "land of the Britons." The Second Life of St. Patrick, in Colgan's collection, has changed Britons into "Picts." In the "Annotations of Tierchan," also preserved in the Book of Armagh, it is said that Palladius was also called

Patricius, and that he suffered martyrdom among the Scots, "as ancient saints relate."

The honour of converting the whole nation to the Holy Roman Catholic faith, was reserved for our great Saint Patrick.

He was born about the year 373 at Nemthur, in France. It is probable that this place was near the present town of Boulogne. St. Patrick has left a work written by himself, which he calls his "Confession," and in this he gives us full information as to his birth-place and parentage. As, however, the names of places change with the lapse of time, although we have the name which the saint himself gave to this locality, it is by no means so easy to identify it; and in a popular life like the present, it is unnecessary, and would indeed be impossible, to give all the arguments of learned men who have contended that the honour belonged to many different places. St. Patrick says that his father had a farm at Bonavem Taburniæ, and it is generally believed now that this was in the north of Gaul, as France was then called.

The saint received the name of Succat in holy baptism. This name signifies "brave in the battle." The name of PATRICK, by which he has been known and venerated for so many centuries, was given to him by Pope Celestine. His father, Calphurnius, was a deacon, and son of Potitus, a priest; his mother was called Conchessa, and she was a niece of the famous St. Martin of Tours. It must be remembered that some priests and deacons of the holy Catholic Church were married men at that time, for many of them were converts from heathenism who had taken wives before they became Christians. Many of their wives became nuns and lived separate from their husbands, who were then free to consecrate themselves to God in the service of religion.

St. Patrick lived with his parents until his sixteenth year. In his "Confession" he accuses himself of having been very heedless about his religious duties; but this statement, no doubt, is caused by his humility, for he himself admits after, that, when in captivity, he was wholly devoted to God and to prayer. We must always remember, in reading the lives of the saints, that they often considered what we would call a trifling fault as a very grievous sin. In his sixteenth year St. Patrick was taken captive and sold as a slave in Ireland. How wonderful are God's ways! Doubtless, even his most pious friends considered this a most terrible misfortune, and yet it proved an inestimable blessing—a blessing for which God will be praised to all eternity.

The Irish pagan kings were a brave and adventurous race : they had made more than one successful raid even on the continent of Europe, and the name of Nial of the Nine Hostages was famous by land and sea.

Our saint was in his sixteenth year when he was

taken captive. He was sold as a slave in that part of Ireland now called Antrim, to four men, one of whom, Milcho, bought up their right from the other three, and employed him in feeding sheep or swine. Exposed to the severity of the weather, day and night, a lonely slave in a strange land, and probably as ignorant of the language as of the customs of his master, his captivity would, indeed, have been a bitter one, had he not brought with him, from a holy home, the elements of most fervent piety. A hundred times in the day, and a hundred times in the night, he lifted up the voice of prayer and supplication to the Lord of the bondman and free, and faithfully served the harsh, and at times cruel, master to whom Providence had assigned him. Perhaps he may have offered his sufferings for those who were serving a master even more harsh and cruel.

After six years he was miraculously delivered. A voice, that was not of earth, addressed him in the stillness of the night, and commanded him to hasten to a certain port, where he would find a ship ready to take him to his own country. "And I came," says the saint, " in the power of the Lord, who directed my course towards a good end; and I was under no apprehension until I arrived where the ship was. It was then clearing out, and I called for a passage. But the master of the vessel got angry, and said to me, 'Do not attempt to come with us.' On hearing this I retired, for the purpose of going to the cabin where I had been received as a guest. And, on my way thither, I began to pray but before I had finished my prayer, I heard one of the men crying out with a loud voice after me, 'Come, quickly; for they are calling you,' and immediately I returned. And they said to me, 'Come, we receive thee on trust. Be our friend, just as it may be agreeable to you.' We then set sail, and after three days reached land." They landed in a place called Treguir, in Brittany, some distance from his native town.

But the coast was wild and desolate, and after they had escaped the perils of the sea, they seemed in no small danger of perishing by hunger on the shore. Happily for them, they had a saint in their company. Our Divine Lord had promised that His disciples should do even greater things than He did; and He who had Himself taken pity on a starving multitude and satisfied their hunger, enabled His servant, St. Patrick, to perform a somewhat similar miracle, and by his prayers he obtained a supply of food for the good sailors. No doubt they rejoiced now for their act of charity to the saint; and the master of the ship, who had at first forbidden Patrick to come with them, must have learned that most blessed lesson, that to befriend the good and holy is the best policy for ourselves even in this world, and it assuredly will promote our highest interests in the next.

St. Patrick's captivity had lasted for about sixteen years, so that he had time to become thoroughly acquainted with the language of the Irish, and with their religion and customs. All this was overruled by God to the one great end. The Catholic missionaries who had previously visited Ireland, must have found their ignorance of the Celtic tongue a great hindrance to their success, for then, as now, that beautiful and expressive language was the only one to which the Celt could listen with pleasure.

It is said that St. Patrick was taken captive a second time, but this captivity only lasted sixty days. Some historians have supposed that this captivity occurred after his visit to St. Martin of Tours. It is at least certain that the saint wished now to dedicate his life to the God who had miraculously delivered him from slavery, by devoting himself to His service, and preaching to poor sinners the means of deliverance from a far worse bondage than that which he had so patiently endured.

As none were allowed to become priests without many years of study and careful preparation, it was necessary for Patrick, or Succat, as he was then called, to spend some time at one or other of the great monasteries established on the continent of Europe, where the monks devoted themselves to the education of youth. This example of the saint must surely encourage those whose secular education has been neglected, and who desire to advance in knowledge to fit themselves for God's holy service. Nothing but a most fervent love of God and most ardent zeal for souls, could have carried the saint through such an arduous course. For years he had not heard a word spoken except in the Celtic tongue, and probably he had almost forgotten the language of his own people. If he had learned even the rudiments of Latin, this was also most likely forgotten, and years of toil in domestic service were in any case a bad preparation for his new life. But Patrick was indeed "brave in battle"—in battle with himself, and in battle for God.

It is important however to remember these circumstances, as they account for what he says in his "Confession" of his want of human learning. Human learning is indeed greatly to be admired and prized, and it is an inestimable blessing if it is sanctified by Divine wisdom ; but learning was not necessary for an apostle, and God seems to have often chosen the unlearned for the evangelization of heathen nations, to show that the success of their work was not to be attributed to them.

The great monastery where St. Patrick studied was at Marmoutier, near Tours, under the direction of his maternal uncle, St. Martin. Here he received the tonsure, and was instructed by his saintly relative in science and religion. Many most interesting facts are recorded of St. Patrick during his residence at Marmoutier, but these must be reserved for a larger work where there will be space for fuller details.

It was here also that St. Patrick was favoured with the vision which made known to him the will of God concerning his mission to Ireland. He thus records this favour in his *Confession:* "I saw, in a vision of the night, a man named Victoricus coming, as if from Ireland, with a large parcel of letters, one of which he handed to me. On reading the beginning of it, I found it contained these words: 'The voice of the Irish,' and while reading it, I thought I heard at the same moment the voice of a multitude of persons near the west of Ireland, which is near the western sea; and they cried out as if with one voice, *We entreat thee, holy youth, to come and henceforth dwell among us.* And I was greatly affected in my heart, and could read no longer, and then I awoke." Like St. Joseph awakened from sleep by the angels commanding him to go into Egypt, and obeying promptly, so also is the blessed Patrick. He hears to obey, and he knows that to prepare himself for the work to which he is appointed is the truest form which his obedience can take.

After the death of St. Martin, St. Patrick left the monastery of Marmoutier, and proceeded to Lerins, which was even then called the *insula beata*, or holy island, from the number of holy men who either dwelt there or came thither for instruction.

St. Honoratus, the founder of this famous school and monastery, was then living, and at the time of St. Patrick's visit, many saintly persons were assembled there. Amongst others we find the names of St. Hilary of Arles, St. Lupas of Troyes, and the famous St. Vincent of Lerins.

St. Patrick is supposed to have remained about nine years at Lerins. It was here he received the STAFF OF JESUS, which was wantonly burned at the time of the so-called Reformation.

St. Bernard mentions this *Bachall Isu*, in his life of St. Malachy, as one of those insignia of the see of Armagh, which were popularly believed to confer upon the possessor a title to be regarded and obeyed as the successor of St. Patrick. Indeed, the great antiquity of this long-treasured relic has never been questioned; nor is there any reason to suppose that it was not some way made a miraculous gift.

St. Patrick now returned to his old master and spiritual guide, St. Germanus, of whom we shall here give some account. Well might the guardian angel of our great saint direct him to one so holy and so full of zeal for souls, and so fervently devoted to the advancement of the holy Catholic Church throughout the world.

St. Fiacc, one of St. Patrick's first converts, wrote a life of the great saint in verse, and he thus describes his intercourse with Germanus:

"The angel Victor sent Patrick over the Alps;
Admirable was his journey—
Until he took his abode with Germanus,
Far away in the south of Letha.
In the isles of the Tyrrhene sea he remained :
In them he meditated;
He read the canon with Germanus—
This, histories made known."

In the year 432 St. Patrick landed in Ireland. It was the first year of the pontificate of St. Sixtus III., the successor to Celestine ; the fourth year of the reign of Laeghairé, son of Nial of the Nine Hostages, King of Ireland. It is generally supposed that the saint landed first at a place called Inbher De, believed to be the mouth of the Bray river, in Wicklow. Here he was repulsed by the inhabitants,—a circumstance which can be easily accounted for from its proximity to the territory of King Nathi, who had so lately driven away his predecessor, Palladius.

St. Patrick returned to his ship, and sailing towards the north, landed at the little island of Holm Patrick, near Skerries, off the north coast of Dublin. After a brief stay he proceeded still farther northward, and finally entering Strangford Lough, landed with his companions in the district of Magh-inis, in the present barony of Lecale. Having penetrated some distance into the interior, they were encountered by Dicho, the lord of the soil, who, hearing of their embarkation, and supposing them to be pirates, had assembled a formidable body of retainers to expel them from his shores. But it is said, that the moment he perceived Patrick, his apprehensions vanished. After some brief converse, Dicho invited the saint and his companions to his house, and soon after received himself the grace of holy baptism. Dicho was St. Patrick's first convert, and the first who erected a Christian church under his direction. The memory of this event is still preserved in the name Saull, the modern contraction of *Sabhall Padruic*, or Patrick's Barn. The saint was especially attached to the scene of his first missionary success, and frequently retired to the monastery which was established there later.

After a brief residence with the new converts, Patrick set out for the habitation of his old master, Milcho, who lived near Slieve Mis, in the present county of Antrim, then part of the territory called Dalriada. It is said, that when Milcho heard of the approach of his former slave, he became so indignant, that, in a violent fit of passion, he set fire to his house, and perished himself in the flames. The saint returned to Saull, and from thence journeyed by water to the mouth of the Boyne, where he landed at a small port called Colp. Tara was his destination; but on his way thither he stayed a night at the house of a man of property, named Seschnan. This man and his whole family were baptized, and one of his sons received the name of Benignus from St. Patrick, on account of the gentleness of his manner. The holy youth attached himself from this moment to his master, and was his successor in the primatial see of Armagh.

St. Patrick arrived at Slane on Holy Saturday, where he caused a tent to be erected, and lighted the paschal fire at nightfall, preparatory to the celebration of the Easter festival. The princes and chieftains of Meath were, at the same time, assembled at Tara, where King Laeghairé was holding a great pagan festival. The object of this meeting has been disputed, some authorities saying that it was convoked to celebrate the Beltinne, or fire of Bal, or Baal; others, that the king was commemorating his own birthday. On the festival of Beltinne it was forbidden to light any fire until a flame was visible from the top of Tara Hill. Laeghairé was indignant that this regulation should have been infringed ; and, probably, the representation of his druids regarding the mission of the great apostle did not tend to allay his wrath. Determined to examine himself into the intention of these bold strangers, he set forth, accompanied by his bards and attendants, to the place where the sacred fire had been kindled, and ordered the apostle to be brought before him, strictly commanding, at the same time, that no respect should be shown to him.

Notwithstanding the king's command, Erc, the son of Dego, rose up to salute him, obtained the grace of conversion, and was subsequently promoted to the episcopate. The result of this interview was the appointment of a public discussion, to take place the next day at Tara, between St. Patrick and the pagan bards.

It was Easter Sunday,—a day ever memorable for this event in the annals of Erin. Laeghairé and his court sat in state to receive the ambassador of the Eternal King. Treacherous preparations had been made, and it was anticipated that Patrick and his companions would scarcely reach Tara alive. The saint was aware of the machinations of his enemies, but that was of no value to him save as it was in performing the great work assigned him, and the success of that work was in the safe keeping of Another. The old writers love to dwell on the meek dignity of the apostle during this day of trial and triumph. He set forth with his companions, from where he had encamped, in solemn procession, singing a hymn of invocation which he had composed, in the Irish tongue, for the occasion, and which is still preserved and well authenticated. He was clothed, as usual, in white robes; but he wore his mitre, and carried in his hand the Staff of Jesus. Eight priests attended him, robed also in white, and his youthful convert Benignus, the son of Seschnan.

Thus, great in the arms of meekness and prayer, did the Christian hosts calmly face the array of pagan pomp and pride. Again the monarch had

commanded that no honour should be paid to the
saint, and again he was disobeyed. His own chief
poet and druid, Dubtach, rose up instantly on the
entrance of the strangers, and saluted the venerable
apostle with affection and respect. The Christian
doctrine was then explained by St. Patrick to his
wondering audience, and such impression made,
that, although Laeghairé lived and died an obstinate pagan, he, nevertheless, permitted the saint to
preach where and when he would, and to receive
all who might come to him for instruction or holy
baptism.

On the following day St. Patrick repaired to
Tailltcn, where the public games were commencing;
and there he remained for a week, preaching to an
immense concourse of people. Here his life was
threatened by Cairbré, a brother of King Laeghairé; but the saint was defended by another of
the royal brothers, named Conall Creevan, who
was shortly after converted. The church of
Donough Patrick, in Meath, was founded by his
desire. It is said that all the Irish churches which
begin with the name Donough were founded by
the saint, the foundation being always marked out
by him on a Sunday, for which Domhnach is the
Irish word.

Having preached for some time in the western
part of the territory of Meath, the saint proceeded
as far as Magh Slecht, where the great idol of the

The Irish Patriot capturing Sir Caystede.

nation, Ceann [or Crom] Cruach was solemnly worshipped.

Nor is the story of Aengus, another royal convert, less interesting. About the year 445, the saint, after passing through Ossory, and converting a great number of people, entered the kingdom of Munster. His destination was Cashel, from whence King Aengus, the son of Natfraech, came forth to meet him with the utmost reverence.

This prince had already obtained some knowledge of Christianity, and demanded the grace of holy baptism.

The saint willingly complied with his request. His courtiers assembled with royal state to assist at the ceremony. St. Patrick carried in his hand, as usual, the Bachall Isu; at the end of this crozier there was a sharp iron spike, by which he could plant it firmly in the ground beside him while preaching, or exercising his episcopal functions. On this occasion, however, he stuck it down into the king's foot, and did not perceive his mistake until—

> "The royal foot transfixed, the gushing blood
> Enrich'd the pavement with a noble flood."

The ceremony had concluded, and the prince had neither moved nor complained of the severe suffering he had endured. When the saint expressed his deep regret for such an occurrence, Aengus merely replied that he believed it to be a part of the ceremony, and did not appear to consider any suffering of consequence at such a moment.

When such was the spirit of the old kings of Erinn who received the faith of Christ from Patrick, we can scarcely marvel that their descendants have adhered to it with such unexampled fidelity.

After the conversion of the princesses Ethnea and Fethlimia, the daughters of King Laeghairé, St. Patrick traversed almost every part of Connaught, and, as our divine Lord promised to those whom He commissioned to teach all nations, proved his mission by the exercise of miraculous powers.

The saint's greatest success was in the land of Tirawley, near the town of Foclut, from whence he had heard the voice of the Irish even in his native land. As he approached this district, he learned that the seven sons of King Amalgaidh were celebrating a great festival. Their father had but lately died, and it was said these youths exceeded all the princes of the land in martial courage and skill in combat. St. Patrick advanced in solemn procession even into the very midst of the assembly, and for his reward obtained the conversion of the seven princes and twelve thousand of their followers. It is said that his life was at this period in some danger, but that Endeus, one of the converted princes, and his son Conall, protected him. After seven years spent in Connaught, he passed into Ulster; there many received the grace of holy baptism, especially in that district now comprised in the county Monaghan.

It was probably about this time that the saint returned to Meath, and appointed his nephew, St. Secundinus or Sechnal, who was bishop of the place, already mentioned as Domnach Sechnail, to preside over the northern churches during his own absence in the southern part of Ireland.

The saint then visited those parts of Leinster which had been already evangelized by Palladius, and laid the foundation of many new churches. He placed one of his companions, Bishop Auxilius, at Killossy, near Naas, and another, Isserinnus, at Kilcullen, both in the present county of Kildare. At Leix, in the Queen's County, he obtained a great many disciples, and from thence he proceeded to visit his friend, the poet Dubtach, who, it will be remembered, paid him special honour at Tara, despite the royal prohibition to the contrary. Dubtach lived in that part of the country called Hy-Kinsallagh, now the county Carlow. It was here the poet Fiacc was first introduced to the saint, whom he afterwards so faithfully followed. Fiacc had been a disciple of Dubtach, and was by profession a bard, and a member of an illustrious house. It was probably at this period that St. Patrick visited Munster, and the touching incident already related occurred at the baptism of Aengus. This prince was singularly devoted to religion, as indeed his conduct during the administration of the sacrament of regeneration could not fail to indicate.

The saint's mission in Munster was eminently successful. Lonan, the chief of the district of Ormond, entertained him with great hospitality, and thousands embraced the faith. Many of the inhabitants of Corca Baiscin crossed the Shannon in their hide-covered boats (curaghs) when the saint was on the southern side, in Hy-Figeinte, and were baptized by him in the waters of their magnificent river. At their earnest entreaty, St. Patrick ascended a hill which commanded a view of the country of the Dalcassians, and gave his benediction to the whole territory. The hill is called Findine in the ancient lives of the saint; but this name is now obsolete. Local tradition and antiquarian investigation make it probable that the favoured spot is that now called Cnoc Patrick, near Foynes Island.

The saint's next journey was in the direction of Kerry, where he prophesied that "St. Brendan, of the race of Hua Alta, the great patriarch of monks, and star of the western world, would be born, and that his birth would take place some years after his own death."

We have now to record the obituary of the only Irish martyr who suffered for the faith while Ireland was being evangelized. While the saint was visiting Ui-Failghe, a territory now comprised in the King's County, a pagan chieftain, named Berraidhe, formed a plan for murdering the apostle. His wicked design came in some way to the knowledge of Odran, the saint's charioteer, who so arranged matters as to take his master's place, and thus received the fatal blow intended for him.

The see of Armagh was founded about the year 455, towards the close of the great Apostle's life. The royal palace of Emania, in the immediate neighbourhood, was then the residence of the kings of Ulster. A wealthy chief, by name Daire, gave the saint a portion of land for the erection of his cathedral on an eminence called *Druim-Sailech*, the Hill of Sallows. This high ground is now occupied by the city of Armagh (Ard Macha). Religious houses for both sexes were established near the church, and soon were filled with ardent and devoted subjects.

The saint's labours were now drawn to a close, and the time of eternal rest was at hand. He retired to his favourite retreat at Saull, and there probably wrote his *Confessions*. It is said that he wished to die in the ecclesiastical metropolis of Ireland, and for this purpose, when he felt his end approaching, desired to be conveyed thither; but even as he was on his journey an angel appeared to him, and desired him to return to Saull. Here he breathed his last, on Wednesday, the 17th of March, in the year of our Lord, 493. The holy viaticum and last anointing were administered to him by St. Tassach.

The intelligence of the death of St. Patrick spread rapidly through the country; prelates and priests flocked from all parts to honour the mortal remains of their glorious father. As each arrived at Saull he proceeded to offer the adorable sacrifice according to his rank. At night the plain resounded with the chanting of psalms; and the darkness was banished by the light of such innumerable torches, that it seemed as if day had hastened to dawn brightly on the beloved remains. St. Fiacc, in his often quoted Hymn, compares it to the long day caused by the standing of the sun at the command of Joshua, when he fought against the Gabaonites.

The hymn which St. Patrick composed when on his journey to Tara has been preserved, but it is too long for insertion here. We shall, however, give one brief extract from it.

"I bind to myself to-day,
 The power of God to guide me;
 The might of God to uphold me;
 The wisdom of God to teach me;
 The eye of God to watch over me;
 The ear of God to hear me;
 The word of God to give me speech;
 The hand of God to protect me;
 The way of God to prevent me;
 The shield of God to shelter me;
 The host of God to defend me—
  Against the snares of demons;
  Against the temptations of vices."

There were four great honours paid to St. Patrick in all the monasteries and churches in Ireland from the time of his death. The first of them was, that the Festival of St. Patrick in spring was honoured for three days with special feasting and rejoicing, except that flesh meat was not allowed to be used, as the 17th of March always fell in Lent. There were also other days kept in his honour; but then, as now, this was his Feast-Day —the day on which he fell asleep in Christ, to use the beautiful language of those ancient times.

The second honour was that there was a proper preface said at his mass.

The third and fourth honours were that his hymn should be sung for the whole time, and his Scotic Hymn always. Thus from the very death of Patrick he was honoured in the land of Erinn, still faithful to his memory.

One of the lessons which he specially inculcated was, obedience to the See of Rome. All history informs us how nobly and at what sacrifice this obedience has been adhered to in Ireland.

The secular history of Ireland, during the mission of St. Patrick, affords but few events of interest or importance. King Laeghairé died, according to the Four Masters, A.D. 458. The popular opinion attributed his demise to the violation of his oath to the Leinster men. It is doubtful whether he died a Christian; but the account of his burial has been taken to prove the contrary.

It is much to be regretted that persons entirely ignorant of the Catholic faith, whether that ignorance be wilful or invincible, should attempt to write lives of Catholic saints, or histories of Catholic countries. Such persons, no doubt unintentionally, make the most serious mistakes, which a well-educated Catholic child could easily rectify.

It is probable that Oiliol Molt, who succeeded King Laeghairé, A.D. 459, lived and died a pagan. Before concluding this chapter I must say a few words about St. Bridget.

Brigid belonged to an illustrious family, who were lineally descended from Eochad, a brother of Conn of the Hundred Battles. She was born at Fochard, near Dundalk, about the year 453, where her parents happened to be staying at the time; but Kildare was their usual place of residence, and there the holy virgin began her saintly career. In her sixteenth year she received the white cloak and religious veil, which was then the distinctive garment of those who were specially dedicated to Christ, from the hands of St. Macaille, the Bishop of Usneach, in Westmeath. Eight young maidens of noble birth took the veil with her. Their first residence was at a place in the King's County, still called Brigidstown. The fame of her sanctity now extended far and wide, and she was earnestly solicited from various parts of the country to found similar establishments. Her first mission was to Munster, at the request of Erc, the holy Bishop of

Slane, who had a singular respect for her virtue. Soon after, she founded a house of her order in the plain of Cliach, near Limerick; but the people of Leinster at last became fearful of losing their treasure, and sent a deputation requesting her return, and offering land for the foundation of a large nunnery. Thus was established, in 483, the famous Monastery of Kildare, or the Church of the Oak.

At the request of the saint, a bishop was appointed to take charge of this important work; and under the guidance of Conlaeth, who heretofore had been an humble anchorite, it soon became distinguished for its sanctity and usefulness. The concourse of strangers and pilgrims was immense; and in the once solitary plain one of the largest cities of the time soon made its appearance. It is singular and interesting to remark, how the call to a life of virginity was felt and corresponded with in the newly Christianized country, even as it had been in the Roman Empire, when it also received the faith. Nor is it less noticeable how the same safeguards and episcopal rule preserved the foundations of each land in purity and peace, and have transmitted even to our own days in the same Church, and in it only, that privileged life.

CHAPTER V.

Some Account of the famous Palace of Tara—The Cursing of Tara—The First Saxon Invasion—The First Danish Invasion—Cruelty of the Danes—The Black and White Gentiles—The Danes Plunder Ireland.

IN the reign of Tuathal a portion of land was separated from each of the four provinces, which met together at a certain place : this portion was considered a distinct part of the country from the provinces. It was situated in the present county Meath.

In the tract separated from Munster, Tuathal built the royal seat of Tlachtga, where the fire of Tlachtga was ordained to be kindled. On the night of All Saints, the Druids assembled here to offer sacrifices, and it was established, under heavy penalties, that no fire should be kindled on that night throughout the kingdom, so that the fire which was used afterwards might be procured from this. To obtain the privilege, the people were obliged to pay over a scraball, or about three-pence, yearly, to the King of Munster.

On the 1st of May a convocation was held in the royal palace of the King of Connaught. He obtained subsidies in horses and arms from those who came to this assembly. On this occasion two fires were lit, between which cattle were driven as a preventative or charm against the murrain and other pestilential distempers. From this custom the feast of St. Philip and St. James was anciently called Beltinne, or the Day of Bel's Fire.

The third palace, erected by Tuathal, was on the portion of land taken from the province of Ulster. Here the celebrated fair of Tailtean was held, and contracts of marriage were frequently made. The royal tribute was raised by exacting an ounce of silver from every couple who were contracted and married at that time. The fair of Tailtean had been instituted some years before, in honour of Tailte, who was buried here. This fair, says Keating, was then kept upon the day known in the Irish language as La Lughnasa, or the day ordained by Lughaidh, and is called in English Lammas-day.

The fourth and the most important of the royal seats was the palace of Temair, or Tara; here, with the greatest state and ceremony, the affairs of the nation were discussed and decided. On these occasions, in order to preserve the deliberations from the public, the most strict secrecy was observed, and women were carefully excluded. Tara was cursed by St. Rodanus of Lothra, in Tipperary, in the reign of Diarmiad, in punishment for violation of sanctuary; and so complete was its subsequent desertion, that in 975 it was described as a desert overgrown with grass and weeds.

But enough still remains to give ample evidence of its former magnificence. An inspection of the site must convince the beholder of the vast extent of its ancient palaces; nor can we, for a moment, coincide with those who are pleased to consider that these palaces consisted merely of a few planks of wood, rudely plastered over, or of hollow mounds of earth. It is true that, from an association of ideas, the cause of so many fallacies, we naturally connect "halls" with marble pavements, magnificently carved pillars, and tesselated floors; but the harp that once resounded through Tara's halls, may have had as appreciating, if not as critical an audience as any which now exists, and the "halls" may have been none the less stately, because their floor was strewn with sand, or the trophies which adorned them fastened to walls of oak.

According to Celtic tradition, as embodied in our annals, Tara became the chief residence of the Irish kings on the first establishment of a monarchical government under Slainge:—

"Slainge of the Firbolgs was he by whom Temair was first raised."

One hundred and fifty monarchs reigned there from this period until its destruction in 563. The *Fees*, or triennial assembly, was instituted by Ollamh Fodhla. The nature of these meetings is explained in a poem, which Keating ascribes to O'Flynn, who died, A.D. 984. It is clear that what was then considered crime was punished in a very peremptory manner; for—

> "Gold was not received as retribution from him,
> But his soul in one hour."

The first Saxon invasion of Ireland took place about the year 623. A treacherous, false-hearted Irishman, after killing the reigning sovereign, fled to England for protection, and sought the assistance of strangers to enable him to obtain the honours he so unlawfully coveted. He met with a well deserved fate, and was slain at the famous battle of Magh Rath. But unfortunately the evil which he did, lived after him, and many unprincipled men were found who followed his perfidious example, and were ready to sacrifice their country for some miserable gain. With but some few exceptions, however, they reaped the just reward of their treachery.

The Danish invasion, one of the most important and memorable events in Irish history, occurred at the commencement of the seventh century. The Danes were brave and cruel, but neither their bravery nor their cruelty could have had much effect on old Ireland, had they not found Irishmen who were equally brave and equally cruel, who helped them to attain their ends. I say those Irishmen were equally brave; no one has ever questioned the valour of the Celt. I say they were equally cruel—nay, they were even more so. The Dane only fought against strangers; the Irish were more cruel because they fought against each other. Had the Irish united as one man against the Danes, they could never have plundered Ireland; had the Irish united as one man against the Saxons, they could never have conquered Ireland.

But why should we blame the men of those days when even in our own time Irishmen will keep up paltry quarrels and differences, instead of uniting in one common band for the good of their ill-fated country. Every Irishman should treat every other Irishman as a friend and a brother. A united people will always be a powerful people. A small body united can effect what a multitude disunited must fail to accomplish.

In the year 795, down came the wild, brave, cruel Danes, upon the Irish coast. They had already attacked the English coasts, "whilst the pious King Bertric was reigning over its western division." Their arrival was sudden and so unexpected, that the king's officer took them for merchants, paying with his life for the mistake. A Welsh chronicle, known by the name of *Brut-y Tywysogion*, or the Chronicle of the Chieftains, has a corresponding record under the year 790 : "Ten years with fourscore and seven hundred was the age of Christ when the pagans went to Ireland." Three MSS. add, " and destroyed Rechren." Another chronicle mentions, that the black pagans, who were the first of their nation to land in Ireland, had previously been defeated in Glamorganshire, and after their defeat they had invaded Ireland, and devastated Rechru.

If by bravery we understand utter recklessness of life, and utter recklessness in inflicting cruelties on others, then the Vikings may be termed brave. The heroism of patient endurance was a bravery but little understood at that period. If the heathen Viking was brave when he plundered and burned monastic shrines—when he massacred the defenceless with wanton cruelty—when he flung little children on the point of spears, and gloated over their dying agonies; perhaps we may also admit those who endured such torments, either in their own persons, or in the persons of those who were dear to them, and yet returned again and again to restore the shrine so rudely destroyed, have also their claims to be termed brave, and may demand some commendation for that virtue from posterity.

As plunder was the sole object of these barbarians, they naturally sought it first where it could be obtained most easily and surely. The islands on the Irish coast were studded with monasteries. Their position was chosen as one which seemed peculiarly suitable for a life of retreat from worldly turmoil, and contemplation of heavenly things. They were richly endowed, for ancient piety deemed it could never give enough to God. The shrines were adorned with jewels, purchased with the wealth which the monks had renounced for their own use : the sacred vessels were costly, the gifts of generous hearts. The Danes commenced their work of plunder and devastation in the year 795. Three years after, A.D. 798, they ravaged Inis-patrick of Man and the Hebrides. In 802 they burned "Hi-Coluim-Cille." In 806 they attacked the island again, and killed sixty-eight of the laity and clergy. In 807 they became emboldened by success, and for the first time marched inland; and after burning Inishmurray, they attacked Roscommon. During the year 812 and 813 they made raids in Connaught and Munster, but not without encountering stout resistance from the native forces. After this predatory and internecine warfare had continued for about thirty years, Turgesius, a Norwegian prince, established himself as sovereign of the Vikings, and made Armagh his head-quarters, A.D. 830. If the Irish chieftains had united their forces, and acted in concert, the result would have been the expulsion of the intruders ; but, unhappily, this unity of purpose in matters political has never existed. The Danes made and broke alliances with the provincial kings at their own convenience, while these princes gladly availed themselves of even temporary assistance from their cruel foes, while engaged in domestic wars which should never have been undertaken. Still the Northmen were more than once driven from the country by the bravery of the native commanders, and they often paid dearly for the cruel wrongs they inflicted on their hapless victims. Sometimes the Danish chiefs mustered all their forces, and left the island for a brief period, to ravage the shores of England or Scotland; but they soon returned, to inflict new barbarities on the unfortunate Irish.

Burning churches or destroying monasteries, was a favourite pastime of these pirates, wherever they could obtain a landing on Christian shores; and the number of religious houses in Ireland, afforded them abundant means of gratifying their barbarous inclinations. But when they became so far masters as to have obtained some permanent settlement, this mode of proceeding was considered either more troublesome or less profitable than that of appropriating to themselves the abbeys and churches. Turgesius, it is said, placed an abbot of his own in every monastery; and as he had already conferred ecclesiastical offices on himself and on his lady, we may presume he was not very particular in his selections. The villages, too, were placed under the rule of a Danish captain; and each family was obliged to maintain a soldier of that nation, who made himself master of the house, using and wasting the food, for lack of which the starving children of the lawful owner were often dying of hunger.

All education was strictly forbidden; books and manuscripts were burned and *drowned:* and the poets, historians, and musicians, imprisoned and driven to the woods and mountains. Martial sports were interdicted, from the lowest to the highest rank. Even nobles and princes were forbidden to wear their usual habiliments, the cast-off clothes of the Danes being considered sufficiently good for slaves.

The clergy, who had been driven from their monasteries, concealed themselves as best they could, continuing still their prayers and fasts, and the fervent recital of the Divine Office. The Irish, true to their faith in every trial, were not slow to attribute their deliverance to the prayers of these holy men.

In 831, Nial Caille led an army against them, and defeated them at Derry; but, in the meanwhile Felim, King of Cashel, with contemptible selfishness, marched into Leinster to claim tribute, and plundered every one except the Danes, who should have been alone considered as enemies at such a time. Even the churches were not spared by him, for he laid waste the termon-lands of Clonmacnois, "up to the church-door." After his death, A.D. 843, a brave and good king came to the rescue of his unfortunate country. While still King of Meath, Meloughlin had freed the nation from Turgesius, one of its worst tyrants, by drowning him in Lough Owel. His death was a signal for general onslaught on the Danes. The people rose simultaneously, and either massacred their enemies, or drove them to their ships. In 846 Meloughlin met their forces at Skreen, where they were defeated; they also suffered a reverse at Kildare.

The Danes themselves were now divided into two parties—the Dubh Galls, or Black Gentiles; and the Finn Galls, or White Gentiles. A fierce conflict took place between them in the year 850, in which the Dubh Galls conquered. In the folowing year, however, both parties submitted to Amlaff, son of the Norwegian king; and thus their power was once more consolidated. Amlaff remained in Dublin; his brothers, Sitric and Ivar, stationed themselves in Waterford and Limerick. A great meeting was now convened by the ecclesiastics of Ireland at Rathugh, for the purpose of establishing peace and concord amongst the native princes. The northern Hy-Nials alone remained belligerent; and to defend themselves, pursued the usual suicidal course of entering into an alliance with the Danes. Upon the death of the Irish monarch, the northern chief, Hugh Finnlaith, succeeded to the royal power; broke his treaty with Amlaff, which had been only one of convenience, and turned his arms vigorously against the foreigners. This prince was married to a daughter of Kenneth M'Alpine, the first sole Monarch of Scotland. After the death of the Irish prince, his wife married his successor, Flann, who, according to the alternate plan of succession, came of the southern Hy-

Nial family, and was a son of Meloughlin, once the formidable opponent of his lady's former husband. During the reign of Flann, Cormac Mac Cullinan, a prelate, distinguished for his learning and sanctity, was obliged to unite the office of priest and king. This unusual combination, however, was not altogether without precedent. The archbishopric of Cashel owes its origin remotely to this great man; as from the circumstance of the city of Cashel having been the seat of royalty in the south, and the residence of the kings of Munster, it was exalted, in the twelfth century, to the dignity of an archiepiscopal see.

Of Cormac, however interesting his history, we can only give a passing word. His reign commenced peaceably; and so wise—perhaps we should rather say, so holy—was his rule, that his kingdom once more enjoyed comparative tranquillity; and religion and learning flourished again as it had done in happier times.

But the kingdom which he had been compelled to rule, was threatened by the very person who should have protected it most carefully; and Cormac, after every effort to procure peace, was obliged to defend his people against the attacks of Flann. Even then a treaty might have been made with the belligerent monarch; but Cormac, unfortunately for his people and himself, was guided by an abbot, named Flahertach, who was by no means so peaceably disposed as his good master. This unruly ecclesiastic urged war on those who were already too willing to undertake it; and then made such representations to the bishop-king, as to induce him to yield a reluctant consent. It is said that Cormac had an intimation of his approaching end. It is at least certain, that he made preparation for death, as if he believed it to be imminent.

On the eve of the fatal engagement he made his confession, and added some articles to his will, in which he left large bounties to many of the religious houses throughout the kingdom. To Lismore he bequeathed a golden chalice and some rich vestments; to Armagh, twenty-four ounces of gold and silver; to his own church of Cashel, a golden and silver chalice, with the famous Saltair. Then he retired to a private place for prayer, desiring the few persons whom he had informed of his approaching fate to keep their information secret, as he knew well the effect such intelligence would have on his army, were it generally known.

Though the king had no doubt that he would perish on the field, he still showed the utmost bravery, and made every effort to cheer and encourage his troops; but the men lost spirit in the very onset of the battle, and probably were terrified at the numerical strength of their opponents. Six thousand Munster men were slain, with many of their princes and chieftains. Cormac was killed by falling under his horse, which missed its footing on a bank, slippery with the blood of the slain. A common soldier, who recognized his remains, cut off his head, and brought it as a trophy to Flann; but the monarch bewailed the death of the good and great prince, and reproved the indignity with which his remains had been treated. This battle was fought at a place called Bealagh Mughna, now Ballaghmoon, in the county of Kildare, a few miles from the town of Carlow.

Flahertach survived the battle, and, after some years spent in penance, became once more minister, and ultimately King of Munster. As he advanced in years, he learned to love peace, and his once irascible temper became calm and equable.

The Rock of Cashel, and the ruins of a small but once beautiful chapel, still preserve the memory of the bishop-king. His literary fame also has its memorials. His Rule is contained in a poem of fourteen stanzas, written in the most pure and ancient style of Gaedhilic, of which, as well as of many other languages, the illustrious Cormac was so profound a master. The Rule is general in several of its inculcations; but it appears to have been written particularly as an instruction to a priest, for the moral and spiritual direction of himself and his flock. He was also skilled in the Ogham writings, as may be gathered from a poem written by a contemporary, who, in paying compliments to many of the Irish kings and chiefs, addresses the following stanzas to Cormac :—

"Cormac of Cashel, with his champions,
Munster is his,—may he long enjoy it!
Around the King of *Raith-Bicli* are cultivated
The letters and the trees."

The death of Cormac is thus pathetically deplored by Dallan, son of Môr :—

"The bishop, the soul's director, the renowned illustrious doctor,
King of Caiseal, King of Farnumha; O God! alas for Cormac!"

Flann's last years were disturbed by domestic dissensions. His sons, Donough and Conor, both rebelled against him; but Nial Glundubh (of the black knee), a northern Hy-Nial chief, led an army against them, and compelled them to give hostages to their father. Flann died the following year, A.D. 914, and was succeeded by the prince who had so ably defended him. Meanwhile, the Danes were not idle. Amlaff has signalized his advent by drowning Conchobhar, "heir apparent of Tara;" by slaying all the chieftains of the Deisi at Cluain-Doimh; by killing the son of Clennfaeladh, King of Muscraighe Breoghain; by smothering Machdaighren in a cave, and by the destruction of Caitill Find (Ketill the White) and his whole garrison. Oisill is the next chief of importance; and he "succeeded in plundering the greatest part of Ireland." It is not recorded how long he was occupied in performing this exploit, but he was eventually slain, and his army cut of, by the men of Erinn.

The deaths of several Danish chieftains are recorded about this period, and referred to the vengeance of certain saints, whose shrines they had desecrated. In A.D. 864 according to the Four Masters, 867 according to O'Flaherty, the Danes were defeated at Lough Foyle, by Hugh Finnliath, King of Ireland. Soon after, Leinster and Munster were plundered by a Scandinavian chief, named Baraid, who advanced as far as *Ciarraighe* (Kerry): "And they left not a cave under ground that they did not explore; and they left nothing, from Limerick to Cork, that they did not ravish." What treasures the antiquarian of the nineteenth century must have lost by this marauder! How great must have been the wealth of the kings and princes of ancient Erinn, where so much remains after so much was taken! In 877 the Black Gentiles took refuge in Scotland, after suffering a defeat in an engagement with the White Gentiles. They were, however consoled by a victory over the men of Alba, in which Constantine, son of Kenneth, was slain, and many others with him. Their success proved beneficial to Ireland, for we are told that a period of "rest to the men of Erinn" ensued. The Danes still held their own in Dublin and at Limerick, occasionally plundered the churches, and now and then had a skirmish with the "men of Erinn;" but for forty years the country was free from the foreign fleets, and therefore, enjoyed a time of comparative quiet.

In the year 913 new fleets arrived. They landed in the harbour of Waterford, where they had a settlement formerly; but though they obtained assistance here, they were defeated by the native Irish, both in Kerry and Tipperary. Sitric came with another fleet in 915, and settled at Cenn-Fuait. Here he was attacked by the Irish army, but they were repulsed with great slaughter. Two years after they received another disastrous defeat at Cill-Mosanhog, near Rathfarnham. A large cromlech, still in that neighbourhood, probably marks the graves of the heroes slain in that engagement. Twelve kings were slain in this battle. Their names are given in the Wars of the Gaedhil, and by other authorities, though in some places the number is increased. Nial Glundubh was amongst the slain. He is celebrated in pathetic verse by the bards. Of the battle was said :—

"Fierce and hard was the Wednesday
On which hosts were strewn under the fall of shields;
It shall be called, till judgment's day,
The destructive burning of Ath-cliath."

The lamentation of Nial was, moreover, said :—

"Sorrowful this day is sacred Ireland,
Without a valiant chief of hostage reign;
It is to see the heavens without a sun,
To view Magh-Neill without Nial."

"There is no cheerfulness in the happiness of men;
There is no peace or joy among the hosts;
No fair can be celebrated
Since the sorrow of sorrow died."

Donough, son of Flann Sinna, succeeded, and passed his reign in obscurity, with the exception of a victory over the Danes at Bregia. Two great chieftains, however, compensated by their prowess for his indifference; these were Muircheartach, son of the brave Nial Glundubh, the next heir to the throne, and Callaghan of Cashel, King of Munster. The northern prince was a true patriot, willing to sacrifice every personal feeling for the good of his country : consequently, he proved a most formidable foe to the Danish invader. Callaghan of Cashel was, perhaps, as brave, but his name cannot be held up to the admiration of posterity. The personal advancement of the southern Hy-Nials was more to him than the political advancement of his country; and he disgraced his name and his nation by leaguing with the invaders. In the year 934 he pillaged Clonmacnois. Three years later he invaded Meath and Ossory, in conjunction with the Danes. Muircheartach was several times on the eve of engagements with the feeble monarch who nominally ruled the country, but he yielded for the sake of peace, or, as the chroniclers quaintly say, "God pacified them." After one of these pacifications, they joined forces, and laid " siege to the foreigners of Ath-cliath, so that they spoiled and plundered all that was under the dominion of the foreigners, from Ath-cliath to Ath-Truisten."

In the twenty-second year of Donough, Muircheartach determined on a grand expedition for the subjugation of the Danes. He had already conducted a fleet to the Hebrides, from whence he returned flushed with victory. His first care was to assemble a body of troops of special valour; and he soon found himself at the head of a thousand heroes, and in a position to commence " his circuit of Ireland." The Danish chief, Sitric, was first seized as a hostage. He then carried off Lorcan, King of Leinster. He next went to the Munster men, who were also prepared for battle; but they too yielded, and gave up their monarch also, "and a fetter was put on him by Muircheartach." He afterwards proceeded into Connaught, where Conchobhar, son of Tadhg, came to meet him, "but no gyve or lock was put upon him." He then returned to Oileach, carrying these kings with him as hostages. Here he feasted them for five months with knightly courtesy, and then sent them to the Monarch Donough.

After these exploits, we cannot be surprised that Muircheartach should be styled the Hector of the west of Europe. But he soon finds his place in the never-ceasing obituary. In two years after his justly famous exploit, he was slain by " Blacaire, son of Godfrey, lord of the foreigners." This event occurred on the 26th of March, A.D. 941, according to the chronology of the Four Masters. The true year, however, is 943. The chroniclers briefly observe, that " Ard-Macha was plundered by the same foreigners, on the day after the killing of Muircheartach."

Donough died in 942, after a reign of twenty-five years. He was succeeded by Congallach, who was killed by the Danes, A.D. 954. Donnell O'Neill, a son of the brave Muircheartach, now obtained the royal power, such as it was; and at his death the throne reverted to Maelseachlainn, or Malachy II., the last of his race who ever held the undisputed sovereignty of Ireland.

CHAPTER VI.

Conversion of the Danes—Brien Boroimé and his brother Mahoun—Defeat of the Danes at Sulcoit—Death of Mahoun—Brian's Revenge—Brian and Malachy unite against the Danes.

MANY of the sea-coast towns were now in possession of the Danes. They had founded Limerick, and, indeed, Wexford and Waterford almost owe them the debt of parentage. Obviously, the ports were their grand securities—a ready refuge if driven by native valour to embark in their fleets; convenient headquarters when marauding expeditions to England or Scotland were in preparation. But the Danes never obtained the same power in Ireland as in the sister country. The domestic dissensions of the men of Erinn, ruinous as they were to the nation, gave it at least the advantage of having a brave and resolute body of men always in arms, and ready to face the foe at a moment's notice, when no selfish policy interfered.

The year 948 has generally been assigned as that of the conversion of the Danes to Christianity; but, whatever the precise period may have been, the conversion was rather of a doubtful character, as we hear of their burning churches, plundering shrines, and slaughtering ecclesiastics with apparently as little remorse as ever. In the very year in which the Danes of Dublin are said to have been converted, they burned the belfry of Slane, while filled with religious who had sought refuge there. Meanwhile the Irish monarchies were daily weakened by divisions and domestic wars. Connaught was divided between two or three independent princes, and Munster into two kingdoms.

The ancient division of the country into five provinces no longer held good; and the Ard-Righ, or chief monarch, was such only in name. Even the great northern Hy-Nials, long the bravest and most united of the Irish clans, were now divided into two portions, the Cinel-Connaill and Cinel-Owen; the former of whom had been for some time excluded from the alternate accession of sovreignty, which was still maintained betwen the two great families of the race of Nial. But, though this arrangement was persevered in with tolerable regularity, it tended little to the promotion of peace, as the northern princes were ever ready to take advantage of the weakness of the Meath men.

The sovereignty of Munster had also been settled on the alternate principle, between the great tribe of Dalcassians, or north Munster race, and the Eoghanists, or southerners. This plan of succession, as may be supposed, failed to work peaceably; and, in 942, Cinneidigh, the father of the famous Brian Boroimhé contested the sovereignty with the Eoghanist prince, Callaghan Cashel; but yielded in a chivalrous spirit, not very common under such circumstances, and joined his former opponent in his contest with the Danes. The author of the Wars of the Gaedhill with the Gall gives a glowing account of the genealogy of Brian and his eldest brother, Mathgamhain. They are described as "two fierce, magnificent heroes, the two stout, able, valiant pillars."

Mahoun was now firmly established on the throne, but his success procured him many enemies. A conspiracy was formed against him under the auspices of Ivar of Limerick, and his son, Dubhcenn. The Eoghanist clans basely withdrew their allegiance from their lawful sovereign, allied themselves with the Danes, and became principals in the plot of assassination. Their motive was as simple as their conduct was vile. The two Eoghanist families were represented by Donovan and Molloy. They were descendants of Oilioll Oluim, from whom Mahoun was also descended, but his family were Dalcassians. Hitherto the Eoghanists had succeeded in depriving the tribes of Dal-Cais of

The Irish Patriot, St. Laurence O'Toole, praying for Ireland.

their fair share of alternate succession to the throne of Munster; they became alarmed at and jealous of the advancement of the younger tribe, and determined to do by treachery what they could not do by force. With the usual headlong eagerness of traitors, they seem to have forgotten Brian, and quite overlooked the retribution they might expect at his hands for their crime. There are two different accounts of the murder, which do not coincide in detail. The main facts, however, are reliable: Mahoun was entrapped in some way to the house of Donovan, and there he was basely murdered, in violation of the rights of hospitality and in defiance of the safe conduct of the bishop, which he secured before his visit.

The traitors gained nothing by their treachery except the contempt of posterity. Brian was not slow in avenging his brother. "He was not a stone in place of an egg, nor a wisp of hay in place of a club; but he was a hero in place of a hero, and valour after valour."

Public opinion was not mistaken in its estimate of his character. Two years after the death of Mahoun, Brian invaded Donovan's territory, drove off his cattle, took the fortress of Cathair Cuan, and slew Donovan and his Danish ally, Harolt. He next proceeded to settle accounts with Molloy. Cogarán is sent to the whole tribe of Ui Eachach, to know "the reason why" they killed Mahoun, and to declare that no *cumhal* or fine would be received, either in the shape of hostages, gold or cattle, but that Molloy must himself be given up. Messages were also sent to Molloy, both general and particular—the general message challenged him to battle at Belach-Lechta; the particular message, which in truth he hardly deserved, was a challenge to meet Murrough, Brian's son, in single combat. The result was the battle of Belach-Lechta, where Molloy was slain, with twelve hundred of his troops, both native and foreign. Brian remained master of the field and of the kingdom, A.D. 978.

Brian was now undisputed King of Munster In 984 he was acknowledged Monarch of Leth Mogha, the southern half of Ireland. Meanwhile Malachy, who governed Leth Cuinn, or the northern half of Ireland, had not been idle. He fought a battle with the Danes in 979, near Tara, in which he defeated their forces, and slew Raguall, son of Amlaibh, King of Dublin. Amlaibh felt the defeat so severely, that he retired to Iona, where he died of a broken heart. Donough O'Neill, son of Muircheartach, died this year, and Malachy obtained the regal dignity. Emboldened by his success at Tara, he resolved to attack the foreigners in Dublin; he therefore laid siege to that city, and compelled it to surrender after three days, liberated two thousand prisoners, including the King of Leinster, and took abundant spoils. At the same time he issued a proclamation, freeing every Irishman then in bondage to the Danes, and stipulating that the race of Nial should henceforth be free from tribute to the foreigners.

It is probable that Brian had already formed designs for obtaining the royal power. The country resounded with the fame of his exploits, and Malachy became aware at last that he should either have him for an ally or an enemy. He prudently chose the former alternative, and in the nineteenth year of his reign (997 according to the Four Masters) he made arrangements with Brian for a great campaign against the common enemy. Malachy surrendered all hostages to Brian, and Brian agreed to recognize Malachy as sole monarch of northern Erinn, "without war or trespass." This treaty was absolutely necessary, in order to offer effective resistance to the Danes. The conduct of the two kings towards each other, had not been of a conciliatory nature previously. In 981 Malachy had invaded the territory of the Dalcassians, and uprooted the great oak-tree of Magh Adhair, under which its kings were crowned—an insult which could not fail to excite bitter feelings both in prince and people. In 989 the monarch occupied himself fighting the Danes in Dublin, to whom he laid siege for twenty nights, reducing the garrison to such straits that they were obliged to drink the salt water when the tide rose in the river. Brian then made reprisals on Malachy, by sending boats up the Shannon, burning the royal rath of

G

Dun Sciath. Malachy, in his turn, recrossed the Shannon, burned Nenagh, plundered Ormond, and defeated Brian himself in battle. He then marched again to Dublin, and once more attacked "the proud invader." It was on this occasion that he obtained the "collar of gold," which Moore has immortalized in his world-famous "Melodies."

When the kings had united their forces, they obtained another important victory at Glen-Mama. Harolt, son of Olaf Cuaran, the then Danish king, was slain, and four thousand of his followers perished with him. The victorious army marched at once to Dublin. Here they obtained spoils of great value, and made many slaves and captives. According to some accounts, Brian remained in Dublin until the feast of St. Brigid (February 1st); other annalists say he only remained from Great Christmas to Little Christmas. Meanwhile there can be but little doubt that Brian had in view the acquisition of the right to be called sole monarch of Ireland. It is a blot on an otherwise noble character—an ugly spot in a picture of more than ordinary interest. Sitric, another son of Olaf's, fled for protection to Aedh and Eochaidh, two northern chieftains; but they gave him up, from motives of fear or policy, to Brian's soldiers, and after due submission he was restored to his former position. Brian then gave his daughter in marriage to Sitric, and completed the family alliance by espousing Sitric's mother, Gormflaith, a lady of rather remarkable character, who had been divorced from her second husband, Malachy. Brian now proceeded to depose Malachy. The account of this important transaction is given in so varied a manner by different writers, that it seems almost impossible to ascertain the truth. The southern annalists are loud in their assertions of the incapacity of the reigning monarch, and would have it believed that Brian only yielded to the urgent entreaties of his countrymen in accepting the proffered crown. But the warlike exploits of Malachy have been too faithfully recorded to leave any doubt as to his prowess in the field; and we may probably class the regret of his opponent in accepting his position with similar protestations made under circumstances in which such regret was as little likely to be real.

The poet Moore, with evident partiality for the subject of his song, declares the magnanimous character of Malachy was the real ground of peace, under such provocation, and that he submitted to the encroachments of his rival rather from motives of disinterested desire for his country's welfare, than from any reluctance or inability to fight his own battle.

But Brian had other chieftains to deal with, of less amiable or more warlike propensities: the proud Hy-Nials of the north were long in yielding to his claims; but even these he at length subdued, compelling the Cinel-Eoghain to give him hostages and carrying off the Lord of Cinel-Connaill bodily to his fortress at Kincora. Here he had assembled a sort of "happy family," consisting of refractory princes and knights, who, refusing hostages to keep the peace with each other, were obliged to submit to the royal will and pleasure, and at least appear outwardly in harmony.

These precautionary measures, however summary, and the energetic determination of Brian to have peace kept either by sword or law, have given rise to the romantic ballad of the lady perambulating Erinn with a gold ring and white wand, and passing unmolested through its once belligerent kingdoms.

Brian now turned his attention to the state of religion and literature, restoring the churches and monasteries which had been plundered and burnt by the Danes. He is said also to have founded the churches of Killaloe and Inniscealtra, and to have built the round tower of Tomgrany, in the present county Clare. A gift of twenty ounces of gold to the church of Armagh,—a large donation for that period,—is also recorded amongst his good deeds.

There is some question as to the precise year in which Brian obtained or usurped the authority and position of Ard-Righ : A.D. 1002, however is the date most usually accepted. He was probably about sixty-one years of age, and Malachy was then about fifty-three.

It will be remembered that Brian had married the Lady Gormflaith. Her brother, Maelmordha, was King of Leinster, and he had obtained his throne through the assistance of the Danes. Brian was Gormflaith's third husband. In the words of the Annals, she had made three leaps—"jumps which a woman should never jump"—a hint that her matrimonial arrangements had not the sanction of canon law. She was remarkable for her beauty, but her temper was proud and vindictive. This was probably the reason why she was repudiated both by Malachy and Brian. There can be no doubt that she and her brother, Maelmordha, were the remote causes of the famous battle of Clontarf. The story is told thus: Maelmordha came to Brian with an offering of three large pine-trees to make masts for shipping. These were probably a tribute which he was bound to pay to his liege lord. The trees had been cut in the great forest of Leinster, called Fidh-Gaibhli. Some other tribes were bringing their tree-tributes at the same time; and as they all journeyed over the mountains together, there was a dispute for precedency. Maelmordha decided the question by assisting to carry the tree of the Ui-Faelain. He had on a tunic of silk which Brian had given him, with a border of gold round it, and silver buttons." One of the buttons came off as he lifted the tree. On his arrival at Kincora, he asked his sister, Gormflaith, to replace it for him; but she at once flung the garment into the fire, and then bitterly reproached her brother with having accepted this token of vassalage. The Sagas say she was "grim" against Brian, which was undoubtedly true. This excited Maelmordha's temper. An opportunity soon offered for a quarrel. Brian's eldest son, Murrough, was playing a game of Chess with his cousin, Conoing; Maelmordha was looking on, and suggested a move by which Murrough lost the game. The young prince exclaimed: "That was like the advice you gave the Danes, which lost them Glen-Mama." "I will give them advice now, and they shall not be defeated," replied the other. "Then you had better remind them to prepare a yew-tree for your reception," answered Murrough.

Early the next morning Maelmordha left the place "without permission and without taking leave. Brian sent a messenger after him to pacify him, but the angry chief, for all reply, "broke all the bones in his head." He now proceeded to organize a revolt against Brian, and succeeded. Several of the Irish princes flocked to his standard. An encounter took place in Meath, where they slew Malachy's grandson, Domhnall, who should have been heir if the usual rule of succession had been observed. Malachy marched to the rescue, and defeated the assailants with great slaughter, A.D. 1013. Fierce reprisals now took place on each side. Sanctuary was disregarded, and Malachy called on Brian to assist him. Brian at once complied. After successfully ravaging Ossory he marched to Dublin, where he was joined by Murrough, who had devastated Wicklow, burning, destroying, and carrying off captives, until he reached *Cill Maighnenn* (Kilmainham). They now blockaded Dublin, where they remained from St. Ciaran's in harvest (Sept. 9th) until Christmas Day. Brian was then obliged to raise the siege, and return home for want of provisions.

CHAPTER VII.

Battle of Clontarf—Brian's Death, and Defeat of the Danes—Rivalry and Reconciliation between Malachy and Brian—Death of Turlough—Bravery of the Dalcassians at Mullaghmast—Death of Malachy.

THE storm was now gathering in earnest; the most active preparations were made on both sides for a mighty and decisive conflict. The Danes had already obtained possession of England, a country which had always been united in its resistance to their power, a country numerically superior to Ireland : why should they not hope to conquer, with at least equal facility, a people who had so many opposing interests, and who rarely sacrificed these interests to the common good? Still they must have had some fear of the result, if we may judge by the magnitude of their preparations. They despatched ambassadors in all directions to obtain reinforcements. Brodir, the earl, and Amlaibh, son of the King of Lochlann, " the two Earls of Cair, and of all the north of Saxon land," came at the head of 2,000 men ; " and there was not one villain of that 2,000 who had not polished, strong, triple-plated armour of refined iron or of cooling, uncorroding brass, encasing their sides and bodies from head to foot." Moreover, the said villains " had no reverence, veneration, or respect, or mercy for God or man, for church or for sanctuary ; they were cruel, ferocious, plundering, hard-hearted, wonderful Dannarbrians, selling and hiring themselves for gold and silver, and other treasure as well." Gormflaith was evidently " head centre" on the occasion ; for we find wonderful accounts of her zeal and efforts in collecting forces. "Other treasures" may possibly be referred to that lady's heart and hand, of which she appears to have been very liberal on this occasion. She despatched her son, Sitric, to Siguard, Earl of the Orkneys, who promised his assistance, but he required the hand of Gormflaith as payment for his services, and that he should be made King of Ireland. Sitric gave the required promise, and found, on his return to Dublin, that it met with his mother's entire approbation. She then despatched him to the Isle of Man, where there were two Vikings, who had thirty ships, and she desired him to obtain their co-operation " at any price." They were the brothers Ospak and Brodir. The latter demanded the same conditions as the Earl Siguard, which were promised quite as readily by Sitric, only he charged the Viking to keep the agreement secret, and above all not to mention it to Siguard.

Brodir, according to the Saga, was an apostate Christian, who had "thrown off his faith, and become God's dastard." He was both tall and strong, and had such long black hair that he tucked it under his belt; he had also the reputation of being a magician. The Viking Ospak refused to fight against "the good King Brian," and, touched by some prodigies, became a convert to Christianity, joined the Irish monarch at Kincora, on the Shannon, and received holy baptism. The author of the Wars of the Gaedhil gives a formidable list of the other auxiliaries who were invited by the Dublin Danes. The Annals of Loch Cè also give an account of the fleet he assembled, and its "chosen braves." Maelmordha had mustered a large army; indeed, he was too near the restless and revengeful Lady Gormflaith to have taken matters quietly, even had he been so inclined.

Meanwhile Brian had been scarcely less successful, and probably not less active. He now marched towards Dublin "with all that obeyed him of the men of Ireland." These were the provincial troops of Munster and Connaught and the men of Meath. His march is thus described in the Wars of the Gaedhil:—"Brian looked out behind him, and beheld the battle phalanx—compact, huge, disciplined, moving in silence, mutely, bravely, haughtily, unitedly, with one mind, traversing the plain towards them; threescore and ten banners over them—of red, and of yellow, and of green, and of all kinds of colours; together with the everlasting, variegated, lucky, fortunate banner, that had gained the victory in every battle, and in every conflict, and in every combat." The portion of the narrative containing this account is believed to be an interpolation, but the description may not be the less accurate. Brian plundered and destroyed as usual on his way to Dublin. When he had encamped near that city, the Danes came out to give him battle on the plain of Magh-n-Ealta. The king then held a council of war, and the result, apparently, was a determination to give battle in the morning. It is said that the Northmen pretended flight in order to delay the engagement. The Njal Saga says the Viking Brodir had found out by his sorcery, "that if the fight were on Good Friday, King Brian would fall, but win the day; but, if they fought before, they would all fall who were against him." Some authorities also mention a traitor in Brian's camp, who had informed the Danes that his forces had been weakened by the absence of his son Donough, whom he had sent to devastate Leinster. Malachy has the credit of this piece of treachery, with other imputations scarcely less disreputable.

The site of the battle has been accurately defined. It took place on the plain of Clontarf, and is called the Battle of the Fishing Weir of Clontarf. The weir was at the mouth of the river Tolka, where the bridge of Ballybough now stands. The Danish line was extended along the coast, and protected at sea by their fleets. It was disposed in three divisions, and comprised about 21,000 men, the Leinster forces being included in the number. The first division or left wing was the nearest to Dublin. It was composed of the Danes of Dublin, and headed by Sitric, who was supported by the thousand mail-clad Norwegians commanded by Carlus and Anrud. In the centre were the Legennians under the command of Maelmordha. The right wing comprised the foreign auxiliaries, under the command of Brodir and Siguard.

Brian's army was also disposed in three divisions. The first was composed of his brave Dalcassians, and commanded by his son Murrough, assisted by his four brothers, Teigue, Donough, Connor, and Flann, and his youthful heir, Turlough, who perished on the field. The second division or centre was composed of troops from Munster, and was commanded by Mothla, grandson of the King of the Deisi, of Waterford, assisted by many native princes. The third battalion was commanded by Maelruanaidh (Mulrooney of the Pater Nosters) and Teigue O'Kelly, with all the nobles of Connaught. Brian's army numbered about twenty thousand men. The accounts which relate the position of Malachy, and his conduct on this occasion, are hopelessly conflicting. It appears quite impossible to decide whether he was a victim to prejudice, or whether Brian was a victim to his not unnatural hostility.

On the eve of the battle, one of the Danish chiefs, Plait, son of King Lochlainn, sent a challenge to Domhnall, son of Emhin, High Steward of Mar. The battle commenced at daybreak. Plait came forth and exclaimed three times, "*Faras Domhnall?*" (Where is Domhnall?) Domhnall replied: "Here, thou reptile." A terrible hand-to-hand combat ensued. They fell dead at the same moment, the sword of each through the heart of the other, and the hair of each in the clenched hand of the other. And the combat of those two was the first combat of the battle.

Before the engagement, Brian harangued his troops, with the crucifix in one hand and a sword in the other. He reminded them of all they had suffered from their enemies, of their tyranny, their sacrilege, their innumerable perfidies; and then, holding the crucifix aloft, he exclaimed: "The great God has at length looked down upon our sufferings, and endued you with the power and the courage this day to destroy for ever the tyranny of the Danes, and thus to punish them for their innumerable crimes and sacrileges by the avenging power of the sword. Was it not on this day that Christ himself suffered death for you?"

He was then compelled to retire to the rear, and await the result of the conflict, but Murrough performed prodigies of valour. Even the Danish historians admit that he fought his way to their standard, and cut down two successive bearers of it.

The mailed armour of the Danes seems to have been a source of no little dread to their opponents. But the Irish battle-axe might well have set even more secure protection at defiance. It was wielded with such skill and force, that frequently a limb was lopped off with a single blow, despite the mail in which it was encased; while the short lances, darts, and slinging-stones proved a speedy means of decapitating or stunning a fallen enemy.

The Dalcassians surpassed themselves in feats of arms. They hastened from time to time to refresh their thirst and cool their hands in a neighbouring brook; but the Danes soon filled it up, and deprived them of this resource. It was a conflict of heroes—a hand-to-hand fight. Bravery was not wanting on either side, and for a time the result seemed doubtful. Towards the afternoon, as many of the Danish leaders were cut down, their followers began to give way, and the Irish forces prepared for a final effort. At this moment the Norwegian prince, Anrud, encountered Murrough, whose arms were paralysed from fatigue; he had still physical strength enough to seize his enemy, fling him on the ground, and plunge his sword into the body of his prostrate foe. But even as he inflicted the death-wound, he received a mortal blow from the dagger of the Dane, and the two chiefs fell together.

The Northmen and their allies were flying hard and fast, the one towards their ships, the others towards the city. But as they fled across the Tolka, they forgot that it was now swollen with the incoming tide, and thousands perished by water who had escaped the sword. The body of Brian's grandson, the boy Turlough, was found in the river after the battle, with his hands entangled in the hair of two Danish warriors, whom he had held down until they were drowned. Sitric and his wife had watched the combat from the battlements of Dublin. It will be remembered that this lady was a daughter of King Brian, and her interests were naturally with the Irish troops. Some rough words passed between her and her lord, which ended in his giving her so rude a blow, that he knocked out one of her teeth. But we have yet to record the crowning tragedy of the day. Brian had retired to his tent to pray, at the commencement of the conflict. When the forces met, he began his devotions, and said to his attendant :— "Watch thou the battle and the combats, whilst I say the psalms." After he had recited fifty psalms, fifty collects, and fifty paternosters, he desired the man to look out and inform him how the battle went, and the position of Murrough's standard. He replied the strife was close and vigorous, and the noise was as if seven battalions were cutting down Tomar's wood; but the standard was safe. Brian then said fifty more psalms, and made the same inquiry. The attendant replied that all was in confusion, but that Murrough's standard still stood erect, and moved westwards towards Dublin. "As long as that standard remains erect," replied Brian, "it shall go well with the men of Erinn." The aged king betook himself to his prayers once more, saying again fifty psalms and collects; then for the last time, he asked intelligence of the field. Latean replied: "They appear as if Tomar's wood was on fire, and its brushwood all burned down;" meaning that the private soldiers of both armies were nearly all slain, and only a few of the chiefs had escaped; adding the most grievous intelligence of all, that Murrogh's standard had fallen. "Alas!" replied Brian, "Erinn has fallen with it: why should I survive such losses, even should I attain the sovereignty of the world?" His attendant then urged him to fly, but Brian replied that flight was useless, for he had been warned of his fate by Aibinn (the banshee of his family), and that he knew that his death was at hand. He then gave directions about his will and his funeral, leaving 240 cows to the "successor of Patrick." Even at this moment his death was impending. A party of Danes approached, headed by Brodir. The king sprang up from the cushion where he had been kneeling, and unsheathed his sword. At first Brodir did not know him, and thought he was a priest from finding him at prayer; but one of his followers informed him that it was the Monarch of Ireland. In a moment the fierce Dane had opened his head with his battle-axe. It is said that Brian had time to inflict a wound on the Viking, but the details of this event are so varied that it is impossible to decide which account is most reliable. The Saga states that Brodir knew Brian, and, proud of his exploit, held up the monarch's reeking head, exclaiming, "Let it be told from man to man that Brodir felled Brian." All accounts agree that the Viking was slain immediately, if not cruelly, by Brian's guards, who thus revenged their own neglect of their master. Had Brian survived this conflict, and had he been but a few years younger, how different might have been the political and social state of Ireland even at the present day! The Danish power was overthrown, and never again obtained an ascendancy in the country. It needed but one strong will, one wise head, one brave arm, to consolidate the nation, and to establish a regular monarchy; for there was mettle enough in the Celt, if only united, to resist foreign invasion for all time to come.

On Easter Monday the survivors were employed in burying the dead and attending to the wounded

The remains of more than thirty chieftains were borne off to their respective territorial churches for interment. But even on that very night dissension arose in the camp. The chieftains of Desmond, seeing the broken condition of the Dalcassian force, renewed their claim to the alternate succession. When they had reached Rath Maisten (Mullaghmast, near Athy) they claimed the sovereignty of Munster, by demanding hostages. A battle ensued, in which even the wounded Dalcassians joined. Their leader desired them to be placed in the fort of Maisten, but they insisted on being fastened to stakes, firmly planted in the ground to support them, and stuffing their wounds with moss, they awaited the charge of the enemy. The men of Ossory, intimidated by their bravery, feared to give battle. But many of the wounded men perished from exhaustion—a hundred and fifty swooned away, and never recovered consciousness again. The majority were buried where they stood; a few of the more noble were carried to their ancestral resting-places. "And thus far the wars of the Gall with the Gaedhil, and the battle of Clontarf."

The Annals state that both Brian and his son, Murrough, lived to receive the rites of the Church, and that their remains were conveyed by the monks to Swords, and from thence, through Duleek and Louth, to Armagh, by Archbishop Maelmuire, the "successor of St. Patrick." Their obsequies were celebrated with great splendour for twelve days and nights by the clergy, after which the body of Brian was deposited in a stone coffin, on the north side of the high altar, in the cathedral. Murrough was buried on the south side. Turlough was interred in the old churchyard of Kilmainham, where the shaft of an ancient cross still marks the site.

Malachy once more assumed the reigns of government by common consent, and proved himself fully equal to the task. A month before his death he gained an important victory over the Danes at Athboy, A.D. 1022. An interregnum of twenty years followed his death, during which the country was governed by two wise men, Cuan O'Lochlann, a poet, and Corcaan Cleireach, an anchoret. The circumstances attending Malachy's death are thus related by the Four Masters :—" The age of Christ 1022. Maelseachlainn Mór, pillar of the dignity and nobility of the west of the world, died in Croinis Locho-Aininn, in the seventy-third year of his age, on the 4th of the nones of September, on Sunday precisely, after intense penance for his sins and transgressions, after receiving the body of Christ and His blood, after being anointed by the hands of Amhalgaidh, successor of Patrick, for he and the successor of Colum-Cille, and the successor of Ciaran, and most of the seniors of Ireland were present [at his death], and they sung masses, hymns, psalms, and canticles for the welfare of his soul."

CHAPTER VIII.

Distinguished Irish Scholars—St. Breudan and St. Ita—St. Brendan visits America—St. Malachy and St. Bernard—St. Columbanus and St. Laurence O'Toole.

DOMESTIC wars were, as usual, productive of the worst consequences, as regards the social state of the country. The schools and colleges, which had been founded and richly endowed by the converted Irish, were now, without exception, plundered of their wealth, and, in many cases, deprived of those who had dispensed that wealth for the common good. It has been already shown that men lived holy lives, and died peaceful deaths, during the two hundred years of Danish oppression; we shall now find that schools were revived, monasteries repeopled, and missionaries sent to convert and instruct in foreign lands. A few monks from Ireland settled in Glastonbury early in the tenth century, where they devoted themselves to the instruction of youth. St. Dunstan, who was famous for his skill in music, was one of their most illustrious pupils; he was a scholar, an artist, and a musician. But English writers, who give him the credit of having brought "Englishmen to care once more for learning, after they had quite lost the taste for it, and had sunk back into ignorance and barbarism," forgot to mention who were his instructors.

Before the death of St. Patrick, Christianity had been firmly established in Ireland, and it is our greatest national honour that from the hour in which the Catholic faith was first taught in Ireland to the present day Irishmen have remained true to their religion. No matter what persecutions they suffered, they braved the storm; and we may believe this singular fact is due to the prayers of our great apostle, St. Patrick, who, we may be assured, watches over the land and the people of his adoption as tenderly and carefully, now as he did in the centuries after his entrance into the eternal reward of his labours.

Ireland was distinguished for her scholars and learned men after the Christian era as well as before it. So famous were those Irish schools and colleges, that the great nobles and lords of France and England sent their sons to be educated here. When shall such a glorious time come again for our native land? It could come, and it would come in a few short years, if Irishmen themselves willed it. In these matters no one can be our masters; our minds are free, and if we attain again the proud and enviable distinction of being a learned nation, it will be all the more to our credit, if we have many difficulties to encounter in attaining our end. Let Irishmen cultivate their own minds by reading good solid literature, and let them seek to have their children well educated; not by making them learn showy and useless accomplishments, but by placing them only at such schools and under such masters as shall give them instruction of real and permanent value for their after life.

I must again refer you to the *Illustrated History of Ireland*, if you wish for full information as to the learning of ancient Erinn; its customs; and the valuable old books which we still possess, which were written hundreds of years ago. But I must here find space for a few words about our Christian missionaries and the learned men who made Ireland famous after the time of St. Patrick.

St. Brendan was one of the most remarkable of our early saints. His early youth was passed under the care of St. Ita, a lady of the princely family of the Desii. By divine command she established the convent of *Cluain Credhuil*, in the present county of Limerick, and there, it would appear, she devoted herself specially to the care of youth. When Brendan had attained his fifth year, he was placed under the protection of Bishop Ercus, from whom he received such instruction as befitted his advancing years. But Brendan's tenderest affection clung to the gentle nurse of his infancy; and to her, in after years, he frequently returned, to give or receive counsel and sympathy.

The legend of his western voyage, if not the most important, is at least the most interesting part of his history. Kerry was the native home of the enterprising saint; and as he stood on its bold and beautiful shores, his naturally contemplative mind was led to inquire what boundaries chained that vast ocean, whose grand waters rolled in mighty waves beneath his feet. His thoughtful piety suggested that where there might be a country there might be life—human life and human souls dying day by day, and hour by hour, and knowing of no other existence than that which at best is full of sadness and decay.

Traditions of a far-away land had long existed on the western coast of ancient Erinn. The brave Tuatha Dé Dananns were singularly expert in naval affairs, and their descendants were by no means unwilling to impart information to the saint.

The venerable St. Enda, the first Abbot of Arran, was then living, and thither St. Brendan journeyed for counsel. Probably he was encouraged in his design by the holy abbot; for he proceeded along the coast of Mayo, inquiring as he went for traditions of the western continent. On his return to Kerry, he decided to set out on the important expedition. St. Brendan's Hill still bears his name; and from the bay at the foot of this lofty eminence he sailed for the "far west." Directing his course towards the south-west, with a few faithful companions, in a well-provisioned bark, he came, after some rough and dangerous navigation, to calm

ST. BRENDAN VISITS AMERICA. 119

seas, where, without aid of oar or sail, he was borne along for many weeks. It is probable that he had entered the great Gulf Stream, which brought his vessel ashore somewhere on the Virginian coasts. He landed with his companions, and penetrated into the interior, until he came to a large river flowing from east to west, supposed to be that now known as the Ohio. Thus, you will see that Ireland looked even in early ages towards America, and that it was probably visited by Irishmen long before its discovery by Columbus.

After many adventures, St. Brendan returned safely to his native land, where he died.

St. Columbanus was born about the year 539. The care of his education was confided to the venerable Senile, who was eminent for his sanctity and knowledge of the Holy Scriptures. It was probably through his influence that the young man resolved to devote himself to the monastic life. For this purpose he placed himself under the direction of St. Comgall, who then governed the great Monastery of Bangor (Banchorr).

It was not until he entered his fiftieth year that he decided on quitting his native land, so that there can be no reason to doubt that his high intellectual attainments were acquired and perfected in Ireland.

With the blessing of his superior, and the companionship of twelve faithful monks, he set forth on his arduous mission ; and arduous truly it proved to be.

In the year 1111 a synod was convened at Fidh Aengussa, or Aengus Grove, near the Hill of Uisneach, in Westmeath. It was attended by fifty bishops, 300 priests, and 3,000 religious. Murtough O'Brien was also permitted to be present, and some of the nobles of his province. The object of the synod was to institute rules of life and manners for the clergy and people. St. Celsus, the Archbishop of Armagh, and Maelmuire or Marianus O'Dunain Archbishop of Cashel, were present. Attention had already been directed to certain abuses in ecclesiastical discipline. Such abuses must always arise from time to time in the Church, through the frailty of her members.

St. Celsus appointed St. Malachy his successor in the Archiepiscopal See of Armagh. Malachy had been educated by the Abbot Imar O'Hagan, who presided over the great schools of that city; and the account given of his early training, sufficiently manifests the ability of his gifted instructor, and the high state of intellectual culture which existed in Ireland. While still young, St. Malachy undertook the restoration of the famous Abbey of Bangor. Here he erected a small oratory of wood, and joined himself to a few devoted men ardent for the perfection of a religious life. He was soon after elected Bishop of Connor. With the assistance of some of his faithful monks he restored what war and rapine had destroyed; and was proceeding peacefully and successfully in his noble

The Irish Patriot giving his Life to save St. Patrick.

work, when he was driven from his diocese by a hostile prince. He now fled to Cormac Mac Carthy, King of Desmond, but he was not permitted to remain here long. The See of Armagh was vacated by the death of St. Celsus, and Malachy was obliged to commence another arduous mission. It is said that it almost required threats of excommunication to induce him to undertake the charge. Bishop Gilbert of Limerick, the Apostolic-Delegate, and Bishop Malchus of Lismore, with other bishops, and several chieftains, visited him in the monastery which he had erected at Ibrach, and at last obtained compliance by promising him permission to retire when he had restored order in his new diocese.

St. Malachy was now appointed Bishop of Down, to which his old see of Connor was united. He had a long desire to visit Rome—a devotional pilgrimage to the men of Erinn from the earliest period. He was specially anxious to obtain a formal recognition of the archiepiscopal sees in Ireland, by the granting of palliums. On his way to the Holy City he visited St. Bernard at Clairvaux, and thus commenced and cemented the friendship which forms so interesting a feature in the lives of the French and Irish saints. It is probable that his account of the state of the Irish Church took a tinge of gloom from the heavy trials he had endured in his efforts to remove its temporary abuses. St. Bernard's ardent and impetuous character, even his very affectionateness, would lead him also to look darkly on the picture: hence the somewhat over-coloured accounts he has given of its state at that eventful period. St. Malachy returned to Ireland after an interview with the reigning Pontiff, Pope Innocent II. His Holiness had received him with open arms, and appointed him Apostolical Legate; but he declined to give the palliums, until they were formally demanded by the Irish prelates.

In virtue of his legatine power, the saint assembled local synods in several places. He rebuilt and restored many churches; and in 1142 he built the famous Cistercian Abbey of Mellifont, near Drogheda. This monastery was liberally endowed by O'Carroll, King of Oriel, and was peopled by Irish monks, whom St. Malachy had sent to Clairvaux, to be trained in the Benedictine rule and observances. But his great act was the convocation of the Synod of Inis Padraig. It was held in the year 1148. St. Malachy presided as Legate of the Holy See; fifteen bishops, two hundred priests, and some religious were present at the deliberations, which lasted for four days. The members of the Synod were unwilling that Malachy should leave Ireland again; but Eugene III., who had been a Cistercian monk, was visiting Clairvaux, and it was hoped he might grant the favour there. The Pope had left the abbey when the saint arrived, who, in a few days after, was seized with mortal sickness, and died on the 2nd November, 1148.

His remains were interred at Clairvaux. His feast was changed from the 2nd of November, All Souls, to the 3rd, by "the seniors," that he might be the more easily revered and honoured.

In 1162 St. Laurence O'Toole was chosen to succeed Greine, or Gregory, the Danish Archbishop of Dublin. He belonged to one of the most noble ancient families of Leinster. His father was chieftain of the district of Hy-Muirahy, a portion of the present county Kildare. St. Laurence had chosen the ecclesiastical state early in life; at the age of twenty-five he was chosen Abbot of St. Kevin's Monastery, at Glendalough. The Danish Bishop of Dublin had been consecrated by the Archbishop of Canterbury, but the saint received the episcopal office from the successor of St. Patrick. A synod was held at Clane the year of his consecration; it was attended by twenty-six prelates and many other ecclesiastics. The college of Armagh was then virtually raised to the rank of a University, as it was decreed that no one, who had not been an alumnus of Armagh, should be appointed lector or professor of theology in any of the diocesan schools in Ireland. Indeed, the clergy at this period were most active in promoting the interests of religion, and most successful in their efforts, little anticipating the storm which was then impending over their country.

CHAPTER IX.

The English Invasion under Henry II.—Treachery of Dermod—The Landing of Strongbow—Marriage of Eva and Strongbow—Siege of Dublin—Arrival of Henry II.—Treaty between Brien and Henry—Henry's rapacity—Insolence of his Courtiers.

WE have now arrived at one of the most important periods of Irish History; to understand it fully we must devote a few pages to the History of England. Although England and Ireland are divided by a narrow channel, which can now be crossed in a few hours, it must be remembered that there were no steam-packets, or swiftly sailing vessels at the time of which we write. It sometimes took several weeks for a vessel to sail from England to Ireland, and at all times the voyage was tedious and more or less dangerous. After the establishment of christianity in Ireland, many English nobles sent their sons to be educated in that country; but as the English were fully occupied with their own domestic wars, they had neither the ability nor inclination to attempt any conquest of Ireland. The Romans conquered and civilized the English, but when their power declined, the English were at war amongst themselves, and had neither time nor ability to make war on others. Until the year 1066 the Saxons had been the masters of England, but in that year they were conquered by the famous William of Normandy, a Norman prince, as his second title implies. He conquered the Saxon Harold at the battle of Hastings, and is known in history as William the Conqueror. The Norman kings continued to govern England for many centuries. The Normans were a brave and restless people, always eager for new conquests, and dividing their time between fighting and feasting. They were a more cultivated race than the Saxons, although they had certainly less solidity of character, and were more skilled in accomplishments than in solid learning. Irishmen often accuse the Saxons as being the cause of all their miseries, but this is a mistake. It was the Normans, not the Saxons, who oppressed and misgoverned Ireland for so many centuries. The term Saxon however was applied to all strangers in Ireland at the period of which we write, and hence the term Saxon became associated with the English race. The Norman kings had quite enough to do to hold their power in England, and to keep their Norman vassals in subjection, for over a hundred years after their conquest of England.

William Rufus, the third son of William the Conquerer, who commenced his reign in 1187, is reported to have said, as he stood on the rocks near St. David's, that he would make a bridge with his ships from that spot to Ireland—a haughty boast, not quite so easily accomplished. His speech was repeated to the King of Leinster who inquired "if the king, in his great threatening, had added, 'if it so please God'?" The reporter replied in the negative. "Then," said he, "seeing this king put teth his trust only in man, and not in God, I fear not his coming." And so the matter ended. But this incident shows that the English kings were only biding their time, and waiting a favourable opportunity to attempt the conquest of Ireland.

After the death of William Rufus, the English were occupied with domestic wars. In the year 1154 Henry II. was crowned King of England, and as that nation was then at peace he naturally turned his thoughts to the long wished for invasion of Ireland. It must be remembered, however, that he might never have attempted this invasion but for the base treachery of an Irishman. The traitor's name was Dermod. He was King of Leinster, but the other kings of Ireland drove him out of the country for his infamous conduct in carrying off the wife of O'Rourke, lord of Breffny. The traitor at once set out for Aquitaine, where Henry then was, and declared himself a vassal of that prince. Dermod's sole object was to secure his dominions in Ireland; the English king was not slow to perceive the advantage he might gain by the traitor's conduct, and who can blame him? He at once wrote a letter declaring that he had taken Dermod under his protection, and authorising all his subjects English, Norman, Welsh, and Scotch, to assist in reinstating him in the kingdom from which he had been so deservedly expelled.

For some time Dermod failed in his efforts to obtain assistance. After some fruitless negociations with the needy and lawless adventurers who thronged the port of Bristol, he applied to the Earl of Pembroke, Richard de Clare. This nobleman had obtained the name of Strongbow, by which he is more generally known, from his skill in archery. Two other young men of rank joined the party; they were sons of the beautiful and infamous Nesta, once the mistress of Henry I., but now the wife of Gerald, Governor of Pembroke and Lord of Carew. The knights were Maurice FitzGerald and Robert FitzStephen. Dermod had promised them the city of Wexford and two cantreds of land as their reward. Strongbow was to succeed him on the throne of Leinster, and to receive the hand of his young and beautiful daughter, Eva, in marriage.

There is considerable uncertainty as to the real date and the precise circumstances of Dermod's arrival in Ireland. According to one account, he returned at the close of the year 1168, and concealed himself during the winter in a monastery of Augustinian Canons at Ferns, which he had founded. The two principal authorities are Giraldus Cambrensis and Maurice Regan; the latter was Dermod Mac Murrough's secretary. According to his account, Robert FitzStephen landed at Bannow, near Waterford, in May, 1169, with an army of three hundred archers, thirty knights, and sixty men-at-arms. A second detachment arrived the next day, headed by Maurice de Prendergast, a Welsh gentleman, with ten knights and sixty archers. Dermod at once assembled his men, and joined his allies. He could only muster five hundred followers; but with their united forces, such as they were, the outlawed king and the needy adventurers laid siege to the city of Wexford. The brave inhabitants of this mercantile town at once set forth to meet them; but fearing the result if attacked in open field by well-disciplined troops, they fired the suburbs, and entrenched themselves in the town. Next morning the assaulting party prepared for a renewal of hostilities, but the clergy of Wexford advised an effort for peace: terms of capitulation were negotiated, and Dermod was obliged to pardon, when he would probably have preferred to massacre. It is said that FitzStephen burned his little fleet, to show his followers that they must conquer or die. Two cantreds of land, comprising the present baronies of Forth and Bargy, were bestowed on him: and thus was established the first English colony in Ireland. The Irish princes and chieftains appear to have regarded the whole affair with silent contempt. The Annals say they "set nothing by the Flemings;" practically, they set nothing by any of the invaders. Could they have foreseen, even for one moment, the consequences of their indifference, we cannot doubt but that they would have acted in a very different manner. Roderic, the reigning monarch, was not the man either to foresee danger, or to meet it when foreseen; though we might pardon even a more sharp-sighted and vigilant warrior, for overlooking the possible consequence of the invasion of a few mercenary troops, whose only object appeared to be the reinstatement of a petty king. Probably, the troops and their captains were equally free from suspecting what would be the real result of their proceedings.

The fair of Telltown was celebrated about this time; and from the accounts given by the Annals of the concourse of people, and the number of horsemen who attended it, there can be little doubt that Ireland was seldom in a better position to resist foreign invasion. But unity of purpose and a competent leader were wanted then, as they have been wanted but too often since. Finding so little opposition to his plans, Mac Murrough determined to act on the offensive. He was now at the head of 3,000 men. With this force he marched into the adjoining territory of Ossory, and made war on its chief, Donough FitzPatrick; and after a brave but unsuccessful resistence, it submitted to his rule. The Irish monarch was at length aroused to some degree of apprehension. He summoned a hosting of the men of Ireland at Tara; and with the army thus collected, assisted by the Lords of Meath, Oriel, Ulidia, Breffni, and some northern chieftains,

he at once proceeded to Dublin. Dermod was
alarmed, and retired to Ferns. Roderic pursued
him thither. But dissension had already broken
out in the Irish camp: the Ulster chiefs returned
home; the contingent was weakened; and, either
through fear, or from the natural indolence of his
pacific disposition, he agreed to acknowledge Mac
Murrough's authority. Mac Murrough gave his
son Cormac as hostage for the fulfilment of the
treaty. A private agreement was entered into
between the two kings, in which Dermod pledged
himself to dismiss his foreign allies as soon as
possible, and to bring no more strangers into the
country. It is more than probable that he had
not the remotest idea of fulfilling his promise; it
is at least certain that he broke it the first moment
it was his interest to do so. Dermod's object
was simply to gain time, and in this he succeeded.

Maurice FitzGerald arrived at Wexford a few
days after, and the recreant king at once proceeded
to meet him; and with this addition to his army,
marched to attack Dublin. The Dano-Celts, who
inhabited this city, had been so cruelly treated by
him, that they dreaded a repetition of his former
tyrannies. They had elected a governor for themselves; but resistance was useless. After a brief
struggle, they were obliged to sue for peace—a
favour which probably would not have been granted
without further massacres and burnings, had not

Dermod wished to bring his arms to bear in another quarter.

Donnell O'Brien, Prince of Thomond, who had married a daughter of Dermod's, had just rebelled against Roderic, and the former was but too willing to assist him in his attempt. Thus encouraged where he should have been treated with contempt, and hunted down with ignominy, his ambition became boundless. He played out the favourite game of traitors; and no doubt hoped, when he had consolidated his own power, that he could easily expel his foreign allies. Strongbow had not yet arrived, though the winds had been long enough "at east and easterly." His appearance was still delayed. The fact was, that the Earl was in a critical position. Henry and his barons were never on the most amiable terms; and there were some very special reasons why Strongbow should prove no exception to the rule.

The first member of the Earl's family who had settled in England was Richard, son of the Norman Earl Brien, a direct descendant of Robert "the Devil," Duke of Normandy, father of William the Conqueror. In return for services at the battle of Hastings, and general assistance in conquering the Saxon, this family obtained a large grant of land in England, and took the title of Earl of Clare from one of their ninety-five lordships in Suffolk. The Strongbow family appears to have inherited a passion for making raids on neighbouring lands, from their Viking ancestors. Strongbow's father had obtained his title of Earl Pembroke, and his property in the present county of that name, from his successful marauding expedition in Wales, in 1138. But as he revolted against Stephen, his lands were seized by that king; and after his death in 1148, his son succeeded to his very numerous titles, without any property commensurate thereto. Richard was not in favour with his royal master, who probably was jealous of the Earl, despite his poverty; but as Strongbow did not wish to lose the little he had in England, or the chance of obtaining more in Ireland, he proceeded at once to the court, then held in Normandy, and asked permission for his new enterprise. Henry's reply was so carefully worded, he could declare afterwards that he either had or had not given the permission, whichever version of the interview might eventually prove most convenient to the royal interests. Strongbow took the interpretation which suited his own views, and proceeded to the scene of action with as little delay as possible. He arrived in Ireland, according to the most generally received account, on the vigil of St. Bartholomew, A.D. 1170, and landed at Dundonnell, near Waterford. His uncle, Hervey de Montmarisco, had already arrived, and established himself in a temporary fort, where he had been attacked by the brave citizens of Wexford. But the besieged maintained their position, killed five hundred men, and made prisoners of seventy of the principal citizens of Waterford. Large sums of money were offered for their ransom, but in vain. They were brutally murdered by the English soldiers, who first broke their limbs, and then hurled them from a precipice into the sea. It was the first instalment of the utterly futile theory, so often put in practice since that day, of "striking terror into the Irish;" and the experiment was quite as unsuccessful as all such experiments have ever been.

While these cruelties were enacting, Strongbow had been collecting forces in South Wales; but, as he was on the very eve of departure, he received a peremptory order from Henry, forbidding him to leave the kingdom. After a brief hesitation he determined to bid defiance to the royal mandate, and set sail for Ireland. The day after his arrival he laid siege to Waterford. The citizens behaved like heroes, and twice repulsed their assailants; but their bravery could not save them in the face of overpowering numbers. A breach was made in the wall; the besiegers poured in; and a merciless massacre followed. Dermod arrived while the conflict was at its height, and for once he has the credit of interfering on the side of mercy. Reginald, a Danish lord, and O'Phelan, Prince of Deisi, were about to be slain by their captors, but at his request they were spared, and the general carnage was suspended. For the sake of common humanity one could wish to think that this was an act of mercy. But Mac Murrough had his daughter Eva with him; he wished to have her nuptials with Strongbow celebrated at once; and he could scarcely accomplish his purpose while men were slaying their fellows in a cold-blooded massacre. The following day the nuptials were performed. The English Earl, a widower, and long past the prime of manhood, was wedded to the fair young Celtic maiden; and the marriage procession passed lightly over the bleeding bodies of the dying and the dead. Thus commenced the union between Great Britain and Ireland : must those nuptials be for ever celebrated in tears and blood !

Immediately after the ceremony, the army set out for Dublin. Roderic had collected a large force near Clondalkin, and Hosculf, the Danish governor of the city, encouraged by their presence, had once more revolted against Dermod. The English army having learned that the woods and defiles between Wexford and Dublin were well guarded, had made forced marches along the mountains, and succeeded in reaching the capital long before they were expected. Their decision and military skill alarmed the inhabitants—they might also have heard of the massacres at Wexford; be this as it may, they determined to negotiate for peace, and commissioned their illustrious Archbishop, St. Laurence O'Toole, to make terms with Dermod. While the discussion was pending, two of the English leaders,

Raymund *le Gros* and Miles de Cogan, obtained an entrance into the city, and commenced a merciless butchery of the inhabitants. When the saint returned he heard cries of misery and groans of agony in all quarters, and it was not without difficulty that he succeeded in appeasing the fury of the soldiers, and the rage of the people who had been so basely treated.

The Four Masters accuse the people of Dublin of having attempted to purchase their own safety at the expense of the national interests, and say that " a miracle was wrought against them," as a judgment for their selfishness. Hosculf, the Danish governor, fled to the Orkneys, with some of the principal citizens, and Roderic withdrew his forces to Meath, to support O'Rourke, on whom he had bestowed a portion of that territory. Miles de Cogan was invested with the government of Dublin, and Dermod marched to Meath, to attack Roderic and O'Rourke, against whom he had an old grudge of the worst and bitterest kind. He had injured him by carrying off his wife, Dervorgil, and men generally hate most bitterly those whom they have injured most cruelly.

Meanwhile MacCarthy of Desmond had attacked and defeated the English garrison at Waterford, but without any advantageous results. Roderic's weakness now led him to perpetrate an act of cruelty, although it could scarcely be called unjust according to the ideas of the times. It will be remembered that he had received hostages from Dermod for the treaty of Ferns. That treaty had been openly violated, and the King sent ambassadors to him to demand its fulfilment, by the withdrawal of the English troops, threatening, in case of refusal, to put the hostages to death. Dermod laughed at the threat. Under any circumstances he was not a man who would hesitate to sacrifice his own flesh and blood to his ambition. Roderic was as good as his word; and the three royal hostages were put to death at Athlone.

In 1171 Dermod Mac Murrough, the author of so many miseries, and the object of so much just reprobation, died at Ferns, on the 4th of May. His miserable end was naturally considered a judgment for his evil life. His obituary is thus recorded: " Diarmaid Mac Murchadha, King of Leinster, by whom a trembling soil was made of all Ireland, after having brought over the Saxons, after having done extensive injuries to the Irish, after plundering and burning many churches, as Ceanannus, Cluain-Iraired, &c., died before the end of a year [after this plundering], of an insufferable and unknown disease; for he became putrid while living, through the miracle of God, Columcille, and Finnen, and the other saints of Ireland, whose churches he had profaned and burned some time before; and he died at Fearnamore, without [making] a will, without penance, without the

THE TRAITOR'S WORK ACCOMPLISHED.

body of Christ, without unction, as his evil deeds deserved."

But the death of the traitor could not undo the traitor's work. Men's evil deeds live after them, however they may repent them on their deathbeds. Strongbow had himself at once proclaimed King of Leinster—his marriage with Eva was the ground of his claim; but though such a mode of succession might hold good in Normandy, it was perfectly illegal in Ireland. The question, however, was not one of right but of might, and it was settled as all such questions invariably are. But Strongbow had a master on the other side of the Channel who had his own views of these complications. His tenure, however, was somewhat precarious. His barons, always turbulent, had now a new ground for aggression, in the weakness to which he had exposed himself by his virtual sanction of the murder of St. Thomas of Canterbury, and he was fain to content himself with a strong injunction commanding all his English subjects then in Ireland to return immediately, and forbidding any further reinforcements to be sent to that country. Strongbow was alarmed, and at once despatched Raymond *le Gros* with apologies and explanations, offering the King all the lands he had acquired in Ireland. Henry does not appear to have taken the slightest notice of these communications, and the Earl determined to risk his displeasure, and remain in Ireland.

His prospects, however, were by no means promising. His Irish adherents forsook him on the death of Dermod; Dublin was besieged by a Scandinavian force, which Hosculf had collected in the Orkneys, and which was conveyed in sixty vessels, under the command of Johan *le Déve* (the Furious). Miles de Cogan repulsed this formidable attack successfully, and captured the leaders. Hosculf was put to death; but he appears to have brought his fate on himself by a proud and incautious boast.

At this period the thoughtful and disinterested Archbishop of Dublin saw a crisis in the history of his country on which much depended. He endeavoured to unite the national chieftains, and rally the national army. His words appeared to have had some effect. Messengers were sent to ask assistance from Godfred, King of the Isle of Man, and other island warriors. Strongbow became aware of his danger, and threw himself into Dublin; but he soon found himself landlocked by an army, and enclosed at sea by a fleet. Roderic O'Connor commanded the national forces, supported by Tiernan O'Rourke and Murrough O'Carroll. St. Laurence O'Toole remained in the camp, and strove to animate the men by his exhortations and example. The Irish army contented themselves with a blockade, and the besieged were soon reduced to extremities from want of food. Strongbow offered terms of capitulation through the Archbishop, proposing to hold the kingdom of Leinster as Roderic's vassal; but the Irish monarch demanded the surrender of the towns of Dublin, Wexford, and Waterford, and required the English invaders to leave the country by a certain day.

While these negotiations were pending, Donnell Cavanagh, son of the late King of Leinster, got into the city in disguise, and informed Strongbow that FitzStephen was closely besieged in Wexford. It was then at once determined to force a passage through the Irish army. Raymond *le Gros* led the van, Miles de Cogan followed; Strongbow, and Maurice FitzGerald, who had proposed the sortie, with the remainder of their force, brought up the rear. The Irish army were totally unprepared for this sudden move ; they fled in panic, and Roderic, who was bathing in the Liffey, escaped with difficulty.

Strongbow again committed the government of Dublin to Miles de Cogan, and set out for Wexford. On his way thither he was opposed by O'Regan, Prince of Idrone; an action ensued, which might have terminated fatally for the army, had not the Irish prince received his death-wound from an English archer. His troops took to flight, and Strongbow proceeded on his journey. But he arrived too late. Messengers met him on the way, to inform him that the fort of Carrig had fallen into the hands of the Irish, who are said to have practised an unjustifiable stratagem to obtain possession of the place. As usual there are two versions of the story. One of these versions, which appears not improbable, is that the besieged had heard a false report of the affair in Dublin; and believing Strongbow and the English army to have been overthrown, they surrendered on the promise of being sent in safety to Dublin. On their surrender, the conditions were violated, FitzStephen was imprisoned, and some of his followers killed. The charge against the besiegers is that they invented the report as a stratagem to obtain their ends, and that the falsehood was confirmed in a solemn manner by the bishops of Wexford and Kildare.

As soon as the Wexford men had heard of Strongbow's approach, they set fire to the town, and fled to Beg-Erin, a stockaded island, at the same time sending him a message, that, if he attempted to approach, they would kill all their prisoners. The Earl withdrew to Waterford in consequence of this threat, and here he learned that his presence was indispensable in England; he therefore set off at once to plead his own cause with his royal master. A third attack had been made on Dublin in the meantime by the Lord of Breffni, but it was repulsed by Miles. With this exception, the Irish made no attempt against the common enemy, and domestic wars were as frequent as usual.

Henry had returned to England, and was now in Newenham, in Gloucestershire, making active preparations for his visit to Ireland. The odium into which he had fallen, after his complicity in the murder of St. Thomas of Canterbury, had rendered his position perilous in the extreme; and probably his Irish expedition would never have been undertaken, had he not required some such object to turn his thoughts and the thoughts of his subjects from the consequences of his crime. He received Strongbow coldly, and at first refused him an interview. After a proper delay, he graciously accepted the Earl's offer of "all the lands he had won in Ireland"—a very questionable gift, considering that there was not an inch of ground there which he could securely call his own. Henry, however, was pleased to restore his English estates; but, with consummate hypocrisy and villany, he seized the castles of the Welsh lords, whom he hated for their vigorous and patriotic opposition, and punished them for allowing the expedition, which he had just sanctioned, to sail from their coasts unmolested.

Henry landed in Ireland on the 18th of October, 1171, at Crook, in the county of Waterford. He was accompanied by Strongbow, William Fitz-Aldelm, Humphrey de Bohun, Hugh de Lacy, Robert Fitz-Barnard, and many other lords. His whole force, which, according to the most authentic English accounts, was distributed in four hundred ships, consisted of 500 knights, and 4,000 men-at-arms. It would appear the Irish had not the least idea that he intended to claim the kingdom as his own, and rather looked upon him as a powerful potentate, who had come to assist the native administration of justice. Even had they suspected his real object, no opposition might have been made to it. The nation had suffered much from domestic dissension; it had yet to learn that foreign oppression was an incomparably greater evil.

MacCarthy of Desmond was the first Irish prince who paid homage to the English king. At Cashel, Donnell O'Brien, King of Thomond, swore fealty, and surrendered the city of Limerick. Other princes followed their example. The "pomp and circumstance" of the royal court, attracted the admiration of a people naturally defferential to authority; the condescension and apparent disinterestedness of the monarch, won the hearts of an impulsive and affectionate race. They had been accustomed to an Ard-Righ, a chief monarch, who, in name at least, ruled all the lesser potentates: why should not Henry be such to them? and why should they suppose that he would exercise a tyranny as yet unknown in the island?

The northern princes still held aloof; but Roderic had received Henry's ambassadors personally, and paid the usual deference which one king owed to another who was considered more powerful. Henry determined to spend his Christmas in Dublin, and resolved on a special display of royal state. His grey bloodshot eyes and tremulous voice, were neither knightly nor kingly qualifications; his savage and ungovernable temper made him appear at times rather like a demon than a man. He was charged with having violated the most solemn oaths when it suited his convenience. A cardinal had pronounced him an audacious liar. Count Thiebault of Champagne had warned an archbishop not to rely on any of his promises, however sacredly made. He and his sons spent their time quarrelling with their subjects. His eldest son, Richard, thus graphically sketched the family characteristics: —" The custom in our family is that the son shall hate the father; our destiny is to detest each other; from the devil we came, to the devil we shall go." And the head of this family had now come to reform the Irish, and to improve their condition—social, secular, and ecclesiastical !

When the Christmas festivities had passed, Henry turned his attention to business, if, indeed, the same festivities had not also been a part of his diplomatic plans, for he was not deficient in kingcraft. In a synod at Cashel he attempted to settle ecclesiastical affairs. In a *Curia Regis*, held at Lismore, he imagined he had arranged temporal affairs. These are subjects which demand our best consideration. It is an historical fact, that the Popes claimed and exercised great temporal power in the Middle Ages; it is admitted also that they used this power in the main for the general good; and that, as monks and friars were the preservers of

K

literature, so Popes and bishops were the protectors of the rights of nations, as far as was possible in such turbulent times. It does not belong to our present subject to theorize on the origin or the grounds of this power; it is sufficient to say that it had been exercised repeatedly both before and after Adrian granted the famous Bull, by which he conferred the kingdom of Ireland on Henry II. The Merovingian dynasty was changed on the decision of Pope Zachary. Pope Adrian threatened Frederick I., that if he did not renounce all pretensions to ecclesiastical property in Lombardy, he should forfeit the crown "received from himself, and through his unction." When Pope Innocent III. pronounced sentence of deposition against Lackland in 1211, and conferred the kingdom of England on Philip Augustus, the latter instantly prepared to assert his claim, though he had no manner of title, except the Papal grant. In fact, at the very moment when Henry was claiming the Irish crown in right of Adrian's Bull, given some years previously, he was in no small trepidation at the possible prospect of losing his English dominions, as an excommunication and an interdict were even then hanging over his head.

It has been already shown that the possession of Ireland was coveted at an early period by the Norman rulers of Great Britain. When Henry II. ascended the throne in 1154, he probably intended to take the matter in hands at once. An Englishman, Adrian IV., filled the Papal chair. The English monarch would naturally find him favourable to his own country. John of Salisbury, then chaplain to the Archbishop of Canterbury, was commissioned to request the favour. No doubt he represented his master as very zealous for the interests of religion, and made it appear that his sole motive was the good, temporal and spiritual, of the barbarous Irish; at least this is plainly implied in Adrian's bull. The Pope could have no motive except that which he expressed in the document itself. He had been led to believe that the state of Ireland was deplorable; he naturally hoped that a wise and good government would restore what was amiss. There is no doubt that there was much which required amendment, and no one was more conscious of this, or strove more earnestly to effect it, than the saintly prelate who governed the archiepiscopal see of Dublin. The Irish clergy had already made the most zealous efforts to remedy whatever needed correction; but it was an age of lawless violence. Reform was quite as much wanted both in England and in the Italian States; but Ireland had the additional disadvantage of having undergone three centuries of ruthless plunder and desecration of her churches and shrines, and the result told fearfully on that land which had once been the home of saints.

Dublin was now made over to the inhabitants of Bristol. Hugh de Lacy, its governor, has been generally considered in point of fact the first Viceroy for Ireland. He was installed in the Norman fashion, and the sword and cap of maintenance were made the insignia of the dignity. Waterford and Wexford were also bestowed on royal favourites, or on such knights as were supposed most likely to hold them for the crown. Castles were erected throughout the country, which was portioned out among Henry's needy followers; and, for the first time in Ireland, a man was called a rebel if he presumed to consider his house or lands as his own property.

In 1179 several Irish bishops were summoned by Alexander III. to attend the third General Council of Lateran. These prelates were St. Laurence of Dublin, O'Duffy of Tuam, O'Brien of Killaloe, Felix of Lismore, Augustine of Waterford, and Brictius of Limerick. Usher says several other bishops were summoned; it is probable they were unable to leave the country, and hence that their names have not been given. The real state of the Irish Church was then made known to the Holy See; no living man could have described it more accurately and truthfully than the sainted prelate who had sacrificed himself for so many years for its good. Even as the bishops passed through England, the royal jealousy sought to fetter them with new restrictions; and they were obliged to take an oath that they would not sanction any infringements on Henry's prerogatives. St. Malachy was now appointed Legate by the Pope, with jurisdiction over the five suffragans, and the possessions attached to his see were confirmed to him. As the bull was directed to Ireland, it would appear that he returned there; but his stay was brief, and the interval was occupied in endeavouring to repress the vices of the Anglo-Norman and Welsh clergy, many of whom were doing serious injury to the Irish Church by their immoral and dissolute lives.

Henry now became jealous of the Archbishop, and perhaps was not overpleased at his efforts to reform these ecclesiastics. Roderic O'Connor had asked St. Laurence to undertake a mission on his behalf to the English court; but the King refused to listen to him, and forbid him to return to Ireland. After a few weeks' residence at the Monastery of Abingdon, in Berkshire, the saint set out for France. He fell ill on his journey, in a religious house at Eu, where his remains are still preserved. When on his deathbed, the monks asked him to make his will; but he exclaimed, "God knows that out of all my revenues I have not a single coin to bequeath." With the humility of true sanctity, he was heard frequently calling on God for mercy, and using the words of the Psalmist, so familiar to ecclesiastics, from their constant perusal of the Holy Scriptures. As he was near his end, he was heard exclaiming, in his own beautiful mother-tongue: "Foolish people, what will become of you? Who will relieve you? Who will heal you?" And well might his paternal heart ache for those who were soon to be left doubly orphans, and for the beloved nation whose sorrows he had so often striven to alleviate.

St. Laurence went to his eternal reward on the 14th of November, 1180. His obsequies were celebrated with great pomp and solemnity, and attended by the Scotch Legate, Alexis, an immense concourse of clergy, and many knights and nobles. His remains were exposed for some days in the church of Notre Dame, at Eu.

Prince John, now preparing for his visit to Ireland, and his singular and unfelicitous attempt at royalty; it would appear that he wished to decline both the honour and the expedition; for, as he was on the eve of his departure, Eraclius, Patriarch of Jerusalem, arrived in England, to enjoin the fulfilment of the king's vow to undertake a crusade to Palestine. As Henry had got out of his difficulties, he declined to fulfil his solemn engagement, and refused permission to his son John, who threw himself at his father's feet, and implored leave to be his substitute. Eraclius then poured forth his indignation upon Henry, with all the energetic freedom of the age. He informed him that God would punish his impieties—that he was worse than any Saracen; and hinted that he might have inherited his wickedness from his grandmother, the Countess of Anjou, who was reported to be a witch, and of whom it was said that she had flown through the window during the most solemn part of Mass, though four squires attempted to hold her.

John sailed from Milford Haven on the evening of Easter Wednesday, 1185. He landed with his troops at Waterford, at noon, on the following day. His retinue is described as of unusual splendour, and, no doubt, was specially appointed to impress the "barbarous" Irish. Gerald Barry, the famous Cambrensis, who had arrived in Ireland some little time before, was appointed his tutor, in conjunction with Ranulf de Glanville. The bitter prejudices of the former against Ireland and the Irish is a matter of history, as well as the indefatigable zeal of the latter in pursuit of his own interests at the expense of justice.

A retinue of profligate Normans completed the court, whom an English authority describes as "great quaffers, lourdens, proud, belly swaines, fed with extortion and bribery." The Irish were looked upon by these worthies as a savage race, only created to be plundered and scoffed at. The Normans prided themselves on their style of dress, and, no doubt, the Irish costume surprised them. Common prudence, however, might have taught them, when the Leinster chieftains came to pay their respects to the young Prince, that they should not add insult to injury; for, not content with open ridicule, they proceeded to pull the beards of the chieftains, and to gibe their method of wearing their hair.

De Lacy has the credit of having done his utmost to render the Prince's visit a failure. But his efforts were not necessary. The insolence of the courtiers, and the folly of the youth himself, were quite sufficient to ruin more promising prospects. In addition to other outrages, the Irish had seen their few remaining estates bestowed on the new comers; and even the older Anglo-Norman and Welsh settlers were expelled to make room for the Prince's favourites—an instalment of the fatal policy which made them eventually "more Irish than the Irish." When the colony was on the verge of ruin, the young Prince returned to England. He threw the blame of his failure on Hugh de Lacy; but the Norman knight did not live long enough after to suffer from the accusation. De Lacy was killed while inspecting a castle which he had just built on the site of St. Columkille's Monastery at Durrow, in the Queen's County. He was accompanied by three Englishmen; as he was in the act of stooping, a youth of an ancient and noble family, named O'Meyey, gave him his deathblow, severed his head from his body, and then fled with such swiftness as to elude pursuit. It is said that he was instigated to perform this deed by Sumagh O'Caharnay (the Fox), with whom he now took refuge.

CHAPTER X.

The English Settlers quarrel with each other—Scandalous Conduct of the Viceroys sent to govern Ireland by the English Kings—The Burkes and Geraldines—The Statute of Kilkenny, and its effects.

IN 1189 Henry II. died at Chinon, in Normandy. He expired launching anathemas against his sons, and especially against John, as he had just discovered that he had joined those who conspired against him. In his last moments he was stripped of his garments and jewels, and left naked and neglected.

Richard I., who succeeded to the throne, was too much occupied about foreign affairs to attend to his own kingdom. He was a brave soldier, and as such merits our respect; but he can scarcely be credited as a wise king. Irish affairs were committed to the care of John, who does not appear to have profited by his former experience. He appointed Hugh de Lacy Lord Justice, to the no small disgust of John de Courcy; but it was little matter to whom the government of that unfortunate country was confided. There were nice distinctions made about titles; for John, even when King of England, did not attempt to write himself king of Ireland. But there were no nice distinctions about property; for the rule seemed to be, that whoever could get it should have it, and whoever could keep it should possess it.

The great difference between the conduct of ecclesiastics who have no family but the Church, and no interests but the interests of religion, is very observable in all history. While English and Norman soldiers were recklessly destroying church property and domestic habitations in the country they had invaded, we find, with few exceptions, that the ecclesiastic, of whatever nation, is the friend and father of the people, wherever his lot may be cast. The English Archbishop resented the wrongs of the Irish Church as personal injuries, and devoted himself to its advancement as a personal interest. We are indebted to Archbishop Comyn for building St. Patrick's Cathedral in Dublin, as well as for his steady efforts to promote the welfare of the nation. After an appeal in person to King Richard and Prince John, he was placed in confinement in Normandy, and was only released by the interference of the Holy See; but Innocent III. had probably by this time discovered that the English monarchs were not exactly the persons to reform the Irish

King John was soon obliged to interfere between his English barons in Ireland, who appear to have been quite as much occupied with feuds among themselves as the native princes. In 1201 Philip of Worcester and William de Braose laid waste the greater part of Munster in their quarrels. John Walter to the latter, for four thousand marks—

The Irish Patriot Lady promoting Religion and Literature.

had sold the lands of the former and of Theobald Walter redeemed his property for five hundred marks; Philip obtained his at the point of the sword. De Braose had large property both in Normandy and in England. He had his chancellor, chancery, and seal, recognizances of all pleas, not even excepting those of the crown, with judgment of life and limb. His sons and daughters had married into powerful families. His wife, Matilda, was notable in domestic affairs, and a vigorous oppressor of the Welsh. A bloody war was waged about the same time between De Lacy, De Marisco, and the Lord Justice. Cathal Crovderg and O'Brien aided the latter in besieging Limerick, while some of the English fortified themselves in their castles, and plundered indiscriminately.

In 1205 the Earldom of Ulster was granted to Hugh de Lacy. The grant is inscribed on the charter roll of the seventh year of King John, and is the earliest record, now extant, of the creation of an Anglo-Norman dignity in Ireland. England was placed under an interdict in 1207, in consequence of the violence and wickedness of its sovereign. He procured the election of John de Grey to the see of Canterbury, a royal favourite, and, if only for this reason, unworthy of the office. Another party who had a share in the election chose Reginald, the sub-prior of the monks at Canterbury. But when the choice was submitted to Pope Innocent III., he rejected both candidates, and fixed on an English Cardinal, Stephen Langton, who was at once elected, and received consecration from the Pope himself. John was highly indignant, as might be expected. He swore his favourite oath, "by God's teeth," that he would cut off the noses and pluck out the eyes of any priest who attempted to carry the Pope's decrees against him into England. But some of the bishops, true to their God and the Church, promulgated the interdict, and then fled to France to escape the royal vengeance. It was well for them they did so; for Geoffrey, Archdeacon of Norwich, was seized, and enveloped, by the royal order, in a sacerdotal vestment of massive lead, and thus thrown into prison, where he was starved to death beneath the crushing weight. We sometimes hear of the cruelties of the Inquisition, of the barbarity of the Irish, of the tyranny of priestcraft; but such cruelties, barbarities, and tyrannies, however highly painted, pale before the savage vengeance which English kings have exercised, on the slightest provocation, towards their unfortunate subjects. But we have not yet heard all the refinements of cruelty which this same monarch exercised. Soon after, John was excommunicated personally. When he found that Philip of France was prepared to seize his kingdom, and that his crimes had so alienated him from his own people that he could hope for little help from them, he cringed with the craven fear so usually found in cruel men, and made the most abject submission. In the interval between the proclamation of the interdict and the fulmination of the sentence of excommunication (A.D. 1210), John visited Ireland. It may be supposed his arrival could not excite much pleasure in the hearts of his Irish subjects, though, no doubt, he thought it a mark of disloyalty that he should not be welcomed with acclamations. A quarter of a century had elapsed since he first set his foot on Irish ground. He had grown grey in profligacy, but he had not grown wiser or better with advancing years.

The year before his arrival, Dublin had been desolated by a pestilence, and a number of people from Bristol had taken advantage of the decrease in the population to establish themselves there. On the Easter Monday after their arrival, when they had assembled to amuse themselves in Cullen's Wood, the O'Byrnes and O'Tooles rushed down upon them from the Wicklow Mountains, and took a terrible vengeance for the many wrongs they had suffered, by a massacre of some three hundred men. The citizens of Bristol sent over new colonists; but the anniversary of the day was long known as Black Monday.

Henry III, succeeded his father, John, while only in his tenth year, William Marshal, Earl of Pembroke, was appointed protector of the kingdom and the king. The young monarch was hastily crowned at Bristol, with one of his mother's golden bracelets.

In 1217 he, or rather his advisers, sent the Archbishop of Dublin to that city to levy a "tallage" or tax for the royal benefit. The Archbishop and the Justiciary were directed to represent to the "Kings of Ireland," and the barons holding directly from the crown, that their liberality would not be forgotten; but neither the politeness of the address nor the benevolence of the promise was practically appreciated, probably because neither was believed to be sincere, and the King's coffers were not much replenished.

Arrangements were now made defining the powers of the Viceroy or Justiciary. The earliest details on this subject are embodied in an agreement between Henry III. and Geoffrey de Marisco, sealed at Oxford, in March, 1220, in presence of the Papal Legate, the Archbishop of Dublin, and many of the nobility.

By these regulations the Justiciary was bound to account in the Exchequer of Dublin for all taxes and aids received in Ireland for the royal purse. He was to defray all expenses for the maintenance of the King's castles and lands out of the revenues. In fact, the people of the country were taxed, either directly or indirectly, for the support of the invaders. The King's castles were to be kept by loyal and proper constables, who were obliged to give hostages. Indeed, so little faith had the English Kings in the loyalty of their own subjects that the Justiciary himself was obliged to give a hostage as security for his own behaviour. Neither does the same viceroy appear to have benefited trade, for he is accused of exacting wine, clothing, and victuals, without payment, from the merchants of Dublin. In 1221, the Archbishop of Dublin, Henry de Londres, was made Governor. He obtained the name of "Scotch Villain,"' from having cast into the fire the leases of the tenants of his see, whom he had cited to produce these documents in his court. The enraged land-holders attacked the attendants, and laid hands on the Archbishop, who was compelled to do them justice from fear of personal violence. When such was the mode of government adopted by the English officials, we can scarcely wonder that the people of Ireland have not inherited very ardent feelings of loyalty and devotion to the crown and constitution of that country.

Such serious complaints were made of the unjust Governor, that Henry was at last obliged to check his rapacity. Probably, he was all the more willing to do so, in consequence of some encroachments on the royal prerogative.

After the death of the Earl of Pembroke, who had obtained the pardon of Hugh de Lacy, a feud arose between the latter and the son of his former friend. In consequence of this quarrel, all Meath was ravaged, Hugh O'Neill having joined De Lacy in the conflict.

Some of the Irish chieftains now tried to obtain

protection from the rapacity of the Anglo-Norman barons, by paying an annual stipend to the crown: but the crown, though graciously pleased to accept anything which might be offered, still held to its royal prerogative of disposing of Irish property as appeared most convenient to royal interests. Though Cathal Crovderg had made arrangements with Henry III, at an immense sacrifice, to secure his property, that monarch accepted his money, but, nevertheless, bestowed the whole province of Connaught shortly after on Richard de Burgo.

For the next ten years the history of the country is the history of deadly feuds between the native princes, carefully fomented by the English settlers, whose interest it was to make them exterminate each other.

The quarrel for the possession of Connaught began in the year 1225. The Anglo-Normans had a large army at Athlone, and Hugh Cathal went to claim their assistance. The Lord Justice put himself at the head of the army; they marched into Connaught, and soon became masters of the situation. Roderic's sons at once submitted, but only to bide their time. During these hostilities the English of Desmond and O'Brien, a Thomond prince, assisted by the Sheriff of Cork, invaded the southern part of Connaught for the sake of plunder. In the previous year, 1224, "the corn remained unreaped until the festival of St. Brigid [1st Feb.], when the ploughing was going on." A famine also occurred, and was followed by severe sickness.

O'Neill had inaugurated Turlough at Carnfree. He appears to have been the most popular claimant. The northern chieftains then returned home. As soon as the English left Connaught, Turlough again revolted. Hugh Cathal recalled his allies; and the opposite party, finding their cause hopeless, joined him in such numbers that Roderic's sons fled for refuge to Hugh O'Neill.

Soon after these events, Hugh O'Connor was captured by his English allies, and would have been sacrificed to their vengeance on some pretence, had not Earl Marshall rescued him by force of arms.

At the close of the year 1227, Turlough again took arms. The English had found it their convenience to change sides, and assisted him with all their forces. Probably they feared the brave Hugh, and were jealous of the very power they had helped him to obtain. Hugh Roderic attacked the northern districts, with Richard de Burgo. Turlough Roderic marched to the peninsula of Rindown, with the Viceroy. Hugh Crovderg had a narrow escape near the Curlieu Mountains, where his wife was captured by the English. The following year he appears to have been reconciled to the Lord Deputy, for he was killed in his house by an Englishman, in revenge for a liberty he had taken with a woman.

As usual, on the death of Hugh O'Connor, the brothers who had fought against him now fought against each other. The Saxon certainly does not deserve the credit of all our national miseries. If there had been a little less home dissension, there would have been a great deal less foreign oppression. The English, however. helped to foment the discord. The Lord Justice took part with Hugh, the younger brother, who was supported by the majority of the Connaught men, although Turlough had already been inaugurated by O'Neill. A third competitor now started up; this was Felim, brother to Hugh O'Connor. Some of the chieftains declared that they would not serve a prince who acknowledged English rule, and obliged Hugh to renounce his allegiance. But this question was settled with great promptitude. Richard de Burgo took the field, desolated the country—if, indeed, there was anything left to desolate—killed Donn Oge Magcraghty, their bravest champion, expelled Hugh, and proclaimed Felim.

Felim fled to the north, and sought refuge with O'Donnell of Tir-Connell. O'Flaherty, who had always been hostile to Felim, joined the English, and, by the help of his boats, they were able to lay waste the islands of Clew Bay. Nearly all the inhabitants were killed or carried off. The victorious forces now laid siege to a castle on the Rock of Lough Key, in Roscommon, which was held for O'Connor by MacDermod. They succeeded in taking it, but soon lost their possession by the quick-witted cleverness of an Irish soldier, who closed the gates on them when they set out on a plundering expedition. The fortress was at once demolished, that it might not fall into English hands again.

It could not fail to be remarked by the Irish annalists, that the first Anglo-Norman settlers had been singularly unfortunate. They can scarcely be blamed for supposing that these misfortunes were a judgment for their crimes. Before the middle of this century (the thirteenth) three of the most important families had become extinct. De Lacy, Lord of Meath, died in 1241, infirm and blind; his property was inherited by his grand-daughters, in default of a male heir. Hugh de Lacy died in 1240, and left only a daughter. The Earl of Pembroke died from wounds received at a tournament. Walter, who succeeded him, also died without issue. The property came eventually to Anselm, a younger brother, who also died childless; and it was eventually portioned out among the females of the family.

In 1248 the young men of Connaught inaugurated the periodical rebellions, which a statesman of modern times has compared to the dancing manias of the Middle Ages. Unfortunately for his comparison, there was a cause for the one, and there was no cause for the other. They acted unwisely, because there was not the remotest possibility of success; and to rebel against an oppression which cannot be remedied, only forges closer chains for the oppressed. But it can scarcely be denied that their motive was a patriotic one. Felim's son, Hugh, was the leader of the youthful band. In 1249, Maurice FitzGerald arrived to crush the movement, or, in modern parlance, "to stamp it out"—not always a successful process; for sparks are generally left after the most careful stamping, which another method might effectually have quenched.

Under the year 1249 the Annals mention a defeat which the Irish suffered at Athenry, which they attribute to their refusal to desist from warfare on Lady Day, the English having asked a truce in honour of the Blessed Virgin. They also record the death of Donough O'Gillapatrick, and say that this was a retaliation due to the English; for he had killed, burned, and destroyed many of them. He is characterized, evidently with a little honest pride, as the third greatest plunderer of the English. The names of the other two plunderers are also carefully chronicled; they were Connor O'Melaghlin and Connor MacCoghlan. The "greatest plunderer" was in the habit of going about to reconnoitre the English towns in the disguise of pauper or poet, as best suited him for the time.

Henry III. died in 1272, after a reign of fifty-six years. He was succeeded by his son, Edward I., who was in the Holy Land at the time of his father's death. In 1254 his father had made him a grant of Ireland, with the express condition that it should not be separated from England. It would appear as if there had been some apprehension of such an event since the time of Prince John. The English monarchs apparently wished the benefit of English laws to be extended to the native population, but their desire was invariably frustrated by such of their nobles as had obtained grants of land in Ireland, and whose object appears to have been the extermination and, if this was not possible, the depression of the Irish race.

Ireland was at this time convulsed by domestic dissensions. Sir Robert D'Ufford, the Justiciary, was accused of fomenting the discord; but he appears to have considered that he only did his duty to his royal master. When sent for into England, to account for his conduct, he "satisfied the King that all was not true that he was charged withal; and for further contentment yielded this reason, that in policy he thought it expedient to wink at one knave cutting off another, and that would save the King's coffers, and purchase peace to the land. Whereat the King smiled, and bid him return to Ireland." The saving was questionable; for to prevent an insurrection by timely concessions, is incomparably less expensive than to suppress it when it has arisen. The "purchase of peace" was equally visionary; for the Irish never appear to have been able to sit down quietly under unjust oppression, however hopeless resistance might be.

In 1280 the Irish who lived near the Anglo-Norman settlers presented a petition to the English King, praying that they might be admitted to the privileges of the English law. Edward issued a writ to the then Lord Justice, D'Ufford, desiring him to assemble the lords spiritual and temporal of the "land of Ireland," to deliberate on the subject. But the writ was not attended to; and even if it had been, the lords "spiritual and temporal" appear to have decided long before, that the Irish should not participate in the benefit of English laws, however much they might suffer from English oppression. A pagan nation pursued a more liberal policy, and found it eminently successful. The Roman Empire was held together for many centuries, quite as much by the fact of her having made all her dependencies to share in the benefits of her laws, as by the strong hand of her cohorts. She used her arms to conquer, and her laws to retain her conquests.[1]

---

[1] *Conquests.*—We really must enter a protest against the way in which Irish history is written by some English historians. In Wright's *History of Ireland* we find the following gratuitous assertion offered to excuse a crime:—"Such a refinement of cruelty *must* have arisen from a suspicion of treachery, or from some other grievous offence with which we are not acquainted." If all the dark deeds in history are to be accounted for in this way, we may bid farewell to historical justice. And yet this work, which is

We now come to an important period of Irish history, in which we find special mention of the two great families of the Burkes and Geraldines. The Burkes were now represented by the Red Earl, Richard de Burgo, and had become very powerful. The Red Earl's grandson, William, who was murdered, in 1333, by the English of Ulster, and whose death was most cruelly revenged, was the third and last of the De Burgo Earls of Ulster. The Burkes of Connaught are descended from William, the younger brother of Walter, the first Earl.

John FitzThomas FitzGerald, Baron of Offaly, was the common ancester of the two great branches of the Geraldines. One of his sons, John, was created Earl of Kildare; the other, Maurice, Earl Desmond.

Wogan was Viceroy during the close of this century, and had ample occupation pacifying the Geraldines and Burkes—an occupation in which he was not always successful. Thomas FitzMaurice, "of the ape," father of the first Earl of Desmond, had preceded him in the office of Justiciary. This nobleman obtained his cognomen from the circumstance of having been carried, when a child, by a tame ape round the walls of a castle, and then restored to his cradle without the slightest injury.

written in the most prejudiced manner, has had large circulation in Ireland, and amongst Irishmen in England. When Irishmen support such works, they must not blame the English for acceptingthem as truthful histories.

The English possessions in Ireland at the close of this century consisted of the "Liberties" and ten counties—Dublin, Louth, Kildare, Waterford, Tipperary, Cork, Limerick, Kerry, Roscommon, and part of Connaught. The "Liberties" were those of Connaught and Ulster, under De Burgo; Meath, divided between De Mortimer and De Verdun; Wexford, Carlow, and Kilkenny, under the jurisdiction of the respective representatives of the Marshal heiresses; Thomond, claimed by De Clare; and Desmond, partly controlled by the FitzGeralds.

Such portions of the country as lay outside the land of which the Anglo-Normans had possessed themselves, were called "marches." These were occupied by troops of natives, who continually resisted the aggressions of the invader, always anxious to add to his territory. These troops constantly made good reprisals for what they had taken, by successful raids on the castle or the garrison. Fleet-footed, and well aware of every spot which would afford concealment, these hardy Celts generally escaped scot-free. Thus occupied for several centuries, they acquired a taste for this roving life; and they can scarcely be reproached for not having advanced in civilization with the age, by those who placed such invincible obstacles to their progress.

The famous invasion of Ireland by Bruce took place on the 16th of May, A.D. 1315. On that day

Edward landed on the coast of Ulster, near Carrickfergus, with six thousand men. He was attended by the heroes of Bannockburn; and as a considerable number of native forces soon joined him, the contingent was formidable. Although a few of the Irish had assisted Edward II. in his war against Scotch independence, the sympathies of the nation were with the cause of freedom; and they gladly hailed the arrival of those who had delivered their own country, hoping they would also deliver Ireland. It was proposed that Edward Bruce should be made King of Ireland. The Irish chieftain, Donnell O'Neill, King of Ulster, in union with the other princes of the province, wrote a spirited but respectful remonstrance to the Holy See, on the part of the nation, explaining why they were anxious to transfer the kingdom to Bruce.

Richard de Burgo, the Red Earl, died in 1326. He took leave of the nobles after a magnificent banquet at Kilkenny. When he had resigned his possessions to his grandson, William, he retired into the Monastery of Athassel, where he expired soon after. In the same year Edward II. attempted to take refuge in Ireland from the vengeance of his people and his false Queen, the "she-wolf of France." He failed in his attempt, and was murdered soon after—A.D. 1327.

The Butler family now appear prominently in Irish history for the first time. It would appear from Carte that the name was originally Walter,

Butler being an addition distinctive of office. The family was established in Ireland by Theobald Walter (Gaultier), an Anglo-Norman of high rank, who received extensive grants of land from Henry II., together with the hereditary office of "Pincerna," Boteler, or Butler, in Ireland, to the Kings of England. In this capacity he and his successors were to attend these monarchs at their coronation, and present them with the first cup of wine. In return they obtained many privileges. On account of the quarrels between this family and the De Burgos, De Berminghams, Le Poers, and the southern Geraldines, royal letters were issued, commanding them, under pain of forfeiture, to desist from warring on each other. The result was a meeting of the factious peers in Dublin, at which they engaged to keep the "King's peace." On the following day they were entertained by the Earl of Ulster; the next day, at St. Patrick's, by Maurice FitzThomas; and the third day, by the Viceroy and his fellow Knights Hospitallers, who had succeeded the Templars at Kilmainham. The Earldoms of Ormonde and Desmond were now created. The heads of these families long occupied an important place in Irish affairs. Butler died on his return from a pilgrimage to Compostella, and was succeeded by his eldest son, Jacques—"a liberal, friendly, pleasant, and stately youth"—who was married this year to King Edward's cousin, Eleanor, daughter of the Earl of Essex. The Desmond peerage was created in 1329, when the County Palatine of Kerry was given to that family.

The years 1333 and 1334 were disgraced by fearful crimes, in which the English and Irish equally participated. In the former year the Earl of Ulster seized Walter de Burgo, and starved him to death in the Green Castle of Innishowen. The sister of the man thus cruelly murdered was married to Sir Richard Mandeville, and she urged her husband to avenge her brother's death. Mandeville took the opportunity of accompanying the Earl with some others to hear Mass at Carrickfergus, and killed him as he was fording a stream. The young Earl's death was avenged by his followers, who slew 300 men. His wife, Maud, fled to England with her only child a daughter, named Elizabeth, who was a year old. The Burkes of Connaught, who were the junior branch of the family, fearing that she would soon marry again, and transfer the property to other hands, immediately seized the Connaught estates, declared themselves independent of English law, and renounced the English language and customs. They were too powerful to be resisted with impunity; and while the ancestor of the Clanrickardes assumed the Irish title of Mac William *Oughter*, or the Upper, Edmund Burke, the progenitor of the Viscounts of Mayo, took the appellation of Mac William *Eighter*, or the Lower. This was not the last time when English settlers identified themselves, not merely from policy, but even from inclination, with the race whom they had once hated and oppressed.

On the 2nd October, A.D. 1394, Richard II. landed on the Irish shores. The country was in its usual state of partial insurrection and general discontent; but no attempt was made to remove the cause of all this unnecessary misery. There was some show of submission from the Irish chieftains, who were overawed by the immense force which attended the King. Art MacMurrough, the heir of the ancient Leinster Kings, was the most formidable of the native nobles; and from his prowess and success in several engagements, was somewhat feared by the invaders. He refused to defer to any one but Richard, and was only prevailed on to make terms when he found himself suddenly shut up in Dublin Castle, during a friendly visit to the court.

The King's account of his reception shows that he had formed a tolerably just opinion of the political state of the country. He mentions, in a letter from Dublin, that the people might be divided into three classes—the "wild Irish, or enemies," the Irish rebels, and the English subjects; and he had just discernment enough to see that the "rebels had been made such by wrongs, and by want of close attention to their grievances," though he had not the judgment or the justice to apply the necessary remedy. His next exploit was to persuade the principal Irish kings to receive knighthood in the

English fashion. They submitted with the worst possible grace, having again and again repeated that they had already received the honour according to the custom of their own country. The dealings of the Anglo-Norman knights, with whom they already had intercourse, were not likely to have inspired them with very sublime ideas of the dignity.

The customs of the Irish nobles were again made a subject of ridicule, as they had been during the visit of Prince John; though one should have supposed that an increased knowledge of the world should have led to a wiser policy, if not to an avoidance of that ignorant criticism, which at once denounces everything foreign as inferior. Richard returned to England in 1395, after nine months of vain display. He appointed Roger Mortimer his Viceroy. Scarcely had the King and his fleet sailed from the Irish shores, when the real nature of the proffered allegiance of seventy-two kings and chieftains became apparent. The O'Byrnes rose up in Wicklow, and were defeated by the Viceroy and the Earl of Ormonde; the MacCarthys rose up in Munster, and balanced affairs by gaining a victory of the English. The Earl of Kildare was captured by Calvagh O'Connor of Offaly, in 1398; and, in the same year, the O'Briens and O'Tooles avenged their late defeat, by a great victory, at Kenlis, in Ossory.

In 1399 King Richard paid another visit to Ireland. His exactions and oppressions had made him very unpopular in England, and it is probable that this expedition was planned to divert the minds of his subjects. If this was his object, it failed signally; for the unfortunate monarch was deposed by Parliament the same year, and was obliged to perform the act of abdication with the best grace he could.

On the accession of Henry IV., his second son, Thomas, Duke of Lancaster, was made Viceroy, and landed at Bullock, near Dalkey, on Sunday, November 13, 1402. As the youth was but twelve years of age, a council was appointed to assist him. Soon after his arrival, the said Council despatched a piteous document from "Le Naas," in which they represent themselves and their youthful ruler as on the very verge of starvation, in consequence of not having received remittances from England. In conclusion, they gently allude to the possibility—of course carefully deprecated—of "peril and disaster" befalling their lord, if further delay should be permitted. The King, however, was not in a position to tax his English subjects; and we find the prince himself writing to his royal father on the same matter, at the close of the year 1402. He mentions also that he had entertained the knights and squires with such cheer as could be procured under the circumstances, and adds: "I, by the advice of my Council, rode against the Irish, your enemies, and did my utmost to harass them."

Probably, had he shared the cheer with "the Irish his enemies," or even showed them some little kindness, he would not have been long placed in so unpleasant a position for want of supplies.

John Duke, the then Mayor of Dublin, obtained the privilege of having the sword borne before the chief magistrate of that city, as a reward for his services in routing the O'Byrnes of Wicklow. About the same time John Dowdall, Sheriff of Louth, was murdered in Dublin, by Sir Bartholomew Vernon and three other English gentlemen, who were outlawed for this and other crimes, but soon after received the royal pardon. In 1404 the the English were defeated in Leix. In 1405 Art MacMurrough committed depredations at Wexford and elsewhere, and 1406 the settlers suffered a severe reverse in Meath.

The Irish of English descent were made to feel their position painfully at the close of this reign, and this might have led the new settlers to reflect, if capable of reflection, that their descendants would soon find themselves in a similar condition. The commons presented a petition complaining of the extortions and injustices practised by the Deputies, some of whom had left enormous debts unpaid. They also represented the injustice of excluding Irish law students from the Inns of Court in London. A few years previous (A.D. 1417), the settlers had presented a petition to Parliament, praying that no Irishman should be admitted to any office or benefice in the Church, and that no bishop should be permitted to bring an Irish servant with him when he came to attend Parliament or Council. This petition was granted; and soon after an attempt was made to prosecute the Archbishop of Cashel, who had presumed to disregard some of its enactments.

CHAPTER XI.

Quarrels between the Houses of York and Lancaster—Their effect upon Ireland—Why the Yorkists were popular—Accession of the English King Henry VII.—Poyning's Parliament, and its effect—The Earl of Kildare accused of Treason—Irish War Cries forbidden.

HENRY VI. succeeded to the English throne while still a mere infant, and, as usual, the "Irish question" was found to be one of the greatest difficulties of the new administration. The O'Neills had been carrying on a domestic feud in Ulster; but they had just united to attack the English, when Edward Mortimer, Earl of March, assumed the government of Ireland (A.D. 1425). He died of the plague the following year; but his successor in office, Lord Furnival, contrived to capture a number of the northern chieftains, who were negotiating peace with Mortimer at the very time of his death. Owen O'Neill was ransomed, but the indignation excited by this act served only to arouse angry feelings; and the northerns united against their enemies, and soon recovered any territory they had lost.

Donough MacMorough was released from the Tower in 1428, after nine years' captivity. It is said the Leinster men paid a heavy ransom for him. The young prince's compulsory residence in England did not lessen his disaffection, for he made war on the settlers as soon as he returned to his paternal dominions. The great family feud between the houses of York and Lancaster, had but little effect on the state of Ireland. Different members of the two great factions had held the office of Lord Justice in that country, but, with one exception, they did not obtain any personal influence there. Indeed, the Viceroy of those days, whether an honest man or a knave, was sure to be unpopular with some party.

The Yorkists and Lancastrians, were descended directly from Edward III. The first Duke of York was Edward's fifth son, Edmund Plantagenet; the first Duke of Lancaster was John of Gaunt, the fourth son of the same monarch. Richard II. succeeded his grandfather, Edward III., as the son of Edward the Black Prince, so famed in English chivalry. His arrogance and extravagance soon made him unpopular; and, during his absence in Ireland, the Duke of Lancaster, whom he had banished, and treated most unjustly, returned to

England, and inaugurated the fatal quarrel. The king was obliged to return immediately, and committed the government of the country to his cousin, Roger de Mortimer, who was next in succession to the English crown, in right of his mother, Philippa, the only child of the Duke of Clarence, third son of Edward III. The death of this nobleman opened the way for the intrusion of the Lancastrians, the Duke of Lancaster having obtained the crown during the lifetime of Richard, to the exclusion of the rightful heir-apparent, Edmund, Earl of March, son of the late Viceroy.

The feuds of the Earl of Ormonde and the Talbots in Ireland, proved nearly as great a calamity to that nation as the disputes about the English succession. A Parliament was held in Dublin in 1441, in which Richard Talbot, the English Archbishop of Dublin, proceeded to lay various requests before the king, the great object of which was the overthrow of the Earl, who, by the intermarrying of his kinsmen with the Irish, possessed great influence among the native septs contiguous to his own territory.

In the year 1447 Ireland was desolated by a fearful plague, in which seven hundred priests are said to have fallen victims, probably from their devoted attendance on the sufferers. In the same year Felim O'Reilly was taken prisoner treacherously by the Lord Deputy; and Finola, the daughter of Calvagh O'Connor Faly, and wife of Hugh Boy

O'Neill, "the most beautiful and stately, the most renowned and illustrious woman of all her time in Ireland, her own mother only excepted, retired from this transitory world, to prepare for eternal life, and assumed the yoke of piety and devotion in the Monastery of Cill-Achaidh."

During the reigns of Edward IV., Edward V., and the usurper, Richard, there was probably more dissensions in England than there ever had been at any time among the native Irish chieftains. Princes and nobles were sacrificed by each party as they obtained power, and regicide might almost be called common. The number of English slain in the Wars of the Roses was estimated at 100,000. Parliament made acts of attainder one day, and reversed them almost on the next. Neither life nor property was safe.

The English power in Ireland was reduced at this time to the lowest degree of weakness. This power had never been other than nominal beyond the Pale; within its precincts it was on the whole all-powerful. But now a few archers and spearmen were its only defence; and had the Irish combined under a competent leader, there can be little doubt that the result would have been fatal to the colony. It would appear as if Henry VII. hoped to propitiate the Yorkists in Ireland, as he allowed the Earl of Kildare to hold the office of Lord Deputy; his brother, Thomas FitzGerald that of Chancellor; and his father-in-law, FitzEustace, that of Lord

Treasurer. After a short time, however, he restored the Earl of Ormonde to the family honours and estates, and thus a Lancastrian influence was secured. The most important events of this reign, as far as Ireland is concerned, are the plots of Simnel and Perkin Warbeck, and the enactments of Poyning's Parliament.

In May, 1492, the Warbeck plot was promulgated in Ireland, and an adventurer landed on the Irish shores, who declared himself to be Richard, Duke of York, the second son of Edward IV., who was supposed to have perished in the tower. His stay in Ireland, however, was brief, although he was favourably received. The French monarch entertained him with the honours due to a crowned head; but this, probably, was purely for political purposes, as he was discarded as soon as peace had been made with England. He next visited Margaret, the Dowager Duchess of Burgundy, who treated him as if he were really her nephew.

Henry now became seriously alarmed at the state of affairs in Ireland, and sent over Sir Edward Poyning, a privy councillor and a Knight of the Garter, to the troublesome colony. He was attended by some eminent English lawyers, and what was of considerably greater importance, by a force of 1,000 men. But neither the lawyers nor the men succeeded in their attempt, for nothing was done to conciliate, and the old policy of force was the rule of action, and failed as usual. The first step was to hunt out the abettors of Warbeck's insurrection, who had taken refuge in the north; but the moment the Deputy marched against them, the Earl of Kildare's brother rose in open rebellion, and seized Carlow Castle. The Viceroy was, therefore, obliged to make peace with O'Hanlon and Magennis, and to return south. After recovering the fortress, he held a parliament at Drogheda, in the month of November, 1494. In this parliament the celebrated statute was enacted, which provided that henceforth no parliament should be held in Ireland until the Chief Governor and Council had first certified to the king, under the Great Seal, as well the causes and considerations as the Acts they designed to pass, and till the same should be approved by the king and Council. This Act obtained the name of "Poyning's Law." It became a serious grievance when the whole of Ireland was brought under English government; but at the time of its enactment it could only affect the inhabitants of the Pale, who formed a very small portion of the population of that country; and the colonists regarded it rather favourably, as a means of protecting them against the legislative oppressions of the Viceroys.

The general object of the Act was nominally to reduce the people to "whole and perfect obedience." The attempt to accomplish this desirable end had been continued for rather more than two hundred years, and had not yet been attained. The Parliament of Drogheda did not succeed, although the Viceroy returned to England afterwards under the happy conviction that he had perfectly accomplished his mission. Acts were also passed that ordnance should not be kept in fortresses without the Vice-regal licence; that the lords spiritual and temporal were to appear in their robes in parliament, for the English lords of Ireland had, "through penuriousness, done away the said robes to their own great dishonour, and the rebuke of all the whole land;" that the "many damnable customs and uses," practised by the Anglo-Norman lords and gentlemen, under the names of "coigne, livery, and pay," should be reformed; that the inhabitants on the frontiers of the four shires should forthwith build and maintain a double ditch, raised six feet above the ground on the side which "meared next unto the Irishmen," so that the said Irishmen should be kept out; that all subjects were to provide themselves with cuirasses and helmets, with English bows and sheaves of arrows; that every parish should be provided with a pair of butts, and the constables were ordered to call the parishioners before them on holidays, to shoot at least two or three games.

The Irish war-cries which had been adopted by the English lords were forbidden, and they were commanded to call upon St. George or the King of England. The Statutes of Kilkenny were confirmed, with the exception of the one which forbid the use of the Irish language. As nearly all the English settlers had adopted it, such an enactment could not possibly have been carried out. Three of the principal nobles of the country were absent from this assembly: Maurice, Earl of Desmond, was in arms on behalf of Warbeck; Gerald, Earl of Kildare, was charged with treason; and Thomas, Earl of Ormonde, was residing in England. The Earl of Kildare was sent to England to answer the charges of treason which were brought against him. Henry had discovered that Poyning's mission had not been as successful as he expected, and, what probably influenced him still more, that it had proved very expensive. He has the credit of being a wise king in many respects, notwithstanding his avariciousness; and he at once saw that Kildare would be more useful as a friend, and less expensive, if he ceased to be an enemy. The result was the pardon of the "rebel," his marriage with the king's first cousin, Elizabeth St. John, and his restoration to the office of Deputy. His quick-witted speeches, when examined before the king, took the royal fancy. He was accused of having burned the Cathedral of Cashel, to revenge himself on the Archbishop, who had sided with his enemy, Sir James Ormonde. There was a great array of witnesses prepared to prove the fact; but the Earl excited shouts of laughter by exclaiming, "I would never have done it had it not been told me the Archbishop was within."

The Archbishop was present, and one of his most active accusers. The king then gave him leave to choose his counsel, and time to prepare his defence. Kildare exclaimed that he doubted if he should be allowed to choose the good fellow whom he would select. Henry gave him his hand as an assurance of his good faith. "Marry," said the Earl, "I can see no better man in England than your Highness, and will choose no other." The affair ended by his accusers declaring that "all Ireland could not rule this Earl," to which Henry replied: "Then, in good faith, shall this Earl rule all Ireland."

In August, 1489, Kildare was appointed Deputy to Prince Henry, who was made Viceroy. In 1498 he was authorized to convene a Parliament, which should not sit longer than half a year. This was the first parliament held under Poyning's Act.

Gerald, the ninth and last Catholic Earl of Kildare, succeeded his father as Lord Deputy in 1513. But the hereditary foes of his family were soon actively employed in working his ruin; and even his sister, who had married into that family, proved not the least formidable of his enemies. He was summoned to London; but either the charges against him could not be proved, or it was deemed expedient to defer them, for we find him attending Henry for four years, and forming one of his retinue at the Field of the Cloth of Gold. Kildare was permitted to return to Dublin again in 1523, but he was tracked by Wolsey's implacable hatred to

The Irish Patriots assembled in a free Parliament.

his doom. In 1533 he was confined in the Tower for the third time. The charges against him were warmly urged by his enemies. Two of his sisters were married to native chieftains; and he was accused with playing fast and loose with the English as a baron of the Pale—with the Irish as a warm ally. Two English nobles had been appointed to assist him, or rather to act the spy upon his movements, at different times. One of these, Sir Thomas Skeffington, became his most dangerous enemy.

In 1515 an elaborate report on the state of Ireland was prepared by the royal command. It gives a tolerably clear idea of the military and political condition of the country. According to this account, the only counties subject to English rule, were Louth, Meath, Dublin, Kildare, and Wexford. Even the residents near the boundaries, of these districts, were obliged to pay "black mail" to the neighbouring Irish chieftains. The king's writs were not executed beyond the bounds described; and within thirty miles of Dublin, the Brehon law was in full force. This document, which is printed in the first volume of the "State Papers" relating to Ireland, contains a list of the petty rulers of sixty different states or "regions," some of which "are as big as a shire; some more, some less." The writer then gives various opinions as to the plans which might be adopted for improving the state of Ireland.

It cannot now be ascertained whether Kildare had incited the Irish chieftains to rebellion or not. In 1520, during one of his periods of detention in London, the Earl of Surrey was sent over as Deputy, with a large force. The new Viceroy was entirely ignorant of the state of Ireland, and imagined he had nothing to do but conquer. As a last resource he suggested the policy of conciliation, which Henry appears to have adopted, as he empowered him to confer the honour of knighthood on any of the Irish chieftains to whom he considered it desirable to offer the compliment, and he sent a collar of gold to O'Neill. About the same time Surrey wrote to inform Wolsey, that Cormac Oge MacCarthy and MaCarthy Reagh were "two wise men, and more conformable to order than some English were;" but he was still careful to keep up the old policy of fomenting discord among the native princes, for he wrote to the king that "it would be dangerful to have them both agreed and joined together, as the longer they continue in war, the better it should be for your Grace's poor subjects here."

Surrey became weary at last of the hopeless conflict, and at his own request he was permitted to return to England and resign his office, which was conferred on his friend, Pierse Butler, of Carrick, subsequently Earl of Ormonde. The Scotch had begun to immigrate to Ulster in considerable numbers, and acquired large territories there; the

Pale was almost unprotected; and the Irish Privy Council applied to Wolsey for six ships of war, to defend the northern coasts, A.D. 1522. The dissensions between the O'Neills and O'Donnells had broken out into sanguinary warfare.

The Earl of Kildare left Ireland, for the third and last time, in February, 1534. Before his departure he summoned a council at Drogheda, and appointed his son, Thomas, to act as deputy in his absence. On the Earl's arrival in London, he was at once seized and imprisoned in the Tower. A false report was carefully circulated in Ireland that he had been beheaded, and that the destruction of the whole family was even then impending. Nor was there anything very improbable in this statement. The English king had already inaugurated his sanguinary career. One of the most eminent English laymen, Sir Thomas More, and one of her best ecclesiastics, Bishop Fisher, had been accused and beheaded, to satisfy the royal caprice. When the king's tutor and his chancellor had been sacrificed, who could hope to escape?

The unfortunate Earl had advised his son to pursue a cautious and gentle policy; but Lord Thomas' fiery temper could ill brook such precaution, and he was but too easily roused by the artful enemies who incited him to rebellion. The reports of his father's execution were confirmed. His proud blood was up, and he rushed madly on the career of self-destruction. On the 11th of June, 1534, he flung down the sword of state on the table of the council-hall at St. Mary's Abbey, and openly renounced his allegiance to the English monarch. Archbishop Cromer implored him with tears to reconsider his purpose, but all entreaties were vain. Even had he been touched by this disinterested counsel, it would probably have failed of its effect; for an Irish bard commenced chanting his praises and his father's wrongs, and thus his doom was sealed. An attempt was made to arrest him, but it failed. Archbishop Allen, his father's bitterest enemy, fled to the Castle, with several other nobles, and here they were besieged by Fitz-Gerald and his followers. The Archbishop soon contrived to effect his escape. He embarked at night in a vessel which was then lying at Dame's Gate; but the ship was stranded near Clontarf, either through accident or design, and the unfortunate prelate was seized by Lord Thomas' people, who instantly put him to death. The young nobleman is said by some authorities to have been present at the murder, as well as his two uncles: there is at least no doubt of his complicity in the crime. The sentence of excommunication was pronounced against him, and those who assisted him, in its most terrible form.

Ecclesiastical intervention was not necessary to complete his ruin. He had commenced his wild career of lawless violence with but few followers, and without any influential companions. The Castle of Maynooth, the great stronghold of the Geraldines, was besieged and captured by his father's old enemy, Sir William Skeffington. In the meanwhile the intelligence of his son's insurrection had been communicated to the Earl, and the news of his excommunication followed quickly. The unfortunate nobleman succumbed beneath the twofold blow, and died in a few weeks. Lord Thomas surrendered himself in August, 1535, on the guarantee of Lord Leonard and Lord Butler, under a solemn promise that his life should be spared. But his fate was in the hands of one who had no pity, even where the tenderest ties were concerned. Soon after the surrender of "Silken Thomas," his five uncles were seized treacherously at a banquet; and although three of them had no part in the rebellion, the nephew and the uncles were all executed together at Tyburn, on the 3rd of February, 1537. If the King had hoped by this cruel injustice to rid himself of the powerful family, he was mistaken. Two children of the late Earl's still existed. They were sons by his second wife, Lady Elizabeth Grey. The younger, still an infant, was, conveyed to his mother in England. The elder, a youth of twelve years of age, was concealed by his aunts, who were married to the chieftains of Offaly and Donegal, and was soon conveyed to France out of the reach of the enemies who eagerly sought his destruction. It is not a little curious to find the ative princes, who had been so cruelly oppressed by his forefathers, protecting and helping the hapless youth, even at the risk of their lives. It is one of many evidences that the antipathy of Celt to Saxon is not so much an antipathy of race or person, as the natural enmity which the oppressed entertains towards the oppressor.

CHAPTER XII.

A full and clear explanation of the causes that led to the so-called Reformation in England—Accession of Henry VIII.—His marriage with Catherine of Arragon—He becomes weary of her, and wishes to marry Anne Boleyn—His scandalous conduct with Anne Boleyn —He revolts against the Holy See, because the Pope will not allow him to have two wives—Conduct of the Protestant Archbishop Cranmer—Henry makes himself head of the Church—The Irish will not become Protestants for either fear or favour.

IN order to understand the period of Irish history at which we have now arrived, it will be necessary to enter into a full explanation of the state of the country at this time, and also to give some account of English history. We all very justly consider a great victory as one of the most important events in the history of any people; and if an entire change occurs in the government of the country, in consequence of this victory, it is carefully recorded with all the events which led to it, and the probable causes which obtained so great a triumph. I am now going to write of one of the greatest, if not the very greatest of victories ever obtained by any nation; and I shall request your careful attention. The victory was obtained by Irishmen. We much fear that many of the conquerors in the bravest conflicts ever recorded, had their share of praise in this world only, and will have but little praise hereafter. But in this victory, to which I must now call your attention, the victors had little praise in this world, but their reward and triumph will be eternal. The victory of which I write was a moral victory—a victory, in which the weak triumphed over the strong: and Irishmen sacrificed their lives and those who were dearer to them even than their lives, sooner than yield to the cruel oppressor who sought to compel them to accept a false religion. The history of the brave and effectual resistance which Irishmen made to the new religion, or rather to the new heresy, is of interest to every Catholic and every thoughtful Protestant. It was introduced by Martin Luther, a wicked monk, who apostatised from his creed in order to marry, and brought into England by Henry VIII., who wished not only to marry as many wives as he pleased, but to kill them as soon as he was tired of them.

Henry VIII. was the second son of Henry VII.,

and was born at Greenwich, June 28, 1491. His
father, Henry VII., had married Elizabeth of York,
and had two sons and two daughters, besides
three children who died young. His eldest son was
called Arthur, his second son, Henry, afterwards
Henry VIII. All this you must remember and
understand thoroughly, that you may know exactly
what led to the introduction of Martin Luther's
heresy into England, and how it then came to
be forced on the Irish by the sword. Arthur,
Henry VII's eldest son, died in 1502. He had
married a Spanish princess, Catherine of Arragon,
in 1501. You will observe that the marriage
took place in November, and the young prince
died in April. The young widow, Catherine of
Arragon, had brought a very large fortune with
her to England; and the old king, Henry VII.,
did not wish to let the money go out of the country, so he made a marriage contract between her
and his second son, Henry, in June, 1502, just
three months after her husband's death. Henry
was only fourteen when this contract was made;
and by his father's advice, he made a secret protest against it, so that if he wished he might
refuse to marry Catherine when he came of age.
Thus you will see the poor young widow was
treated very treacherously. Henry did not become king for seven years after, and then he was
free to choose whether he would abide by the contract or not. He chose, however, to marry Cathe-

rine, and they were crowned afterwards with great splendour, June 24, 1509.

For several years Henry was very popular with his subjects. The English arms were victorious in many engagements in France and Scotland; and all promised a long, prosperous, and comparatively peaceful reign. Henry had one daughter by Catherine, named Mary, who was afterwards Queen of England. He lived, to all appearances, very happily and contentedly with his wife, until the year 1526. About this time a lady named Anne Boleyn came to court as maid of honour to the queen. This lady was very beautiful, very vain, and very ambitious. She began to have great influence with the king, and when he found that she had been engaged to Lord Percy, he insisted that the engagement should be broken off. She was willing enough to be the king's mistress, but she determined if possible to be his queen also, and used every effort to attain her end. There are always plenty of flatterers round a prince ready to urge him on to evil, and to help him in every way to attain his ends, whatever they may be; such persons hoping to advance their interests by making themselves useful to their master. It cannot be known for certain now whether it was Henry himself or one of his bad advisers who suggested that he should get a divorce. It matters but little from whom the suggestion came, for Henry was only too ready to act upon it.

Henry was at this time a Catholic, at least in name; but it should be remembered, and remembered carefully, that when a man sets the commands of God and the Church at defiance by living in constant sin and absenting himself from the sacraments, he becomes in great danger of losing his faith. God may withdraw that great grace from him if he proves himself unworthy of it. Henry probably knew this very well; he was clever and, it would appear, highly educated. He had even defended the Holy See against the attacks of Martin Luther, and wrote a work on the Seven Sacraments, which he published in 1521, and for which he obtained the title of Defender of the Faith. But while he was himself despising and contemning the sacraments, it was little use for him to write in their defence. How little he really cared for the sacraments is shown by the way in which he violated the solemn engagements of the Sacrament of Matrimony.

His object now was to get rid of his wife quietly, and to marry Anne Boleyn. But in order to do this he wanted a dispensation from the Holy See. He had already got a dispensation to marry Catherine, although it was believed that her marriage with his brother Arthur had never been consummated, this dispensation was necessary, as she was legally his sister-in-law. Now, however, he pretended that his conscience would not allow him to live with her any longer; and this was the excuse he made to the Pope for wanting the dispensation. His conscience, however, did not prevent him from living with Anne Boleyn for three years before he married her; and her child, afterwards Queen Elizabeth, was in consequence illegitimate.

It is probable the Pope was very well aware of the whole state of affairs. But Henry knew that he was a very powerful monarch, and he thought to frighten the Pope into complying with his desires. He had yet to learn that Popes can neither be frightened nor cajoled, and that they would give up their lives and their liberties, were it possible, fifty times over, sooner than yield to the wicked will of any king or prince.

The Pope, however, very wisely sent a legate to England to inquire into the matter, as this mark of respect was due to Henry. But the Pope's advisers saw plainly the great injustice of the whole proceeding, and that Henry only wished to gratify his passions. Cardinal Wolsey died soon after, and the Pope's legate found that he had only been summoned to England to give judgment in the king's favour, and that if he refused to do it, the king was determined to take his own course. Still, be it remembered, Henry was a professing Catholic. If the Pope had given him a dispensation to commit sin, as so many Protestants ignorantly think that popes and priests can do, he would certainly have remained a Catholic. The

Pope knew very well what would be likely to happen. Already many German princes had become Protestants, and followed Martin Luther's example of profligacy; but even to save the whole kingdom of England from becoming Protestant the Pope would not sanction sin. All this, you must remember, is not my opinion, or my view of the Reformation; it is a matter of HISTORY; and it is a subject with which every Irishman should be very fully acquainted.

After Wolsey's death, Henry got a new adviser, a man named Cromwell, whom you must not confound with the cruel and infamous Oliver Cromwell, who devastated Ireland many years after. This Cromwell was a follower of Anne Boleyn's family, and of course anxious that she should become queen. He had spent a long time on the continent, where he served as a common soldier, and he had learned the new doctrines taught by Martin Luther and his followers. He now came to the assistance of Henry, and suggested that he should set the Pope at defiance, that he should declare himself head of the Church, and then as head of the Church, he could legalize the sin which the Pope's authority would not allow. Henry at once acted on the advice; it flattered his vanity to place himself, as far as he could, in the position of the Pope in England, and he was very anxious to get rid of his wife. Cromwell was ordered to make the necessary arrangements, which may be simply explained thus. The English kings, though some of them had been really good Catholics, were always anxious for an increase of power, and particularly wished to get some kind of power over the bishops and clergy. They had made laws at different times to try and effect this object. One of these laws was called the statute of *præmunire*. This statute made it necessary, under certain circumstances, for ecclesiastics to obtain a patent from the crown before exercising the office of Papal legate.

When Cardinal Wolsey was appointed Papal legate he was granted this patent to enable him to exercise his office, but when Henry turned against him he had him accused of having accepted the office without obtaining the necessary permission. Of course, this permission had nothing whatever to do with the spiritual power of ecclesiastics; for no English king, however wicked, thought of assuming to himself any spiritual power until Henry VIII. made himself head of the Church. Wolsey pleaded guilty of the crime against the State, although he knew very well that he was not guilty, but he thought that by pleading guilty the king would have mercy on him. Henry, however, was too cruel and too selfish to show him any consideration. The Cardinal was now dead, and Henry, or his minister Cromwell, thought of this very clever plan to attain his wicked ends. He now proceeded to charge the clergy with having recognised Wolsey's authority, and thus infringed the statute.

But you will remember that as Wolsey had not been guilty of this offence against the law of the land, they were not guilty. This, however, was nothing to the king, and the unfortunate clergy knew but too well with whom they had to deal.

The clergy at once consulted together, and offered the king the enormous sum of one hundred thousand pounds, if he would forgive their pretended offence. It would have been far better had they firmly resisted the king, and had they united in doing so, they would probably have carried the day. The king graciously accepted the offer, but refused to forgive the clergy unless they introduced a clause into the preamble of their grant, acknowledging him as "the protector and only supreme head of the Church and clergy of England." The clergy were not a little astonished at this demand; they did not know, then, that it was the real object which Henry had in prosecuting them, and they probably never foresaw, or even suspected, the fearful consequences which the admission of his claim would involve. The clergy debated the matter for three days in convocation, and at last agreed to do what the king wished, provided he would allow them to insert the clause " in so far as the law of Christ will allow." This, of course, quite did away with the meaning intended by the king in his clause; for both the clergy and the king knew very well that Christ's law had made St. Peter and the Popes, his successors, the heads of his

Church, and that this place and authority could never be given to any king or prince, or layman.

The king, however, accepted the money and the clause. He feared to press the clergy too far, and hoped that the clause, even as it stood, would become generally known amongst the people of England, and that they would get used to the idea of his being called the head of the Church. This, then, was the commencement of what has been so foolishly called the "Glorious Reformation" in England. The king, Henry VIII., wished to get rid of his lawful wife, and to make Anne Boleyn his queen, a bad woman, by whom he had a child before he made even the pretence of marrying her. The Pope would not give his consent to the king's committing this sin, and when Henry could not get the Pope's consent, either by bribes or threats, he was determined to commit the sin, and made himself Pope, as far as he could do so, that he might be at liberty to commit sin. Surely Protestants have no cause for being proud of a religion which commenced in such a disgraceful manner. But it must be remembered that although Henry made himself head of the Church to legalize his sin, he did not as yet wish to renounce all the articles of the Holy Catholic Faith. He went on in sin and in heresy step by step. Mass was still said, and the sacraments administered in England, and the English people had not yet formally renounced the Faith of the one True Church.

In the year 1532 Wareham the last Catholic Archbishop of Canterbury died, worn out by the troubles of the times, and grief at the national apostasy even then impending. Henry knew that a great deal depended on whom he put into his place, and he found a man exactly suited to his purpose. This man, Thomas Cranmer, of whom English Protestants are so proud, and whom they consider justly the great promoter of the Protestant Reformation in England. But if they knew more about this wretched man, and his real character, they would be ashamed of him and of his religion. This man, like Cromwell, had been a dependant on the Boleyn family, and got himself into power by encouraging her adultery with the king. How then could he be fit, even if guilty of no other crime, for the awful and solemn charge of guiding and teaching the church of God. But there was worse still. His friend and companion, Cromwell, made no pretence of religion; his religion was to get himself on in the world. But Cranmer was always canting about his conscience, and boasting of his piety. He gave a fine specimen of both when he was made Archbishop; for he swore inviolable fidelity to the Holy See, although he knew perfectly well that Henry got him consecrated Archbishop that he might overturn the power of the Pope in England.

This is no mere statement of mine; if it were, it would not be history, and I am now writing a history, and not opinions. On the morning of the day on which Cranmer was consecrated he called four witnesses, unprincipled men like himself, into St. Stephen's chapel, and there declared that he did not intend to keep the oath he was about to make. He then went and celebrated the Holy Sacrifice of the Mass, although he did not believe in it, for he was at heart a follower of Martin Luther, and all this time he was privately married, although the king knew nothing of it. Had the king known it, probably he would not have had Cranmer made an Archbishop; for though he liked to be free to commit sin himself, he did not wish the clergy to do it, unless in some special matter where his own personal convenience was concerned.

Cranmer was now fairly afloat on the ocean of duplicity, and he continued his career until his death. A fortnight after his consecration he wrote a letter to the king, calling on him "for the good of his soul" to grant him his royal license to examine the question of his marriage.

This, then, is a true, though somewhat severe, account of the origin of the Church by law established. These proceedings hastened the decision of the Holy See; and on the 20th of March, 1534, the sentence was pronounced, which declared the marriage with Catherine to be valid and indissoluble, and charged the king to restore her to her rights, under pain of excommunication. But when that sentence reached the court, England had been already severed from the communion of the Church. Acts of Parliament had been passed by which all jurisdiction in spiritual things was transferred from the Holy See to the Crown; the king was formally declared the only supreme head of the Church of England; and his subjects were called on to acknowledge his supremacy and the lawfulness of his late marriage, under the penalties attached to treason. "In the course of one short session," says Lingard, "the whole papal power was swept away." If the reader ask how such measures could have been made into laws, we can only reply that Cromwell prepared the bill, and that the houses of Parliament passed them. Resistance to the royal will was a thing they never dared to dream of; and one man alone, of all the lords spiritual, refused to take the oaths. This was John Fisher, Bishop of Rochester—a name which no Catholic can pronounce but with sentiments of the profoundest veneration.

Those who would not submit to the king's assumed spiritual authority paid for their loyalty to the Catholic faith by the sacrifice of their lives. Amongst the most illustrious victims were Sir Thomas More, and Bishop Fisher. They were executed in 1535, simply and solely for denying the king's supremacy in religious matters.

As the king had put himself in the place of the Pope, he was obliged to appoint a Vicar-General, and he gave this office to Cromwell. The next move of these worthies was to suppress the monasteries, and to get possession of all the money which the good monks and nuns had distributed so freely to the poor. Of course the king was determined to establish the new religion firmly in England before he attempted to do anything in Ireland. He probably cared very little what the Irish said or thought about it, but there were monasteries and convents in Ireland also, and he could not rob them of their property without some excuse.

The Irish parliament which was composed solely of persons whom the English government had permitted to be elected, were sure to do exactly what the English government wished. Hence they were quite ready to imitate the English parliament by declaring the king's marriage with Catherine of Arragon null and void, and by sanctioning his marriage with Anne Boleyn. All this was done in the year 1536.

But Henry soon found that there was something more than mere Acts of Parliament necessary in order to establish the new religion in faithful Catholic Ireland. He therefore looked out for some apostate priest who might do for Ireland what the wicked Cranmer had done for England. He found the kind of man he wanted, but he found also that no amount of persecution or bribery would induce the Irish to become Protestants. A few persons here and there might be tempted to renounce the old faith, sooner than suffer death, or lose their temporal possessions, but, AS A NATION, THE IRISH PEOPLE ALWAYS HAVE, AND PLEASE GOD ALWAYS WILL REMAIN TRUE TO THE ONE HOLY CATHOLIC FAITH.

The person selected by Henry VIII. for the very useless attempt of trying to make Protestants of the Irish was an apostate priest named Browne. He had been Archbishop Cranmer's secretary, and was also a great friend of Cromwell's. Early in March 1535, he was appointed by Henry VIII., Archbishop of Dublin, and he was consecrated by Cranmer. Thus a wicked king, who had made himself head of the Church, took upon himself to appoint bishops, and a still more wicked archbishop, who pretended to be a Catholic, while in private he declared himself a Protestant, took upon himself to ordain the new prelate, of course having no other authority to do so except what he could get from Henry VIII. Dr. Browne knew all this very well, and never made any pretence of having any divine authority for his office. So far at least he was honest. He knew well enough that he was no successor of St. Patrick, and no true son of the one holy Catholic Church, yet from him, and from this sole and single will of the profligate monarch, Henry VIII., all the Protestant clergy of Ireland derive their sole authority.

Indeed Henry took very good care there should be no mistake about the matter. A letter of his to this same Dr. Browne is still in existence, and in this letter he thus issues his royal commands and declares his royal opinion:

"Do then your duty towards us in the advancement of our affairs there, and in the signifaction hither, from time to time, of the state of the same, and we shall put your former negligence in oblivion. If this will not serve to induce you to it, but that you will still persevere in your fond folly and ungrateful ungentleness, that you cannot remember what we have done, and how much above many others you be bound in all the points before touched, to do your duty; let it sink into your remembrance that we be as able for the not doing thereof, to remove you again, and to put another man of more virtue and honesty in your place, both for our discharge against God, and for the comfort of our good subjects there; as we were at the beginning to prefer you, upon hope that you would in the same do your office, as to your profession and our opinion conceived of you appertaineth."

Soon after his arrival in Ireland, Dr. Browne received a formal letter from Lord Cromwell, acquainting him with "the royal will and pleasure of his Majesty; that his subjects in Ireland, even as those of England, should obey his commands in spiritual matters as in temporal, and renounce their allegiance to the See of Rome."

The Irish people, however, were not so very obliging, and had no idea whatever of renouncing their allegiance to the See of Rome, and so the unfortunate prelate who wished very much both to please Henry VIII. and to keep his archbishopric, found himself in a very unpleasant position, and he writes thus to his great patron, Cromwell.

"My most honoured Lord,—Your humble servant, receiving your mandate as one of his highness's commissioners, hath endeavoured, almost to the danger and hazard of his temporal life to procure the nobility and gentry of this nation to due obedience, in owning of this highness their supreme head as well spiritual as temporal, and do find much oppugning therein, especially by my brother, Armagh, who hath been the main oppugner, and so hath withdrawn most of his suffragans and clergy within his see and jurisdiction. He made a speech to them, laying a curse on the people whosoever should own his highness's supremacy, saying that isle — as it is in their Irish chronicles—insula sacra, belongs to none but the Bishop of Rome, and that it was the Bishop of Rome that gave it to the king's ancestors. There be two messengers, by the priests of Armagh and by that archbishop, now lately sent to the Bishop of Rome. Your lordship may inform his highness that it is convenient to call a parliament in his nation, to pass the supremacy by act; for they do not much matter his highness's commission, which your lordship sent us over. This island hath been for a long time held in ignorance by the Romish orders. The common people of this isle are more zealous in their blindness than the saints and martyrs were in truth, at the beginning of the gospel. I send to you, my very good lord, these things, that your lordship and his highness may consult what is to be done. It is feared O'Neill will be ordered by the Bishop of Rome to oppose your lordship's order from the king's highness, for the natives are very much in numbers within his powers. I do pray the Lord Christ to defend your lordship from your enemies.—Dublin, 4th Kal. Dec., 1535."

As it was now found the Irish people would not apostatize, the most cruel persecutions commenced, and every religious order in Ireland, Franciscans, Dominicans, and Augustinians, sent numbers of holy souls to join the royal army of martyrs in heaven. It will be impossible here to give details of all their martyrdoms, and of the fidelity and generosity of the Irish, where all, with but few exceptions, from the highest in the land to the very poorest, were willing to lay down their lives cheerfully for the faith which had been taught them by their glorious apostle, St. Patrick. I refer those who wish for further information to the *Illustrated History of Ireland*.

The reformers now began to upbraid each other with the very crimes of which they had accused the clergy in England. When mention is made of the immense sums of money which were obtained by the confiscation of religious houses at this period, it has been commonly and naturally sup posed, that the religious were possessors of immense wealth, which they hoarded up for their own benefit; and although each person made a vow of poverty, it is thought that what was possessed collectively, was enjoyed individually. But this false impression arises from a mistaken idea of a monastic life, and from a misapprehension as to the kind of property possessed by the religious.

A brief account of some of the property forfeited in Ireland, will explain this important matter. We do not find in any instance that religious communities had large funds of money. If they had extensive tracts of land, they were rather the property of the poor, who farmed them, than of the friars, who held them in trust. Any profit they produced made no addition to the fare or the clothing of the religious, for both fare and clothing were regulated by certain rules framed by the original founders, and which could not be altered. These rules invariably required the use of the plainest diet and of the coarsest habits. A considerable portion—indeed, by far the most considerable portion—of conventual wealth, consisted in the sacred vessels and ornaments. These had been bestowed on the monastic churches by benefactors, who considered that what was used in the service of God should be the best which man could offer. The monk was none the richer if he offered the sacrifice to the Eternal Majesty, each morning in a chalice of gold, encrusted with the most precious jewels; but if it were right and fitting to present that chalice to God for the service of his Divine Majesty, who shall estimate the guilt of those who presumed to take the gift from Him to whom it had been given? We know how terrible was the judgment which came upon a heathen monarch who dared to use the vessels which had belonged to the Jewish Temple, and we may well believe that a still more terrible judgment is prepared for those who desecrate Christian churches, and that it will be none the less sure because, under the new dispensation of mercy, it comes less swiftly.

All the gold and silver plate, jewels, ornaments, lead, bells, &c., were reserved by special command for the king's use. The church-lands were sold to the highest bidder, or bestowed as a reward on those who had helped to enrich the royal coffers by sacrilege. Amongst the records of the sums thus obtained, we find £326 2s. 11d., the price of divers pieces of gold and silver, of precious stones, silver ornaments, &c.; also £20, the price of 1,000 lbs. of wax. The sum of £1,710 2s. was realized from the sale of sacred vessels belonging to thirty-nine monasteries. The profits on the spoliation of St. Mary's Dublin, realized £385. The destruction of the Collegiate Church of St. Patrick must have procured an enormous profit, as we find that Cromwell received £60 for his pains in effecting the same. It should also be remembered that the value of a penny then was equal to the value of a shilling now, so that we should multiply these sums at least by ten to obtain an approximate idea of the extent of this wholesale robbery.

The spoilers now began to quarrel over the spoils. The most active or the most favoured received the largest share; and Dr. Browne grumbled loudly at not obtaining all he asked for. But we have not space to pursue the disedifying history of their quarrels. The next step was to accuse each other. In the report of the Commissioners appointed in 1538 to examine into the state of the country, we find complaints made of the exaction of undue fees, extortions for baptisms and marriages, &c. They also (though this was not made an accusation by the Commissioners) received the fruits of benefices in which they did not officiate, and they were accused of taking wives and dispensing with the sacrament of matrimony. The king, whatever personal views he might have on this subject, expected his clergy to live virtuously; and in 1542 he wrote to the Lord Deputy, requiring an Act to be passed "for the continency of the clergy," and some "reasonable plan to be devised for the avoiding of sin." However, neither the Act nor the reasonable plan appears to have succeeded. In 1545 Dr. Browne writes: "Here reigneth insatiable ambition; here reigneth continually coigne and livery, and callid extortion." Five years later, Sir Anthony St. Leger, after piteous complaints of the decay of piety and the increase of immorality, epitomizes the state of the country thus : "I never saw the land so far out of good order." Pages might be filled with such details; but the subject shall be dismissed with a brief notice of the three props of the Reformation and the king's supremacy in Ireland. These were Dr. Browne of Dublin, Dr. Staples of Meath, and Dr. Bale of Ossory. The latter, writing of the former in 1553, excuses the corruption of his own reformed clergy, by stating that "they would at no hand obey; alleging for their vain and idle excuse, the lewd example of the Archbishop of Dublin, who was always slack in things pertaining to God's glory." He calls him "an epicurious archbishop, a brockish swine, and a dissembling proselyte," and accuses him in plain terms of "drunkenness and gluttony." Dr. Browne accuses Dr. Staples of having preached in such a manner, "as I think the three-mouthed Cerberus of hell could not have uttered it more viperously." And Dr. Mant, the Protestant panegyrist of the Reformation and the Reformers, admits that Dr. Bale was guilty of "uncommon warmth of temperament"—a polite appellation for a most violent temper; and of "unbecoming coarseness"—a delicate definement of a profligate life. His antecedents were not very creditable. After flying from his convent in England, he was imprisoned for preaching sedition in York and London. He obtained his release by professing conformity to the new creed. He eventually retired to Canterbury, after his expulsion from Kilkenny by the Catholics, and there he died, in 1563.

CHAPTER XIII.

The Insurrection of Silken Thomas—Joy of the Irish at the Accession of Queen Mary—Accession of Queen Elizabeth—Martyrs during her Reign—Shane O'Neill—Help obtained from Spain—Failure of this attempt for Freedom—O'Neill's Insurrection—The Siege of Dunboy.

WE must now return to secular history. In 1537, the English tried to bribe the Irish chieftains into submission to their rule by making O'Conor Faly a baron, thinking that Irishmen would so hate him afterwards, that he would be forsaken by them and obliged to persevere in allegiance to the Saxon. But the plan failed, for O'Brien, Caher's brother, expelled the new-made lord and took possession of his territory. In 1538 there was a great Geraldine league formed by the O'Neill's, O'Donnell's, O'Briens, O'Rourkes, and the Earl of Desmond, but they failed to effect any good for their oppressed country, simply and solely from their want of unanimity of purpose. It does, indeed, seem as if Irishmen never would, and never could learn the most important of all lessons for the oppressed, to meet in vigorous unity against the oppressor.

On the 1st of July, 1543, Murrough O'Brien was

created Earl of Thomond and Baron of Inchiquin; and De Burgo, known by the soubriquet of Ulich-na-gceann ("of the heads"), from the number of persons whom he decapitated in his wars, was created Earl of Clanrickarde and Baron of Dunkellin. These titles were conferred by the king, with great pomp, at Greenwich; but the Irish chieftains paid for the honour, if honour it could be called where honour was forfeited, by acknowledging the royal supremacy.

The Four Masters record the following events under the year 1545:—A dispute between the Earl of Ormonde and the Lord Justice. Both repaired to the King of England to decide the quarrel, and both swore that only one of them should return to Ireland. "And so it fell out; for the Earl died in England, and the Lord Justice returned to Ireland." Sir Richard Cox asserts that the Earl and thirty-five of his servants were poisoned, at a feast at Ely House, Holborn, and that he and sixteen of them died; but he does not mention any cause for this tragedy. It was probably accidental, as the Earl was a favourer of the reformed religion, and not likely to meet with treachery in England. The Irish annalists do not even allude to the catastrophe; the Four Masters merely observe, that "he would have been lamented, were it not that he had greatly injured the Church by advice of the heretics."

Great dearth prevailed this year, so that sixpence

of the old money was given for a cake of bread in Connaught, or six white pence in Meath.

In 1546 they mention a rising of the Geraldines, "which did indescribable damages; and two invasions of the Lord Justice in Offaly, who plundered and spoiled, burning churches and monasteries, crops and corn. They also mention the introduction of a new copper coin into Ireland, which the men of Ireland were obliged to use as silver.

The immense sums which Henry had accumulated by the plunder of religious houses, appear to have melted away, like snow-wreaths in sunshine, long before the conclusion of his reign. His French and Scotch wars undoubtedly exhausted large supplies; his mistresses made large demands for their pleasures and their needy friends; yet there should have been enough, and to spare, for all these claims.

Yet in 1545 a benevolence was demanded, though benevolences had been declared illegal by Act of Parliament. This method of raising money had been attempted at an early period of this reign; but the proposal met with such spirited opposition from the people, that even royalty was compelled to yield. A few years later, when the fatal result of opposition to the monarch's will and pleasure had become apparent, he had only to ask and obtain. Yet neither per-centage, nor tenths, nor sacrilegious spoils, sufficed to meet his expenses: and, as a last expedient, the coin was debased, and irreparable injury inflicted on the country.

On the 28th of January, 1547, Edward VI. was crowned King of England. The Council of Regency appointed by Henry was set aside, and Seymour, Duke of Somerset, appointed himself Protector. St. Leger was continued in the office of Lord Deputy in Ireland; but Sir Edward Bellingham was sent over as Captain-General, with a considerable force, to quell the ever-recurring disturbances. His energetic character bore down all opposition, as much by the sheer strength of a strong will as by force of arms. In 1549 the Earl of Desmond refused to attend a Council in Dublin, on the plea that he wished to keep Christmas in his own castle. Bellingham, who had now replaced St. Leger as Lord Deputy, set out at once, with a small party of horse, for the residence of the refractory noble, seized him as he sat by his own fire-side, and carried him off in triumph to Dublin.

In 1551 the Lord Deputy, Crofts, who succeeded Sir Thomas Cusack, led an army into Ulster against the Scotch settlers, who had long been regarded with a jealous eye by the English Government; but he was defeated both at this time and on a subsequent occasion. No Parliament was convened during this short reign, and the affairs of the country were administered by the Privy Council.

The most important native chieftain of the age was Shane O'Neil. His father, surnamed Con Baccagh ("the lame") had procured the title of

Baron of Dungannon, and the entail of the earldom of Tyrone, from Henry VII., for his illegitimate son, Ferdoragh. He now wished to alter this arrangement; but the ungrateful youth made such charges against the old man, that he was seized and imprisoned by the Deputy. After his death, Shane contended bravely for his rights. The French appear to have made some attempt about this period to obtain allies in Ireland, but the peace which ensued between that country and England soon terminated such intrigues.

All efforts to establish the new religion during this reign were equally unsuccessful. On Easter Sunday, A.D. 1551, the liturgy was read for the first time in the English tongue, in Christ Church Cathedral. As a reward for his energy in introducing the reform in general, and the liturgy in particular, Edward VI. annexed the primacy of all Ireland to the See of Dublin by Act of Parliament. There was one insuperable obstacle, however, in the way of using the English tongue, which was simply that the people did not understand it. Even the descendants of the Anglo-Normans were more familiar with the Celtic dialect, and some attempt was made at this time to procure a Latin translation of the Protestant communion service.

Dr. Dowdall had been appointed, in 1543, to the primatial See of Armagh, by Henry VIII., who naturally hoped he would prove a ready instrument in his service; but, to the surprise of the court, he put himself at the head of the Catholic party, and was one of the most faithful opposers of the introduction of the Protestant form of prayer.

Mary succeeded to the crown in 1553. A Protestant writer explains the difference between the religious persecutions of her reign, and those which occurred during the reign of Henry VIII., with admirable discrimination and impartiality. "The religious persecutions which prevailed in this reign proceeded altogether from a different cause from that which stands as an everlasting blot on the memory of Henry VIII. In Henry's instance, people were tortured and murdered in the name of religion, but the real cause was their opposition to the will of an arbitrary tyrant; whereas those who suffered under Mary, were martyred because the Queen conscientiously believed in those principles to which she clung with such pertinacity." One of the principal of these victims was Archbishop Cranmer, who had already caused several persons to suffer in the flames for differing from his opinions, and thus almost merited his fate. It is a curious fact that several Protestants came to Ireland during this reign, and settled in Dublin; they were subsequently the founders of respectable mercantile families.

Although the English people had adopted the reformed religion nationally, there were still a few persons whom neither favour nor indifference could induce to renounce the ancient faith; and this brief respite from persecution tended to confirm and strengthen those who wavered. In Ireland, always Catholic, the joy was unbounded. Archbishop Dowdall immediately prepared to hold a provincial synod at Drogheda, where enactments were made for depriving the conforming prelates and priests. Happily their number were so few that there was but little difficulty in making the necessary arrangements. The only prelates that were removed were Browne, of Dublin; Staples of Meath; Lancaster, of Kildare; and Travers of Leighlin. Goodacre died a few months after his intrusion into the See of Armagh; Bale of Ossory, fled beyond the seas; Casey, of Limerick, followed his example. All were English except the latter, and all, except Staples, were professing Protestants at the time of their appointment to their respective sees. Bale, who owed the Kilkenny people a grudge, for the indignant reception with which they greeted him on his intrusion into the see, gives a graphic account of the joy with which the news of Edward's death was received. The people "flung up their caps to the battlements of the great temple;" set the bells ringing; brought out incense and holy water, and formed once more a Catholic procession, chanting the *Sancta Maria, ora pro nobis*, as of old. In fact, " on the accession of Mary to the throne, so little had been done in the interest of the Reformation, that there was little or nothing to undo. She issued a license for the celebration of Mass in Ireland, where no other service was, or had been celebrated worth mentioning, and where no other supreme head had been ever in earnest acknowledged but the Pope."

In the year 1553 Gerald and Edward, the sons of the late Earl of Kildare, returned from exile, and were restored to the family honours and possessions. The Four Masters say that "there was great rejoicing because of their arrival, for it was thought that not one of the decendants of the Earls of Kildare or of the O'Connors Faly would ever again come to Ireland." They also mention that Margaret, daughter of O'Connor Faly, went to England, " relying on the number of her friends and relatives there, and her knowledge of the English language, to request Queen Mary to restore her father to her." Her petition was granted, but he was soon after seized again by the English officials, and cast into prison.

Shane O'Neil made an unsuccessful attempt to recover his paternal dominions, in 1557. The following year his father died in captivity, in Dublin, and he procured the murder of Ferdoragh, so that he was able to obtain his wishes without opposition. Elizabeth had now ascended the English throne (A.D. 1558), and, as usual, those in power, who wished to retain office, made their religion suit the views of the new ruler. The Earl of Sussex still continued Viceroy, and merely reversed his previous acts. Sir Henry Sydney also made his worldly interests and his religious views coincide. A Parliament was held in Dublin, in 1560, on the 12th of January. It was composed of seventy-six members, the representatives of ten counties, the remainder being citizens and burgesses of those towns in which the royal authority was predominant. "It is little wonder," observes Leland, "that, in despite of clamour and opposition, in a session of a few weeks, the whole ecclesiastical system of Queen Mary was entirely reversed." Every subject connected with this assembly and its enactments demands the most careful consideration, as it has been asserted by some writers—who, however, have failed to give the proofs of their assertion—that the Irish Church and nation conformed at this time to the Protestant religion. This, certainly, was not the opinion of the Government officials who were appointed by royal authority to enforce the Act, and who would have been only too happy could they have reported success to their mistress.

A recent writer, whose love of justice has led him to take a position in regard to Irish ecclesiastical history which has evoked unpleasant remarks from those who are less honest, writes thus:— "There was not even the show of free action in the ordering of that parliament, nor the least pretence that liberty of choice was to be given to it.

Notwithstanding the solemn promise of the Lord Deputy, the penal statutes against Catholics were carried out. In 1563 the Earl of Essex issued a proclamation, by which all priests, secular and regular, were forbidden to officiate, or even to reside in Dublin. Fines and penalties were strictly enforced for absence from the Protestant service; before long, torture and death were inflicted. Priests and religious were, as might be expected, the first victims. They were hunted into mountains and caves; and the parish churches and few monastic chapels which had escaped the rapacity of Henry VIII., were sacrificed to the sacrilegious emissaries of Elizabeth. Curry gives some account of those who suffered for the faith in this reign. He says: "Among many other Roman Catholic bishops and priests, who were put to death, for the exercise of their function in Ireland, Globy O'Boyle, Abbot of Boyle, and Owen O'Mulkeran, Abbot of the Monastery of the Holy Trinity, were hanged and quartered by Lord Grey, in 1580."

Dr. Adam Loftus, the Protestant Archbishop of Armagh, was one of the most violent persecutors of the Catholics. In his first report to the Queen, dated May 17, 1565, he describes the nobility of the Pale as all devoted to the ancient creed; and he recommends that they should be fined "in a good round sum," which should be paid to her Majesty's use, and "sharply dealt withal." An original method of conversion, certainly! But it did not succeed. On the 22nd September, 1590, after twenty-five years had been spent in the fruitless attempt to convert the Irish, he writes to Lord Burleigh, detailing the causes of the general decay of the Protestant religion in Ireland, and suggesting " how the same may be remedied." He advises that the ecclesiastical commission should be put in force, "for the people are poor, and fear to be fined." He requests that he and such commissioners as are "well affected in religion, may be permitted to imprison and fine all such as are obstinate and disobedient;" and he has no doubt, that "within a short time they will be reduced to good conformity." He concludes : "And *this course of reformation*, the sooner it is begun the better it will prosper; and the longer it is deferred, the more dangerous it will be." When Catholics remember that such words were written, and such deeds were enacted, by the head of the Protestant Church in Ireland, and sanctioned by the head of the Protestant Church in England, they may surely be content to allow modern controversialists the benefit of their pleasant dream that Catholic bishops conformed. If they had conformed to such doctrines and such practices, it can scarcely be seen what advantage the Anglican Establishment could gain from their patronage.

Seven years later, when the same prelate found that the more the Church was persecuted the more she increased, he wrote to advise pacification : "The

The Irish Patriot Bishop offering his life for Ireland.

rebels are increased, and grown insolent. I see no cure for this cursed country but pacification [he could not help continuing], until, hereafter, when the fury is passed, her Majesty may, with more convenience, correct the heads of those traitors." The prelate was ably seconded by the Lord Deputy. Even Sir John Perrot, who has the name of being one of the most humane of these governors, could not refrain from acts of cruelty where Catholics were concerned.

Father Dominic à Rosario, the author of "The Geraldines," scarcely exceeded truth when he wrote these memorable words: "This far-famed English Queen has grown drunk on the blood of Christ's martyrs; and, like a tigress, she has hunted down our Irish Catholics, exceeding in ferocity and wanton cruelty the emperors of pagan Rome." We shall conclude this painful subject for the present with an extract from O'Sullivan Beare: "All alarm from the Irish chieftains being ceased, the persecution was renewed with all its horrors. A royal order was promulgated, that all should renounce the Catholic faith, yield up the priests, receive from the heretical minister the morality and tenets of the Gospel. Threats, penalties, and force were to be employed to enforce compliance. Every effort of the Queen and her emissaries was directed to despoil the Irish Catholics of their property, and exterminate them. More than once did they attempt this, for they knew that not otherwise

could the Catholic religion be suppressed in our
island, *unless by the extermination of those in whose
hearts it was implanted;* nor could their heretical
teachings be propagated, while the natives were
alive to detest and execrate them."

In 1561 Sussex returned from England with reinforcements for his army, and marched to Armagh,
where he established himself in the cathedral.
From thence he sent out a large body of troops to
plunder in Tyrone, but they were intercepted by the
redoubtable Shane O'Neill, and suffered so serious a
defeat as to alarm the inhabitants of the Pale, and
even the English nation. Fresh supplies of men
and arms were hastily despatched from England,
and the Earls of Desmond, Ormonde, Kildare,
Thomond, and Clanrickarde assembled round the
Viceregal standard to assist in suppressing the
formidable foe. And well might they fear the
lion-hearted chieftain! A few years later, Sidney
describes him as the only strong man in Ireland.
The Queen was warned, that unless he were speedily
put down, she would lose Ireland, as her sister had
lost Calais. He had gained all Ulster by his sword,
and ruled therein with a far stronger hand,
and on a far firmer foundation, than ever any
English monarch had obtained in any part of
Ireland.

As this man was too clever to be captured, and
too brave to be conquered, a plan was arranged,
with the full concurrence of the Queen, by which

he might be got rid of by poison or assassination. Had such an assertion been made by the Irish annalists, it would have been scouted as a calumny on the character of " good Queen Bess ;" but the evidence of her complicity is preserved in the records of the State Paper Office. I shall show presently that attempts at assassination were a common arrangement for the disposal of refractory Irish chieftains during this reign.

The proposal for this diabolical treachery, and the arrangements made for carrying it out, were related by Sussex to the Queen. He writes thus: "In fine, I brake with him to kill Shane, and bound myself by my oath to see him have a hundred marks of land to him and to his heirs for reward. He seemed desirous to serve your Highness, and to have the land, but fearful to do it, doubting his own escape after. I told him the ways he might do it, and how to escape after with safety; which he offered and promised to do." The Earl adds a piece of information, which, no doubt, he communicated to the intended murderer, and which probably decided him on making the attempt: "I assure your Highness he may do it without danger if he will; and if he will not do what he may in your service, there will be done to him what others may."

Her Majesty, however, had a character to support; and whatever she may have privately wished and commanded, she was obliged to disavow complicity publicly. In two despatches from court she expresses her "displeasure at John Smith's horrible attempt to poison Shane O'Neill in his wine." In the following spring John Smith was committed to prison, and "closely examined by Lord Chancellor Cusake." What became of John is not recorded, but it is recorded that "Lord Chancellor Cusake persuaded O'Neill to forget the poisoning."

In October, 1562, Shane was invited to England, and was received by Elizabeth with marked courtesy. His appearance at court is thus described: "From Ireland came Shane O'Neill, who had promised to come the year before, with a guard of axe-bearing galloglasses, their heads bare, their long curling hair flowing on their shoulders, their linen garments dyed with saffron, with long open sleeves, with short tunics, and furry cloaks, whom the English wondered at as much as they do now at the Chinese or American aborigines." Shane's visit to London was considered of such importance, that we find a memorandum in the State Paper Office, by "Secretary Sir W. Cecil, March, 1562," of the means to be used with Shane O'Neill, in which the first item is, that "he be procured to change his garments, and go like an Englishman." But this was precisely what O'Neill had no idea of doing. Sussex appears to have been O'Neill's declared and open enemy. There is more than one letter extant from the northern chief to the

Deputy. In one of these he says: "I wonder very much for what purpose your Lordship strives to destroy me." In another, he declares that his delay in visiting the Queen had been caused "by the amount of obstruction which Sussex had thrown in his way, by sending a force of occupation into his territory without cause; for as long as there shall be one son of a Saxon in my territory against my will, from that time forth I will not send you either settlement or message, but will send my complaint through some other medium to the Queen." In writing to the Baron of Slane, he says that "nothing will please him [the Deputy] but to plant himself in my lands and my native territory, as I am told every day that he desires to be styled Earl of Ulster."

The Lord Chancellor Cusake appears, on the contrary, to have constantly befriended him. On 12th January, 1568, he writes of O'Neill's "dutifulness and most commendable dealing with the Scots;" and soon after three English members of the Dublin Government complain that Cusake had entrapped them into signing a letter to the unruly chieftain. There is one dark blot upon the escutcheon of this remarkable man. He had married the daughter of O'Donnell, Lord of one of the Hebrides. After a time he and his father-in-law quarrelled, and Shane contrived to capture O'Donnell and his second wife. He kept this lady for several years as his mistress ; and his own wife is said to have died of shame and horror at his conduct, and at his cruel treatment of her father. English writers have naturally tried to blacken his character as deeply as possible, and have represented him as a drunkard and a profligate; but there appears no foundation for the former accusation. The foundation for the latter is simply what we have mentioned, which, however evil in itself, would scarcely appear so very startling to a court over which Henry VIII. had so long presided.

After many attempts at assassination, *Shane-an-Diomais* [John the Ambitious] fell a victim to English treachery. Sir William Piers, the Governor of Carrickfergus, invited some Scotch soldiers over to Ireland, and then persuaded them to quarrel with him and kill him. They accomplished their purpose by raising a disturbance at a feast, when they rushed on the northern chieftain, and despatched him with their swords. His head was sent to Dublin, and his old enemies took the poor revenge of impaling it on the Castle walls.

The Earl of Sussex was recalled from Ireland in 1564, and Sir Henry Sidney was appointed Viceroy. The Earls of Ormonde and Desmond had again quarrelled, and, in 1562, both Earls were summoned to court by the Queen. Elizabeth was related to the Butlers through her mother's family, and used to boast of the loyalty of the house of Ormonde. The Geraldines adhered to the ancient faith, and suffered for it. A battle was fought at Affane, near

Cappoquin, between the two parties, in which Desmond was wounded and made prisoner. The man who bore him from the field asked, tauntingly: "Where is now the proud Earl of Desmond?" He replied, with equal pride and wit: "Where he should be; upon the necks of the Butlers."

CHAPTER XIV.

Spenser's Castle—Sidney's Official Account of Ireland—Miserable State of the Protestant Church—The Catholic Church and its Persecuted Rulers—The Viceroy's Administration—A Packed Parliament and its Enactments—Claim of Sir P. Carew—An Attempt to plant in Ulster—Smith's Settlement in the Ards—His Description of the Native Irish—He tries to induce Englishmen to join him—Smith is killed, and the attempt to plant fails—Essex next tries to colonize Ulster—He dies in Dublin—Sidney returns to Ireland—His Interview with Granuaile—Massacre at Mullamast—Spenser's Account of the State of Ireland.

AT the close of the month of January, 1567, the Lord Deputy, Sir Henry Sidney, set out on a visitation of Munster and Connaught. In his official account he writes thus of Munster: "Like as I never was in a more pleasant country in all my life, so never saw I a more waste and desolate land. Such horrible and lamentable spectacles are there to behold—as the burning of villages, the ruin of churches, the wasting of such as have been good towns and castles; yea, the view of the bones and skulls of the dead subjects, who, partly by murder, partly by famine, have died in the fields—as, in truth, hardly any Christian with dry eyes could behold."

In 1576 Sidney complains of the state of the Protestant Church, and addresses himself, with almost blasphemous flattery, to the head of that body, "as to the only sovereign salvegiver to this your sore and sick realm, the lamentable state of the most noble and principal limb thereof—the Church I mean—as foul, deformed, and as cruelly crushed as any other part thereof, only by your generous order to be cured, or at least amended. I would not have believed, had I not, for a greater part, viewed the same throughout the whole realm." He then gives a detailed account of the state of the diocese of Meath, which he declares to be the best governed and best peopled diocese in the realm; and from his official report of the state of religion there, he thinks her Majesty may easily judge of the spiritual condition of less favoured districts. He says there are no resident parsons or vicars, and only a very simple or sorry curate appointed to serve them; of these only eighteen could speak English, the rest being "Irish ministers, or rather Irish rogues, having very little Latin, and less learning or civility." In many places he found the walls of the churches thrown down, the chancels uncovered, and the windows and doors ruined or spoiled—fruits of the iconoclastic zeal of the original reformers, and of the rapacity of the nobles, who made religion an excuse for plunder. He complains that the sacrament of baptism was not used amongst them, and he accuses the "prelates themselves" of despoiling their sees, declaring that, if he told all, he should make "too long a libel of his letter. But your Majesty may believe it, that, upon the face of the earth where Christ is professed, there is not a Church in so miserable a case."

It should be observed, however, that Sir Henry Sidney's remarks apply exclusively to the Protestant clergy. Of the state of the Catholic Church and clergy he had no knowledge, neither had he any interest in obtaining information. His account of the Protestant clergy who had been intruded into the Catholic parishes, and of the Protestant bishops who had been placed in the Catholic dioceses, we may presume to be correct, as he had no interest or object in misrepresentation.

It is also a matter of fact, that although the Protestant services were not attended, and the lives of the Protestant ministers were not edifying, that the sacraments were administered constantly by the Catholic clergy. It is true they date their letters "from the place of refuge," which might be the wood nearest to their old and ruined parish-church, or the barn or stable of some friend, who dared not shelter them in his house; yet this was no hindrance to their ministrations; for we find

Dr. Loftus complaining to Sir William Cecil that the persecuted Bishop of Meath, Dr. Walsh, was "one of great credit amongst his countrymen, and upon whom (as touching cause of religion) they wholly depend." Sir Henry Sidney's efforts to effect reformation of conduct in the clergy and laity, do not seem to have been so acceptable at court as he might have supposed. His strong measures were followed by tumults; and the way in which he obtained possession of the persons of some of the nobles was not calculated to enhance his popularity. He was particularly severe towards the Earl of Desmond, whom he seized in Kilmallock, after requiring his attendance on pretence of wishing him to assist in his visitation of Munster. In October, 1567, the Deputy proceeded to England to explain his conduct, taking with him the Earl of Desmond and his brother, John, whom he also arrested on false pretences. Sidney was, however, permitted to return in September, 1568. He landed at Carrickfergus, where he received the submission of Turlough O'Neill, who had been elected to the chieftaincy on the death of Shane the Proud.

The first public act of the Lord Deputy was to assemble a parliament, in which all constitutional rules were simply set at defiance (January 17th, 1569). In this parliament—if, indeed, it could be called such—Acts were passed for attainting Shane O'Neill, for suppressing the name, and for annexing Tyrone to the royal possessions.

Sidney now began to put his plan of local governments into execution; but this arrangement simply multiplied the number of licenced oppressors. Sir Edward Fitton was appointed President of Connaught, and Sir John Perrot, of Munster. Both of these gentlemen distinguished themselves by "strong measures," of which cruelty to the unfortunate natives was the predominant feature. Perrot boasted that he would "hunt the fox out of his hole," and devoted himself to the destruction of the Geraldines. Fitton arrested the Earl of Clanrickarde, and excited a general disturbance. In 1570 the Queen determined to lay claim to the possessions in Ulster, graciously conceded to her by the gentlemen who had been permitted to vote according to her royal pleasure in the so-called parliament of 1569. She bestowed the district of Ards, in Down, upon her secretary, Sir Thomas Smith. It was described as "divers parts and parcels of her Highness' Earldom of Ulster that lay waste, or else was inhabited with a wicked, barbarous, and uncivil people." There were, however, two grievous misstatements in this document. Ulster did not belong to her Highness, unless, indeed, the Act of a packed parliament could be considered legal; and the people who inhabited it were neither "wicked, barbarous, nor uncivil." The tract of country thus unceremoniously bestowed on an English adventurer, was in the possession of Sir Rowland Savage. His first ancestor was one of the most distinguished of the Anglo-Norman settlers who had accompanied De Courcy to Ireland. Thus, although he could not claim the prescriptive right of several thousand years for his possession, he certainly had the right of possession for several centuries. The next attempt was made by Walter Devereux, Earl of Essex, who received part of the seignories of Clannaboy and Ferney, provided he could expel the "rebels" who dwelt there. Essex mortgaged his estates to the Queen to obtain funds for the enterprise. He was accompanied by Sir Henry Kenlis, Lord Dacres, and Lord Norris's three sons.

Sir William FitzGerald, the then Lord Deputy, complained loudly of the extraordinary powers granted to Essex; and some show of deference to his authority was made by requiring the Earl to receive his commission from him. Essex landed in Ireland in 1573, and the usual career of tyranny and treachery was enacted. The native chieftains resisted the invasion of their territories, and endeavoured to drive out the men whom they could only consider as robbers. The invaders, when they could not conquer, stooped to acts of treachery. Essex soon found that the conquest of Ulster was not quite so easy a task as he had anticipated. Many of the adventurers who had assumed his livery, and joined his followers, deserted him; and Brian O'Neill, Hugh O'Neill, and Turlough O'Neill, rose up against him. Essex then invited Conn O'Donnell to his camp; but, as soon as he secured him, he seized his Castle of Lifford, and sent the unfortunate chieftain a prisoner to Dublin.

In 1574 the Earl and Brian O'Neill made peace. A feast was prepared by the latter, to which Essex and his principal followers were invited; but after this entertainment had lasted for three days and nights, "as they were agreeably drinking and making merry, Brian, his brother, and his wife were seized upon by the Earl, and all his people put unsparingly to the sword—men, women, youths, and maidens—in Brian's own presence. Brian was afterwards sent to Dublin, together with his wife and brother, where they were cut in quarters. Such was the end of their feast. This wicked and treacherous murder of the lord of the race of Hugh Boy O'Neil, the head and the senior of the race of Eoghan, son of Nial of the Nine Hostages, and of all the Gaels, a few only excepted, was a sufficient cause of hatred and dispute to the English by the Irish."

In 1586 a thousand soldiers were withdrawn from Ireland to serve in the Netherlands; and as the country was always governed by force, it could scarcely be expected not to rebel when the restraint was withdrawn. O'Neill manifested alarming symptoms of independence. He had married a daughter of Sir Hugh O'Donnell, and Sir Hugh refused to admit an English sheriff into his territory.

The Government had, therefore, no resource but war or treachery. War was impossible, when so large a contingent had been withdrawn; treachery was always possible; and even Sir John Perrot stooped to this base means of attaining his end. The object was to get possession of Hue Roe O'Donnell, a noble youth, and to keep him as hostage. The treachery was accomplished thus: a vessel laden with Spanish wine was sent to Donegal on pretence of traffic. It anchored at Rathmullen, where it had been ascertained that Hugh Roe O'Donnell was staying with his foster-father, MacSweeney. The wine was distributed plentifully to the country people; and when MacSweeny sent to make purchases, the men declared there was none left for sale, but if the gentlemen came on board they should have what was left. Hugh and his companions easily fell into the snare. They were hospitably entertained, but their arms were carefully removed, the hatches were shut down, the cable cut, and the ship stood off to sea. The guests who were not wanted were put ashore, but the unfortunate youth was taken to Dublin, and confined in the Castle.

In 1588 Sir John Perrot was succeeded by Sir William FitzWilliam, a nobleman of the most opposite character and disposition. Perrot was generally regretted by the native Irish, as he was considered one of the most humane of the Lord Deputies. The wreck of the Spanish Armada occurred during this year, and was made at once an excuse for increased severity towards the Catholics, and for acts of grievous injustice.

In 1590 Hugh of the Fetters, an illegitimate son of the famous Shane O'Neill, was hanged by the Earl of Tyrone, for having made false charges against him to the Lord Deputy. This exercise of authority excited considerable fear, and the Earl was obliged to clear himself of blame before Elizabeth. After a brief detention in London, he was permitted to return to Ireland, but not until he had signed certain articles in the English interest, which he observed precisely as long as it suited his own convenience. About this time his nephew, Hugh O'Donnell, made an ineffectual attempt to escape from Dublin Castle, but he was recaptured, and more closely guarded. This again attracted the attention of Government to the family; but a more important event was about to follow. O'Neill's wife was dead, and the chieftain was captivated by the beauty of Sir Henry Bagnal's sister. How they contrived to meet and to plight their vows is not known, though State Papers have sometimes revealed as romantic particulars. It has been discovered, however, from that invaluable source of information, that Sir Henry was furious, and cursed himself and his fate that his " bloude, which had so often been spilled in repressinge this rebellious race, should nowe be mingled with so treacherous a stocke and kindred." He removed the lady from Newry to her sister's house, near Dublin, who was the wife of Sir Patrick Barnwell. The Earl followed Miss Bagnal thither. Her brother-in-law received him courteously; and while the O'Neill engaged the family in conversation, a confidential friend rode off with the lady, who was married to O'Neill immediately after.

Hugh O'Donnell made another attempt to escape from confinement at Christmas, A.D. 1592. He succeeded on this ocassion, though his life was nearly lost in the attempt. Turlough Roe O'Hagan, his father's faithful friend, was the principal agent in effecting his release. Henry and Art O'Neill, sons of Shane the Proud, were companions in his flight. They both fell exhausted on their homeward journey. Art died soon after, from the effects of fatigue and exposure, and Hugh recovered but slowly. He continued ill during the remainder of the winter, and was obliged to have his toes amputated. As soon as he was sufficiently recovered, a general meeting of his sept was convened, when he was elected to the chieftaincy, and inaugurated in the usual manner. He then commenced incursions on the territories occupied by the English; but as the Earl of Tyrone was anxious to prevent a premature rebellion, he induced the Lord Deputy to meet him at Dundalk, where he obtained a full pardon for his escape from Dublin Castle, and a temporary pacification was arranged.

In 1593 he collected another army; Turlough Luineach resigned his chieftaincy to the Earl of

Tyrone; and Ulster became wholly the possession of its old chieftains—the O'Neill and O'Donnell. An open rebellion broke out soon after, in consequence of the exactions of two English officers on the territories of Oge O'Rourke and Maguire. Several trifling engagements took place. The Earl of Tyrone was placed in a difficult position. He was obliged to join the English side while his heart and inclinations were with his own people; but he contrived to send a messenger to Hugh Roe, who had joined Maguire's party, requesting him not to fight against him. He was placed in a still greater difficulty at the siege of Enniskillen, which took place the following year. He compromised matters by sending his brother, Cormac O'Neill, with a contingent, to fight on the national side. Cormac met the English soldiers, who had been sent to throw provisions into the town, almost five miles from their destination, and routed them with great slaughter. The site of the engagement was called the "Ford of the Biscuits," from the quantity of those provisions which he obtained there. An Irish garrison was left at Enniskillen, and the victorious party, after retaliating the cruelties which had been inflicted on the natives, marched into northern Connaught to attack Sir Richard Bingham.

Many Catholics suffered most cruelly for their faith about this time. One of the principal of these sufferers, and one of those who was most barbarously tortured, was Archbishop O'Hurley. He was martyred in Stephen's-green on the 6th of May, 1584. The details of his heroic endurance form one of the most glorious epochs in the history of our country. Many brave and true men have shed their blood in her defence—all honour to their memories; but amongst the bravest and the truest have been the priests of Ireland, who suffered, as far as cruel torture goes, far—far more agonising pain than could be inflicted even by the cruelest soldiers on the field of battle.

In 1598 another conference was held, the intervening years having been spent in mutual hostilities, in which, on the whole, the Irish had the advantage. O'Neill's tone was proud and independent; he expected assistance from Spain, and he scorned to accept a pardon for what he did not consider a crime. The Government was placed in a difficult position. The prestige of O'Neill and O'Donnell was becoming every day greater. On the 7th of June, 1598, the Earl laid siege to the fort of the Blackwater, then commanded by Captain Williams, and strongly fortified. Reinforcements were sent to the besieged from England, but they were attacked *en route* by the Irish, and lost 400 men at Dungannon. At last the Earl of Ormonde and Bagnal determined to take up arms—the former marching against the Leinster insurgents; the latter, probably but too willing, set out to encounter his old enemy and brother-in-law. He commanded a fine body of men, and had but little doubt on which side victory should declare itself.

The contingent set out for Armagh on the 14th of August, and soon reached the Yellow Ford, about two miles from that city, where the main body of the Irish had encamped. They were at once attacked on either flank by skirmishers from the hostile camp; but the vanguard of the English army advanced gallantly to the charge, and were soon in possession of the first entrenchments of the enemy. Although Bagnal's personal valour is unquestionable, he was a bad tactician. His leading regiment was cut to pieces before a support could come up; his divisions were too far apart to assist each other. Bagnal raised the visor of his helmet for one moment, to judge more effectually of the scene of combat, and that moment proved his last. A musket-ball pierced his forehead, and he fell lifeless to the ground. Almost at the same moment an ammunition waggon exploded in his ranks—confusion ensued. O'Neill took advantage of the panic; he charged boldly; and, before one o'clock, the rout had become general.

The English officers and their men fled to Armagh, and shut themselves up in the cathedral; but they had left twenty-three officers and 1,700 rank and file dead or dying on the field. O'Neill retired for a time to recruit his forces, and to rest his men; and a revolt was organized under his auspices in Munster, with immense success. O'Donnell was making rapid strides; but a new Viceroy was on his way to Ireland, and it was hoped by the royalist party that he would change the aspect of affairs.

Essex arrived on the 15th of April, 1599. He had an army of 20,000 foot and 2,000 horse—the most powerful, if not the best equipped force ever sent into the country. He at once issued a proclamation, offering pardon to all the insurgents who should submit; and he despatched reinforcements to the northern garrison towns, and to Wicklow and Naas. He then marched southward, not without encountering a sharp defeat from Rory O'More. He attacked the Geraldines, without much success, in Fermoy and Lismore, having, on the whole, lost more than he had accomplished by the expedition. An engagement took place between O'Donnell and Sir Conyers Clifford, in the pass of Balloghboy, on the 16th of August, in which Conyers was killed, and his army defeated. His body was recognized by the Irish, towards whom he had always acted honourably, and they interred the remains of their brave and noble enemy with the respect which was justly due to him.

Essex wrote to England for more troops, and his enemies were not slow to represent his incapacity, and to demand his recall; but he had not yet lost grace with his royal mistress, and his request was granted. The Viceroy now marched into the northern provinces. When he arrived at the Lagan, where it bounds Louth and Monaghan, O'Neill appeared on the opposite hill with his army, and sent the O'Hagan, his faithful friend and attendant, to demand a conference. The interview took place on the following day; and O'Neill, with chivalrous courtesy, dashed into the river on his charger, and there conversed with the English Earl, while he remained on the opposite bank. It was supposed that the Irish chieftain had made a favourable impression on Essex, and that he was disposed to conciliate the Catholics. He was obliged to go to England to clear himself of these charges; and his subsequent arrest and execution would excite more sympathy, had he been as amiable in his domestic relations as he is said to have been in his public life.

O'Neill had now obtained a position of considerable importance, and one which he appears to have used invariably for the general good. The fame of his victories had spread throughout the Continent. It was well known now that the Irish had not accepted the Protestant Reformation, and it appeared as if there was at last some hope of permanent peace in Ireland.

James, son of Gerald, Earl of Desmond, who had long been imprisoned in London, was now sent to Ireland, and a patent, restoring his title and estates, was forwarded to Carew, with private instructions that it should be used or not, as might be found expedient. The people flocked with joy to meet the heir of the ancient house, but their enthusiasm was soon turned into contempt. He arrived on a Saturday, and on Sunday went to the Protestant service, for he had been educated in the new religion in London. His people were amazed; they fell on their knees, and implored him not to desert the faith of his fathers; but he was ignorant of their language as well as of their creed. Once this was understood, they showed how much dearer that was to them than even the old ties of kindred, so revered in their island; and his return from prayers was hailed by groans and revilings. The hapless youth was found to be useless to his employers; he was therefore taken back to London, where he died soon after of a broken heart.

Attempts were made to assassinate O'Neill in 1601. £2,000 was offered to anyone who would capture him alive; £1,000 was offered for his head; but none of his own people could be found to play the traitor even for so high a stake. The "Sugane Earl" was treacherously captured about the end of August, and was sent to London in chains, with Florence MacCarthy. But the long-expected aid from Spain had at last arrived. The fleet conveyed a force of 3,000 infantry, and entered the harbour of Kinsale on the 23rd of September, under the command of Don Juan d'Aquila. The northern chieftains set out at once to meet their allies when informed of their arrival; and O'Donnell, with characteristic impetuosity, was the first on the road. Carew attempted to intercept him, but despaired of coming up with " so swift-footed a general," and left him to pursue his way unmolested.

The Lord Deputy was besieging Kinsale, and Carew joined him there. The seige was continued through the month of November, during which time fresh reinforcements came from Spain; and on the 21st of December O'Neill arrived with all his force. Unfortunately, the Spanish general had become thoroughly disgusted with the enterprise; and, although the position of the English was such that the Lord Deputy had serious thoughts of raising the siege, he insisted on decisive measures; and O'Neill was obliged to surrender his opinion, which was entirely against this line of action. A sortie was agreed upon for a certain night; but a youth in the Irish camp, who had been in the President's service formerly, warned him of the intended attack. This was sufficient in itself to cause the disaster which ensued. But there were other misfortunes. O'Neill and O'Donnell lost their way; and, when they reached the English camp at dawn, found the soldiers under arms, and prepared for an attack. Their cavalry at once charged, and the new comers in vain struggled to maintain their ground, and a retreat which they attempted was turned into a total rout.

A thousand Irish were slain, and the prisoners were hanged without mercy. The loss on the

English side was but trifling. It was a fatal blow to the Irish cause. Heavy were the hearts and bitter the thoughts of the brave chieftains on that sad night. O'Neill no longer hoped for the deliverance of his country; but the more sanguine O'Donnell proposed to proceed at once to Spain, to explain their position to King Philip. He left Ireland in a Spanish vessel three days after the battle—if battle it can be called; and O'Neill marched rapidly back to Ulster with Rory O'Donnell, to whom Hugh Roe had delegated the chieftaincy of Tir-Connell.

D'Aquila, whose haughty manners had rendered him very unpopular, now surrendered to Mountjoy, who received his submission with respect, and treated his army honourably. According to one account, the Spaniard had touched some English gold, and had thus been induced to desert the Irish cause; according to other authorities, he challenged the Lord Deputy to single combat, and wished them to decide the question at issue. In the meantime, O'Sullivan Beare contrived to get possession of his own Castle of Dunboy, by breaking into the wall at the dead of night, while the Spanish garrison were asleep, and then declaring that he held the fortress for the King of Spain, to whom he transferred his allegiance. Don Juan offered to recover it for the English by force of arms; but the Deputy, whose only anxiety was to get him quietly out of the country, urged his immediate departure. He left Ireland on the 20th of February; and the suspicions of his treachery must have had some foundation, for he was placed under arrest as soon as he arrived in Spain.

The siege of Dunboy is one of the most famous and interesting episodes in Irish history. The castle was deemed almost impregnable from its situation; and every argument was used with Sir George Carew to induce him to desist from attacking it. But the Lord Deputy had resolved that it should be captured. The Lord President considered the enterprise would be by no means difficult, for "he declared that he would plant the ordnance without the losse of a man; and within seven dayes after the battery was begun, bee master of all that place." There was cosiderable delay in the arrival of the shipping which conveyed the ordnance, and operations did not commence until the 6th of June. The defence of the castle was entrusted by O'Sullivan to Richard MacGeoghegan. The chief himself was encamped with Tyrrell in the interior of the country. The soldiers were tempted, and the governor was tempted, but neither flinched for an instant from their duty. The garrison only consisted of 143 fighting men, with a few pieces of cannon. The besieging army was about 3,000 strong, and they were amply supplied with ammunition. On the 17th of June, when the castle was nearly shattered to pieces, its brave defenders offered to surrender if they were allowed to depart with their arms; but the only reply vouchsafed was to hang their messenger, and to commence an assault.

The storming party were resisted for an entire day with undaunted bravery. Their leader was mortally wounded, and Taylor took the command. The garrison at last retreated into a cellar, into which the only access was a narrow flight of stone steps, and where nine barrels of gunpowder were stored. Taylor declared he would blow up the place if life were not promised to those who surrendered. Carew refused, and retired for the night, after placing a strong guard over the unfortunate men. The following morning he sent cannon-ball in amongst them, and Taylor was forced by his companions to yield without conditions. As the English soldiers descended the steps, the wounded MacGeoghegan staggered towards the gunpowder with a lighted candle, and was in the act of throwing it in when he was seized by Captain Power, and in another moment he was massacred. Fifty-eight of those who had surrendered were hanged immediately; a few were reserved to see if they could be induced to betray their old companions, or to renounce their faith; but, as they "would not endeavour to merit life," they were executed without mercy. One of these prisoners was a Father Dominic Collins. He was executed in Youghal, his native town—a most unwise proceeding; for his fate was sure to excite double sympathy in the place where he was known, and, consequently, to promote double disaffection, O'Sullivan Beare assigns the 31st of October as the day of his martyrdom.

The fall of Dunboy was a fatal blow to the national cause. The news soon reached Spain. Hugh O'Donnell had been warmly received there; but the burst of grief which his people uttered, when they saw him departing from his native land, was his death-keen, for he did not long survive his voluntary expatriation.

Donnell O'Sullivan now found his position hopeless, and commenced his famous retreat to Leitrim. He set out with about 1,000 followers, of whom only 400 were fighting men; the rest were servants, women, and children. He fought all the way, and arrived at his destination with only thirty-five followers.

O'Neill now stood merely on the defensive. The land was devastated by famine; Docwra, Governor of Derry, had planted garrisons at every available point; and Mountjoy plundered Ulster. In August he prepared to attack O'Neill with a large army; and, as he informs Cecil, "by the grace of God, as near as he could, utterly to waste the country of Tyrone." O'Neill had now retired to a fastness at the extremity of Lough Erne, attended by his brother, Cormac Art O'Neill, and MacMahon. Mountjoy followed him, but could not approach nearer than twelve miles; he therefore returned to Newry. In describing this march to Cecil, he says, "O'Hagan protested to us, that between Tullaghoge and Toome there lay, unburied, 1,000 dead."

The news of O'Donnell's death had reached Ireland; and his brother submitted to the Deputy. In 1603 Sir Garret More entered into negotiations with O'Neill, which ended in his submitting also. The ceremony took place at Mellifont, on the 31st of March. Queen Elizabeth had expired, more miserably than many of the victims who had been executed in her reign, on the 24th of March; but the news was carefully concealed until O'Neill had made terms with the Viceroy.

CHAPTER XV.

The Reign of James I.—His Treachery towards the Irish—Persecution of the Catholics—The Plantation of Ulster—Accession of Charles I.—His Treachery—The Plantation of Connaught—Irish Parliament at Kilkenny—The Pope sends over the Legate Rinuccinni—His Plans are defeated by intrigues—He returns to Italy.

REAT was the joy of the Irish nation when James the First of England and the Sixth of Scotland ascended the throne.

The Irish Catholics, only too ready to rejoice in the faintest gleam of hope, took possession of their own churches, and hoped they might practise their religion openly, but they were soon undeceived. The penal statutes were renewed, and enforced with increased severity. Several members of the Corporation and some of the principal citizens of Dublin were sent to prison ; similar outrages on religious liberty were perpetrated at Waterford, Ross, and Limerick. In some cases these gentlemen were only asked to attend the Protestant church once ; but they nobly refused to act against their conscience even once, though it should procure them freedom from imprisonment, or even from death.

In 1611 the Bishop of Down and Connor was executed in Dublin. He had been seized, in 1587, by Perrot, and thrown into prison. He was released in 1593, and, according to Dr. Loftus, he took the oath of supremacy. This statement, however, is utterly incredible ; for he devoted himself to his flock immediately after his release, and continued to administer the sacraments to them, at the risk of his life, until June, 1611, when he was again arrested in the act of administering the sacrament of confirmation to a Catholic family. Father O'Luorchain was imprisoned with him, and they were both sentenced and executed together.

Communications with Rome were still as frequent and as intimate as they had ever been since Ireland received the faith at the hands of the great Apostle. The Irish were always children of Patrick and children of Rome ; and the Holy See watched still more tenderly over this portion of the Church while it was suffering and persecuted. Paul V. wrote a special letter to the Irish Catholics, dated from "St. Mark's, 22nd of September, 1606," in which he mourns over their afflictions, commends their marvellous constancy, which he says can only be compared to that of the early Christians, and exhorts them specially to avoid the sin of attending Protestant places of worship—a compliance to which they were strongly tempted, when even one such act might procure exemption, for a time at least, from severe persecution or death.

O'Neill and O'Donnell may be justly considered the last of the independent native chieftains. When the latter died in exile, and the former accepted the coronet of an English earl, the glories of the olden days of princes, who held almost regal power, had passed away for ever.

In May, 1603, O'Neill had visited London in company with Lord Mountjoy and Rory O'Donnell. The northern chieftains were graciously received; and it was on this occasion that O'Neill renounced his ancient name for his new titles. O'Donnell was made Earl of Tyrconnell at the same time. The first sheriffs appointed for Ulster were Sir Edward Pelham and Sir John Davies. The latter has left it on record, as his deliberate opinion, after many years experience, "that there is no nation of people under the sun that doth love equal and indifferent justice better than the Irish, or will rest better satisfied with the execution thereof, *although it be against themselves, so that they may have the protection and benefits of the law, when, upon just cause, they do desire it.*"

A plot was now got up to entrap O'Neill and O'Donnell. Their complicity in it has long been questioned, though Dr. O'Donovan appears to think that Moore has almost decided the question against them.

The Four Masters give a touching account of the flight of the Earl, and exclaim : " Woe to the heart that meditated, woe to the mind that conceived, woe to the council that decided on the project of their setting out on the voyage !" The exiles left Rathmullen on the 14th of September, 1607. O'Neill had been with the Lord Deputy shortly before; and one cannot but suppose that he had then obtained some surmise of premeditated treachery, for he arranged his flight secretly and swiftly, pretending that he was about to visit London. O'Neill was accompanied by his countess, his three sons, O'Donnell, and other relatives. They first sailed to Normandy, where an attempt was made by the English Government to arrest them, but Henry IV. would not give them up. In Rome they were received as confessors exiled for the faith, and were liberally supported by the Pope and the King of Spain. They all died in a few years after their arrival, and their ashes rest in the Franciscan Church of St. Peter-in-Montorio.

The Red Hand of the O'Neills had hitherto been

a powerful protection to Ulster. The attempts "to plant" there had turned out failures; but now that the chiefs were removed, the people became an easy prey. O'Dogherty, Chief of Innishowen, was insulted by Sir George Paulett, in a manner which no gentleman could be expected to bear without calling his insulter to account; and the young chieftan took fearful vengeance for the rude blow which he had received from the English sheriff.

There can be little doubt, from Sir Henry Docwra's own account, that O'Dogherty was purposely insulted, and goaded into rebellion. He was the last obstacle to the grand scheme, and he was disposed of. Ulster was now at the mercy of those who chose to accept grants of land; and the grants were made to the highest bidders, or to those who had paid for the favour by previous services. Sir Arthur Chichester evidently considered that he belonged to the latter class; for we find him writing at considerable length to the Earl of Northampton, then a ruling member of King James' cabinet, to request that he may be appointed President of Ulster.

The plan of the plantation was agreed upon in 1609. It was the old plan which had been attempted before, though with less show of legal arrangement, but with quite the same proportion of legal iniquity. The simple object was to expel the natives, and to extirpate the Catholic religion.

The six counties to be planted were Tyrone, Derry, Donegal, Armagh, Fermanagh, and Cavan. These were parcelled out into portions varying from 2,000 to 4,000 acres, and the planters were obliged to build bawns and castles, such as that of Castle Monèa, co. Fermanagh.

Chichester now proposed to call a parliament. The plantation of Ulster had removed some difficulties in the way of its accomplishment. The Protestant University of Dublin had obtained 3,000 acres there, and 400,000 acres of tillage land had been partitioned out between English and Scotch proprietors. It was expressly stipulated that their tenants should be English or Scotch, and Protestants; the Catholic owners of the land were, in some cases, as a special favour, permitted to remain, if they took the oath of supremacy, if they worked well for their masters, and if they paid double the rent fixed for the others. Sixty thousand acres in Dublin and Waterford, and 385,000 acres in Westmeath, Longford, King's County, Queen's County, and Leitrim, had been portioned out in a similar manner.

Chichester retired from the government of Ireland in 1616. In 1617 a proclamation was issued for the expulsion of the Catholic clergy, and the city of Waterford was deprived of its charter in consequence of the spirited opposition which its Corporation offered to the oath of spiritual supremacy. In 1622 Viscount Falkland came over as Lord Deputy; and Usher, who was at heart a Puritan, preached a violent sermon on the occasion, in which he suggested a very literal application of the text, " He beareth not the sword in vain." If a similar application of the text had been made by a Catholic divine, it would have been called intolerance, persecution, and a hint that the Inquisition was at hand; as used by him, it was supposed to mean putting down Popery by the sword.

James I. died on the 27th March, 1625, and left his successor no very pleasant prospects in any part of his kingdom.

On the accession of Charles I., in 1625, it was so generally supposed he would favour the Catholic cause, that the earliest act of the new parliament in London was to vote a petition, begging the King to enforce the laws against recusants and Popish priests. The Viceroy, Lord Falkland, advised the Irish Catholics to propitiate him with a voluntary subsidy. They offered the enormous sum of £120,000, to be paid in three annual instalments, and in return he promised them certain "graces." The contract was ratified by royal proclamation, in which the concessions were accompanied by a promise that a Parliament should be held to confirm them. The first instalment of the money was paid, and the Irish agents returned home to find themselves cruelly deceived and basely cheated.

The Protestant Archbishop of Dublin, Dr. Bulkely, was foremost in commencing the persecution. He marched, with the Mayor and a file of soldiers, to the Franciscan Church in Cook-street, on St. Stephen's Day, 1629, dispersed the congregation, seized the friars, profaned the church, and broke the statue of St. Francis. The friars were rescued by the people, and the Archbishop had "to take to his heels and cry out for help," to save himself. Eventually the Franciscans established their novitiates on the Continent, but still continued their devoted ministrations to the people, at the risk of life and liberty.

"Charles' faith" might now safely rank with Grey's; and the poor impoverished Irishman, who would willingly have given his last penny, as well as the last drop of his blood, to save his faith, was again cruelly betrayed where he most certainly might have expected that he could have confided and trusted. One of the "graces" was to make sixty years of undisputed possession of property a bar to the claims of the crown; and certainly if there ever was a country where such a demand was necessary and reasonable, it was surely Ireland. There had been so many plantations, it was hard for anything to grow; and so many settlements, it was hard for anything to be settled. Each new monarch, since the first invasion of the country by Henry II., had his favourites to provide for and his friends to oblige. The island across the sea was considered "no man's land," as the original inhabitants were never taken into account, and were simply ignored, unless, indeed, when they made their presence very evident by open resistance to this wholesale robbery. It was no wonder, then, that this "grace" should be specially solicited. It was one in which the last English settler in Ulster had quite as great an interest as the oldest Celt in Connemara. The Burkes and the Geraldines had suffered almost as much from the rapacity of their own countrymen as the natives, on whom their ancestors had inflicted such cruel wrongs. No man's property was safe in Ireland, for the tenure was depending on the royal will; and the caprices of the Tudors were supplemented by the necessities of the Stuarts.

But the "grace" was refused, although, probably, there was many a recent colonist who would have willingly given one-half of his plantation to have secured the other to his descendants. The reason of the refusal was soon apparent. As soon as parliament was dissolved, a Commission of "Defective Titles" was issued for Connaught. Ulster had been settled, Leinster had been settled, Munster had been settled; there remained only Connaught, hitherto inaccessible, now, with advancing knowledge of the art of war, and new means of carrying out that art, doomed to the scourge of desolation.

It was now discovered that the lands and lordships of De Burgo, adjacent to the Castle of Athlone, and, in fact, the whole remaining province, belonged to the crown. It would be impossible here to give details of the special pleading on which this statement was founded; and I must again refer you to the Illustrated History of Ireland for full particulars; it is an illustration of what I have observed before, that the tenure of the English settler was quite as uncertain as the tenure of the Celt. The jury found for the King; and, as a reward, the foreman, Sir Lucas Dillon, was graciously permitted to retain a portion of his own lands. The juries of Mayo and Sligo were equally complacent; but there was stern resistance made in Galway, and stern reprisals were made for the resistance. The jurors were fined £4,000 each, and were imprisoned, and their estates seized until that sum was paid. The sheriff was fined £1,000, and being unable to pay that sum, he died in prison. And all this was done with the full knowledge and the entire sanction of the "royal martyr."

The country was discontented, and the Lord Deputy demanded more troops, "until the intended plantation should be settled." He could not see why the people should object to what was so very much for their own good, and never allowed himself to think that the disturbance had anything to do with the land question. The new proprietors were of the same opinion. Those who were or who feared to be dispossessed, and those who felt that their homes, whether humble or noble, could not be called their own, felt differently; but their opinion was as little regarded as their sufferings.

The kingdom of England was never in a more critical state than at this period. The King was such only in name, and the ruling powers were the Puritan party, who already looked to Cromwell as their head. The resistance which had begun in opposition to tyrannical enactments, and to the arbitrary exercise of authority by the King and his High Church prelates, was fast merging into, what it soon became, an open revolt against the Crown, and all religion which did not square with the very peculiar and ill-defined tenets of the rebellious party. In 1641 the Queen's confessor was sent to the Tower, and a resolution was passed by both houses never to consent to the toleration of the Catholic worship in Ireland, or in any other part of his Majesty's dominions. The country party had determined to possess themselves of the command of the army, and whatever struggles the King might make to secure the only support of his throne, it was clear that the question was likely to be decided in their favour. The conduct of Holles, Pym, Hampden, and Stroud, was well known even in Ireland; and in Ireland fearful apprehensions were entertained that still more cruel sufferings were preparing for that unfortunate country.

An insurrection was organized, and its main supports were some of the best and bravest of the old race, who had been driven by political and religious persecutions to other lands, where their bravery had made them respected, and their honourable dealings had made them esteemed.

The movement in Ireland was commenced by Roger O'More, a member of the ancient family of that name, who had been so unjustly expelled from their ancestral home in Leix; by Lord Maguire, who had been deprived of nearly all his ancient patrimony at Fermanagh, and his brother Roger; by Sir Phelim O'Neill, of Kinnare, the elder branch of whose family had been expatriated; by Turlough O'Neill, his brother, and by several other gentlemen similarly situated. O'More was the chief promoter of the projected insurrection. He was eminently suited to become a popular leader, for he was a man of great courage, fascinating address, and imbued with all the high honour of the old Celtic race. In May, 1641, Nial O'Neill arrived in Ireland with a promise of assistance from Cardinal Richelieu; and the confederates arranged that the rising should take place a few days before or after All Hallows, according to circumstances. In the meanwhile the exiled Earl of Tyrone was killed; but his successor, Colonel Owen Roe O'Neill, then serving in Flanders, entered warmly into all their plans.

The King was now obliged to disband his Irish forces, and their commanders were sent orders for that purpose. They had instructions, however, to keep the men at home and together, so that they might easily be collected again if they could be made available, as, strange to say, the so-called "Irish rebels" were the only real hope which Charles had to rely on in his conflict with his disloyal English subjects. An understanding was soon entered into between these officers and the Irish party. They agreed to act in concert; and one of the former, Colonel Plunket, suggested the seizure of Dublin Castle. The 23rd of October was fixed on for the enterprise; but, though attempted, the attempt was frustrated by a betrayal of the plot, in consequence of an indiscretion of one of the leaders.

The rage of the Protestant party knew no limits. The Castle was put in a state of defence, troops were ordered in all directions, and proclamations were issued. In the meantime the conspirators at a distance had succeeded better, but, unfortunately, they were not aware of the failure in Dublin until it was too late. Sir Phelim O'Neill was at the head of 30,000 men. He issued a proclamation stating that he intended " no hurt to the King, or hurt of any of his subjects, English or Scotch;" but that his only object was the defence of Irish liberty. He added, that whatever hurt was done to anyone should be personally repaired. This proclamation was dated from " Dungannon, the 23rd of October, 1641," and signed " PHELIM O'NEILL.'

The massacre of Island Magee took place about this period; and though the exact date is disputed, and the exact number of victims has been questioned, it cannot be disproved that the English and Scotch settlers at Carrickfergus sallied forth at night, and murdered a number of defenceless men, women, and children. That there was no regular or indiscriminate massacre of Protestants by the Catholics at this period, appears to be proved beyond question by the fact, that no mention of such an outrage was made in any of the letters of the Lords Justices to the Privy Council. It is probable, however, that the Catholics did rise up in different places to attack those by whom they had been so severely and cruelly oppressed; and although there was no concerted plan of massacre, many victims, who may have been personally innocent, paid the penalty of the guilty. In such evidence as is still on record ghost stories predominate; and even the Puritans seem to have believed the wildest tales of the apparition of Protestants, who demanded the immolation of the Catholics who had murdered them.

CHAPTER XVI.

English Adventurers speculate on Irish Disaffection—Coote's Cruelties—Meeting of Irish Noblemen and Gentlemen—Discontent of the People—The Catholic Priests try to save Protestants from their Fury—A National Synod to deliberate on the State of Irish Affairs—The General Assembly is convened at Kilkenny—A Mint is established—A Printing Press set up—Relations are entered into with Foreign States, and a method of Government is organized—Differences of opinion between the Old Irish and Anglo-Irish—A Year's Treaty is made—Arrival of Rinuccinni—He lands at Kenmare—His account of the Irish People—His Reception at Kilkenny—His Opinion of the State of Affairs—Divisions of the Confederates—Ormonde's Intrigues—The Battle of Benburb—Divisions and Discord in Camp and Senate—A Treaty signed and published by the Representatives of the English King—Rinuccinni returns to Italy.

O'NEILL now took the title of "Lord-General of the Catholic army in Ulster."

A proclamation was issued by the Irish Government, declaring he had received no authority from the King; and the ruling powers were often heard to say, "that the more were in rebellion, the more lands should be forfeited to them." A company of adventurers were already formed in London on speculation, and a rich harvest was anticipated. Several engagements took place, in which the insurgents were on the whole successful. It was now confidently stated that a general massacre of the Catholics was intended; and, indeed the conduct of those engaged in putting down the rising was very suggestive of such a purpose. In Wicklow Sir Charles Coote put many innocent persons to the sword, without distinction of age or sex; and on one occasion, when he met a soldier carrying an infant on the point of his pike, he was charged with saying that "he liked such frolics."

Before taking an open step, even in self-defence, the Irish noblemen and gentlemen sent another address to the King; but their unfortunate messenger, Sir John Read, was captured, and cruelly racked by the party in power—their main object being to obtain something from his confessions which should implicate the King and Queen. Patrick Barnwell, an aged man, was also racked for a similar purpose. The Lord's Justices now endeavoured to get several gentlemen into their possession, on pretence of holding a conference. Their design was suspected, and the intended victims escaped; but they wrote a courteous letter, stating the ground of their refusal. A meeting of the principal Irish noblemen and gentlemen was now held on the Hill of Crofty, in Meath.

After they had been a few hours on the ground, the leaders of the insurgent party came up, and were accosted by Lord Gormanstown, who inquired why they came armed into the Pale. O'More replied that they had "taken up arms for the freedom and liberty of their consciences, the maintenance of his Majesty's prerogative, in which they understood he was abridged, and the making the subjects of this kingdom as free as those of England." Lord Gormanstown answered: "Seeing these be your true ends, we will likewise join with you therein."

On the 1st of January, 1642, Charles issued a proclamation against the Irish rebels, and wished to take the command against them in person; but his parliament was his master, and they were glad enough of the excuses afforded by the troubles in Ireland to increase the army, and to obtain a more direct personal control over its movements. They voted away Irish estates, and uttered loud threats of exterminating Popery; but they had a more important and interesting game in hand at home, which occupied their attention, and made them comparatively indifferent to Irish affairs.

Sir Phelim O'Neill was not succeeding in the north. He had been obliged to raise the siege of Drogheda, and the English had obtained possession of Dundalk. £1,000 was offered for his head, and £600 for the heads of some of his associates.

A synod met at Kilkenny, on the 10th of May, 1642. It was attended by the Archbishops of Armagh, Cashel, and Tuam, and the Bishops of Ossory, Elphin, Waterford, and Lismore, Kildare, Clonfert, and Down and Connor. Proctors attended for the Archbishop of Dublin, and for the Bishops of Limerick, Emly, and Killaloe. There were present, also, sixteen other dignitaries and heads of religious orders. They issued a manifesto explaining their conduct; and, forming a Provisional Government, concluded their labours, after three days spent in careful deliberation.

Owen Roe O'Neill and Colonel Preston arrived in Ireland in July, 1642, accompanied by a hundred officers, and well supplied with arms and ammunition. Sir Phelim O'Neill went at once to meet O'Neill, and resigned the command of the army; and all promised fairly for the national cause. The Scots, who had kept up a war of their own for some time against both the King and the Catholics, were wasting Down and Antrim; and O'Neill was likely to need all his military skill and all his political wisdom in the position in which he was placed.

Preston had landed in Wexford, and brought a still larger force; while all the brave expatriated Irishmen in foreign service, hastened home the moment there appeared a hope that they could strike a blow with some effect for the freedom of their native land.

The General Assembly projected by the national synod in Kilkenny, held its first meeting on October 14, 1642—eleven spiritual and fourteen temporal peers, with 226 commoners, representing the Catholic population of Ireland. It was, in truth, a proud and glorious day for the nation. For once, at least, she could speak through channels chosen by her own free will; and for once there dawned a hope of legislative freedom of action for the long-enslaved people. The old house is still shown where that assembly deliberated—a parliament all but in name. The table then used, and the chair occupied by the Speaker, are still preserved as sad mementos of freedom's blighted cause. The house used was in the market-place. The peers and commoners sat together; but a private room was allotted for the lords to consult in. Dr. Patrick Darcy, an eminent lawyer, represented the Chancellor and the judges. Mr. Nicholas Plunket was chosen as speaker; the Rev. Thomas O'Quirke, a learned Dominican friar, was appointed Chaplain to both houses.

The Assembly at once declared that they met as a provisional government, and not as a parliament. The preliminary arrangements occupied them until the 1st of November. From the 1st until the 4th the committee were engaged in drawing up a form for the Confederate Government; on the 4th it was sanctioned by the two houses. Magna Charta, and the common and statute law of England, in all points not contrary to the Catholic religion, or inconsistent with the liberty of Ireland, were the basis of the new government. The administrative authority was vested in a Supreme Council, which was then chosen, and of which Lord Mountgarret was elected President.

The Assembly broke up on the 9th of January,

1643, after sending a remonstrance to the King, declaring their loyalty and explaining their grievances. The complicated state of English politics proved the ruin of this noble undertaking, so auspiciously commenced. Charles was anxious to make terms with men whom he knew would probably be the only subjects on whose loyalty he could thoroughly depend. His enemies—and the most cursory glance at English history during this period proves how many and how powerful they were—desired to keep open the rupture, and, if possible, to bring it down from the high stand of dignified remonstrance to the more perilous and lower position of a general and ill-organized insurrection. The Lords Justices Borlase and Parsons were on the look-out for plunder; but Charles had as yet sufficient power to form a commission of his own, and he sent the Marquis of Ormonde and some other noblemen to treat with the Confederates. Ormonde was a cold, calculating, and, if we must judge him by his acts, a cruel man; for, to give only one specimen of his dealings, immediately after his appointment he butchered the brave garrison of Timolin, who had surrendered on promise of quarter.

The Confederates were even then divided into two parties. That section of their body principally belonging to the old English settlers, were willing to have peace on almost any terms; the ancient Irish had their memories burthened with so many centuries of wrong, that they demanded something like certainty of redress before they would yield. Ormonde was well aware of the men with whom, and the opinions with which, he had to deal, and he acted accordingly. In the various engagements which occurred, the Irish were, on the whole, successful. They had gained an important victory near Fermoy, principally through the headlong valour of a troop of mere boys, who dashed down with wild impetuosity on the English, and showed what metal there was still left in the country. Envoys were arriving from foreign courts, and Urban VIII. had sent Father Scarampi with indulgences and a purse of 30,000 dollars, collected by Father Wadding. It was, therefore, most important that the movement should be checked in some way; and, as it could not be suppressed by force, it was suppressed by diplomacy.

On the 15th of September, 1643, a cessation of arms for one year was agreed upon; and the tide which had set in so gloriously for Irish independence, rolled back its sobbing waves slowly and sadly towards the English coast, and never returned again with the same hopeful freedom and overpowering strength.

In August, 1644, the cession was again proroged by the General Assembly until December, and subsequently for a longer period. Thus, precious time, and the fresh energies and interests of the Confederates were hopelessly lost.

The Irish Patriots at the Boyne loyal to their false-hearted King.

In the meantime Belling, the Secretary of the Supreme Council, was sent to Rome, and presented to Innocent X., by father Wadding, as the envoy of the Confederate Catholics, in February, 1645. On hearing his report, the Pope sent John Babtist Rinucinni, Archbishop of Fermo, to Ireland as Nuncio-Extraordinary. This prelate set out immediately; and, after some detention at St. Germains, for the purpose of conferring with the English Queen, who had taken refuge there, he purchased the frigate of *San Pietro* at Rochelle, stored it with arms and ammunition; and, after some escapes from the parliamentary cruisers, landed safely in Kenmare Bay, on the 21st of October, 1645.

The General Assembly met in Kilkenny, in January, 1646, and demanded the release of Glamorgan. He was bailed out; but the King disowned the commission, as Rinuccinni had expected, and proved himself therby equally a traitor to his Catholic and Protestant subjects. Ormonde took care to foment the division between the Confederate party, and succeeded so well that a middle party was formed, who signed a treaty consisting of thirty articles. This document only provided for the religious part of the question, that Roman Catholics should not be bound to take the oath of supremacy. An act of oblivion was passed, and the Catholics were to continue to hold their possessions until a settlement could be made by Act of Parliament. Even in a political point of view, this treaty was a failure; and one should have thought that Irish chieftains and Anglo-Irish nobles had known enough of Acts of Parliament to have prevented them from confiding their hopes to such an uncertain future.

The division of the command in the Confederate army had been productive of most disastrous consequences. The rivalry between O'Neill, Preston, and Owen Roe, increased the complication; but the Nuncio managed to reconcile the two O'Neill's, and active preparations were made by Owen Roe for his famous nothern campaign. The Irish troops intended for Charles had remained in their own country; the unfortunate monarch had committed his last fatal error by confiding himself to his Scotch subjects, who sold him to his own people for £400,000. Ormonde now refused to publish the treaty which had been just concluded, or even to enforce its observance by Monroe, although the Confederates had given him £3,000 to get up an expedition for that purpose.

In the beginning of June, A.D. 1646, Owen Roe O'Neill marched against Monroe, with 5,000 foot and 500 horse. Monroe received notice of his approach; and although his force was far superior to O'Neill's, he sent for reinforcements of cavalry from his brother, Colonel George Monroe, who was stationed at Coleraine. But the Irish forces advanced more quickly than he expected; and on the 4th of June they had crossed the Blackwater, and encamped at Benburb. The approach was anticipated; and, on the 5th of June, 1646, the most magnificent victory ever recorded in the annals of Irish history was won. The Irish army prepared for the great day with solemn religious observances. The whole army approached the sacraments of penance and holy communion, and thus were prepared alike for death or victory. O'Neill's skill as a military tactician is beyond all praise. For four long hours he engaged the attention of the enemy, until the glare of the burning summer sun had passed away, and until he had intercepted the reinforcements which Monroe expected. At last the decisive moment had arrived. Monroe thought he saw his brother's contingent in the distance; O'Neill knew that they were some of his own men who had beaten that very contingent. When the Scotch General was undeceived, he resolved to retire. O'Neill saw his advantage, and gave the command to charge. With one wild cry of vengeance for desecrated altars and desolated homes, the Irish soldiers dashed to the charge, and Monroe's ranks were broken, and his men driven to flight. Even the General himself fled so precipitately, that he left his hat, sword, and cloak after him, and never halted until he reached Lisburn. Lord Montgomery was taken prisoner, and 3,000 of the Scotch were left on the field. Of the Irish, only seventy men were killed, and 200 wounded. It was a great victory; and it was something more—it was a glorious victory; although Ireland remained, both as to political and religious freedom, much as it had been before.

Rinuccinni now took a high hand. He entered Kilkenny in state, on the 18th of September, and committed the members of the Supreme Council as prisoners to the Castle, except Darcy and Plunket. A new Council was appointed, or self-appointed, on the 20th, of which the Nuncio was chosen President. The imprisonment of the old Council was undoubtedly a harsh and unwise proceeding, which can scarcely be justified; but the times were such that prompt action was demanded, and the result alone, which could not be foreseen, could justify or denounce its consequences.

The Generals were again at variance; and, although the new Council had decided on attacking Dublin, their plans could not be carried out. Preston was unquestionably playing fast and loose; and when the Confederate troops did march towards Dublin, his duplicity ruined the cause which might even then have been gained. A disgraceful retreat was the result. An Assembly was again convened at Kilkenny; the old Council was released; the Generals promised to forget their animosities; but three weeks had been lost in angry discussion; and although the Confederates bound themselves by oath not to lay down their arms until their demands were granted, their position was weakened to a degree which the selfishness of the contending parties made them quite incapable of estimating.

The fact was, the Puritan faction in England was every day gaining an increase of power; while every hour that the Confederate Catholics wasted in discussion or division was weakening their moral strength.

In the meantime, Inchiquin was distinguishing himself by his cruel victories in the south of Ireland. The massacre of Cashel followed. When the walls were battered down, the hapless garrison surrendered without resistance, and were butchered without mercy. The people fled to the cathedral, hoping there, at least, to escape; but the savage general poured volleys of musket-balls through the doors and windows, and his soldiers, rushing in afterwards, piked those who were not yet dead. Twenty priests were dragged out as objects of special vengeance; and the total number of those who were thus massacred amounted to 3,000.

Inchiquin had been treating with the Supreme Council for a truce; but Rinuccinni, who detested his duplicity, could never be induced to listen to his proposals. On the 27th of May, the Nuncio promulgated a sentence of excommunication against all cities and villages where it should be received, and, at the same time, he withdrew to the camp of Owen Roe O'Neill, against whom Inchiquin and

Preston were prepared to march. It was a last and desperate resource, and, as might be expected, it failed signally of its intended effects. Various attempts to obtain a settlement of the question at issue, by force of arms, were made by the contending parties; but O'Neill baffled his enemies, and the Nuncio withdrew to Galway.

Ormonde arrived in Ireland soon after, and was received at Cork, on the 27th of September, 1648, by Inchiquin. He then proceeded to Kilkenny, where he was received in great state by the Confederates. On the 17th of January, 1649, he signed a treaty of peace, which concluded the seven years' war. This treaty afforded the most ample indulgences to the Catholics, and guaranteed fairly that civil and religious liberty for which alone they had contended; but the ink upon the deed was scarcely dry, ere the execution of Charles I., on the 30th of January, washed out its enactments in royal blood; and civil war, with more than ordinary complications, was added to the many miseries of our unfortunate country.

Rinuccinni embarked in the *San Pietro* once more, and returned to Italy, February 23, 1649. Had his counsels been followed, the result might have justified him, even in his severest measures; as it is, we read only failure in his career; but it should be remembered, that there are circumstances under which failure is more noble than success.

CHAPTER XVII.

Cromwell arrives in Ireland—His cruel Massacres—His Treachery at Drogheda—The Siege of Limerick—The Irish to Connaught—The Irish sold as Slaves—The Wolf, the Priest, and the Tory—Origin and Causes of Agrarian Outrages — Accession of Charles II.— His Injustice—Execution of the Most Rev. D. Plunket—The Battle of the Boyne.

CROMWELL'S command in Ireland extends from the middle of August, 1649, to the end of May, 1650, about nine months in all, and is remarkable for the number of sieges of walled towns crowded into that brief period.

Of the spirit in which these several sieges were conducted, it is impossible to speak without a shudder. It was, in truth, a spirit of hatred and fanaticism, altogether beyond the control of the revolutionary leader. At Drogheda, the work of slaughter occupied five entire days. Of the brave garrison of 3,000 men, not thirty were spared, and these "were in hands for the Barbadoes;" old men, women, children, and priests, were unsparingly put to the sword. Wexford was basely betrayed by Captain James Stafford, commander of the castle, whose midnight interview with Cromwell, at a private house without the walls, tradition still recounts with horror and detestation. This port was particularly obnoxious to the parliament, as, from its advantageous position on the Bristol Channel, its cruisers greatly annoyed and embarrassed their commerce.

The unexpected death of O'Neill favoured still farther Cromwell's southern movements. The gallant, but impetuous Bishop of Clogher, Heber M'Mahon, was the only northern leader who could command confidence enough to keep O'Neill's force together, and on him, therefore, the command devolved. O'Ferrall, one of Owen's favourite officers, was despatched to Waterford, and mainly contributed to Cromwell's repulse before that city; Hugh O'Neill covered himself with glory at Clonmel and Limerick; Daniel O'Neill, another nephew of Owen, remained attached to Ormond, and accompanied him to France; but within six months from the loss of their Fabian chief, who knew as well when to strike as to delay, the brave Bishop of Clogher sacrificed the remnant of "the Catholic Army" at the pass of Scariffhollis, in Donegal, and, two days after, his own life by a martyr's death, at Omagh. At the date of Cromwell's departure—when Ireton took command of the southern army—there remained to the Confederates only some remote glens and highlands of the North and West, the cities of Limerick and Galway, with the county of Clare, and some detached districts of the province of Connaught.

The last act of Cromwell's proper campaign was the seige of Clonmel, where he met the stoutest resistance he had anywhere encountered. The Puritans, after effecting a breach, made an attempt to enter, chanting one of their scriptural battle-songs. They were, by their own account, " obliged to give back a while," and finally night settled down upon the scene. The following day, finding the place no longer tenable, the garrison silently withdrew to Waterford, and subsequently to Limerick. The inhabitants demanded a parley, which was granted; and Cromwell takes credit, and deserves it, when we consider the men he had to humour, for having kept conditions with them.

From before Clonmel he returned at once to England, where he was received with royal honours.

Henry Ireton, son-in-law of Cromwell, by a marriage contracted about two years before, was now in command, and in August following Cromwell's departure, Waterford and Duncannon were taken by him; and there only remained to the Confederates the fortresses of Sligo, Athlone, Limerick, and Galway, with the country included within the irregular quadrangle they describe.

Political events of great interest happened during the two short years of Ireton's command. The Assembly, which met at Jamestown in August, and again at Loughrea in November, 1650, made the retirement of Ormond from the Government a condition of all future efforts in the royal cause, and that nobleman, deeply wounded by this condition, had finally sailed from Galway.

The decisive battle of Worcester, fought on the 3rd of September, 1651, drove Charles II. into that nine years' exile, from which he only returned on the death of Cromwell. It may be considered the last military event of importance in the English civil war. In Ireland the contest was destined to drag out another campaign, before the walls of the two gallant cities, Galway and Limerick.

Ireton now prepared to lay siege to the latter. To effect this, Coote made a feint of attacking Sligo; and when he had drawn off Clanrickarde's forces to oppose him, marched back hastily, and took Athlone. By securing this fortress he opened a road into Connaught; and Ireton, at the same time, forced the passage of the river at O'Briensbridge, and thus was enabled to invest Limerick. Muskerry marched to its relief; but he was intercepted by Lord Broghill, and his men were routed with great slaughter. The castle at the salmon weir was first attacked; and the men who defended it were butchered in cold blood, although they had surrendered on a promise of quarter. At length treachery accomplished what valour might have prevented. The plague was raging in the city, and many tried to escape; but were either beaten back into the town, or killed on the spot by Ireton's troopers. The corporation and magistrates were in favour of a capitulation; but the gallant Governor, Hugh O'Neill, opposed it earnestly. Colonel Fennell, who had already betrayed the pass at Killaloe, completed his perfidy by seizing St. John's Gate and Tower, and admitting Ireton's men by night. On the following day the invader was able to dictate his own terms. 2,500 soldiers laid down their arms in St. Mary's Church, and marched out of the city, many dropping dead on their road of the fearful pestilence. Twenty-four persons were exempted from quarter. Amongst the number were a Dominican prelate, Dr. Terence O'Brien, Bishop of Emly, and a Franciscan, Father Wolfe. Ireton had special vengeance for the former, who had long encouraged the people to fight for their country and their faith, and had refused a large bribe which the Cromwellian General had offered him if he would leave the city. The ecclesiastics were soon condemned; but ere the bishop was dragged to the gibbet, he turned to the dark and cruel man who had sacrificed so many lives, and poured such torrents of blood over the land, summoning him, in stern and prophetic tones, to answer at God's judgment-seat for the evils he had done. The bishop and his companion were martyred on the Eve of All Saints, October 31st, 1651. On the 26th of November Ireton was a corpse. He caught the plague eight days after he had been summoned to the tribunal of eternal justice; and he died raving wildly of the men whom he had murdered, and accusing every one but himself of the crime he had committed.

Several of the leading gentry of Limerick were

also executed; and the traitor Fennell met the reward of his treachery, and was hanged. Hugh O'Neill was saved through the remonstrances of some of the parliamentary officers, who had the spirit to appreciate his valour and his honourable dealing.

The Long Parliament declared, in its session of 1652, that the rebellion in Ireland " was subdued and ended," and proceeded to legislate for that kingdom as a conquered country. On the 12th of August they passed their Act of Settlement, the authorship of which was attributed to Lord Orrery, in this respect the worthy son of the first Earl of Cork. Under this Act, there were four chief descriptions of persons whose status was thus settled: 1st. All ecclesiastics and royalist proprietors were exempted from pardon of life or estate. 2nd. All royalist commissioned officers were condemned to banishment, and the forfeit of two-thirds of their property, one-third being retained for the support of their wives and children. 3rd. Those who had not been in arms, but who could be shown, by a parliamentary commission, to have manifested " a constant, good affection," to the war, were to forfeit one-third of their estates, and receive " an equivalent" for the remaining two-thirds west of the Shannon. 4th. All husbandmen and others of the inferior sort, " not possessed of lands or goods exceeding the value of £10," were to have a free pardon, on condition also of transporting themselves across the Shannon.

THE BANISHMENT TO CONNAUGHT. 291

This is the official proclamation which was issued on the subject: " The Parliament of the Commonwealth of England, having, by an Act lately passed (entitled an Act for the Settling of Ireland), declared that it is not their intention to extirpate this whole nation .... it is ordered that the Governor and Commissioners of Revenue .... do cause the said Act of Parliament, with this present declaration, to be published and proclaimed in their respective precincts, by beat of drum and sound of trumpet, on some market-day, within ten days after the same shall come unto them within their respective precincts."

Connaught was selected as the place of banishment for two reasons: first, because it was the most wasted province of Ireland; and, secondly, because it could be, and in fact was, most easily converted into a national prison, by erecting a *cordon militaire* across the country, from sea to sea. To make the imprisonment more complete, a belt four miles wide, commencing one mile to the west of Sligo, and thence running along the coast and the Shannon, was to be given to the soldiery to plant. Thus, any Irishman who attempted to escape, would be sure of instant capture and execution.

Children under age, of both sexes, were captured by thousands, and sold as slaves to the tobacco-planters of Virginia and the West Indies. Secretary Thurloe informs Henry Cromwell that the

"Committee of the Council have authorized 1,000 girls and as many youths to be taken up for that purpose." Sir William Petty mentions 6,000 Irish boys and girls shipped to the West Indies. Some contemporary accounts make the total number of children and adults so transported 100,000 souls. To this decimation, we may add 34,000 men of fighting age, who had permission to enter the armies of foreign powers, at peace with the Commonwealth.

Charles II. commenced his reign in 1660, under the most favourable auspices. In England public affairs were easily settled. Those who had been expelled from their estates by the Cromwellian faction, were driven out by the old proprietors; but in Ireland the case was very different. Even the faithful loyalists, who had sacrificed everything for the King, and had so freely assisted his necessities out of their poverty, were now treated with contempt, and their claims silenced by proclamation; while the men who had been most opposed to the royal interests, and most cruel in their oppression of the natives, were rewarded and admitted into favour. Coote and Broghill were of this class. Each tried to lessen the other in the opinion of their royal master as they ran the race for favour, and each boasted of services never accomplished, and of loyalty which never existed. The two enemies of each other and of the nation were now appointed Lords Justices of Ireland.

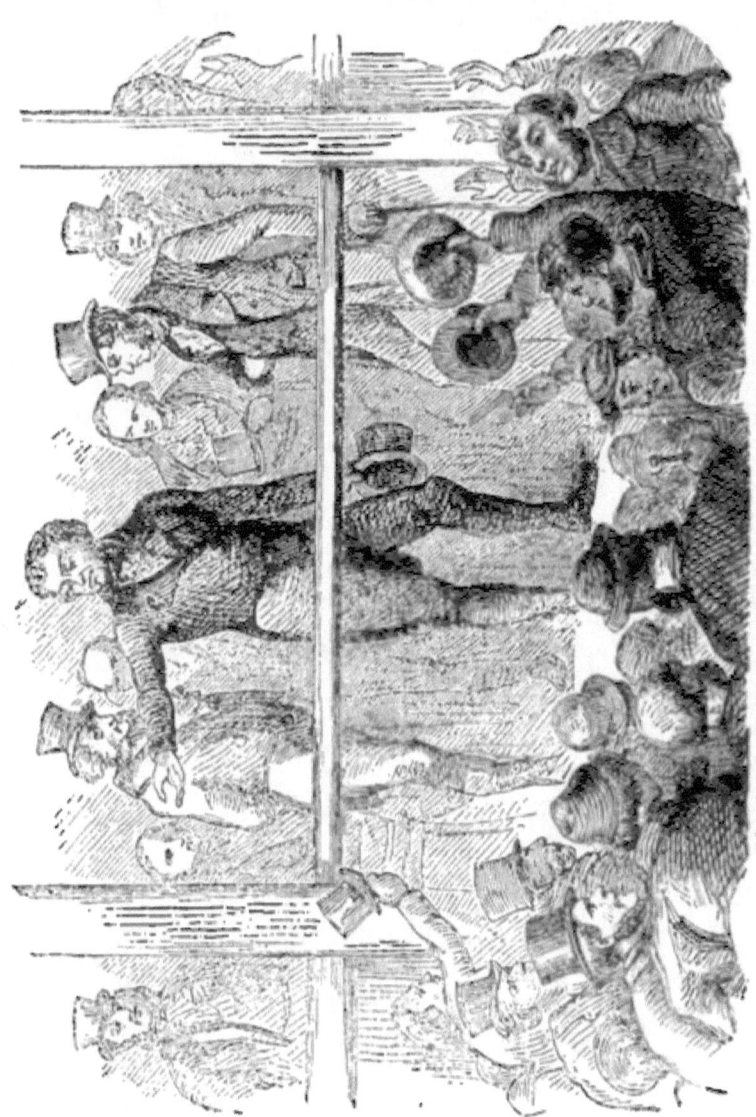

The Irish Patriot agitating peacefully for Ireland.

In 1679, the example of successful villany in England, of Oates, pensioned and all-powerful, brought an illustrious victim to the scaffold. This was Oliver Plunkett, a scion of the noble family of Fingal, who had been Archbishop of Armagh since the death of Dr. O'Reilly, in exile, in 1699.

Such had been the prudence and circumspection of Dr. Plunkett, during his perilous administration, that the agents of Lord Shaftesbury, sent over to concoct evidence for the occasion, were afraid to bring him to trial in the vicinage of his arrest, or in his own country. Accordingly, they caused him to be removed from Dublin to London, contrary to the laws and customs of both kingdoms.

Dr. Plunkett, after ten months' confinement without trial in Ireland, was removed, 1680, and arraigned at London, on the 8th of June, 1681, without having had permission to communicate with his friends or to send for witnesses. The prosecution was conducted by Maynard and Jeffries, in violation of every form of law, and every consideration of justice. A "crown agent," whose name is given as Gorman, was introduced by "a stranger," in court, and volunteered testimony in his favour. The earl of Essex interceded with the King on his behalf, but Charles answered, almost in the words of Pilate—"I cannot pardon him, because I dare not. His blood be upon your conscience; you could have saved him if you pleased." The Jury, after a quarter of an hour's deliberation, brought in their verdict of guilty, and the brutal chief-justice condemned him to be hung, emboweled, and quartered, on the 1st day of July, 1681. The venerable martyr bowed his head to the bench, and exclaimed: *Deo Gratias!* Eight years from the very day of his execution, on the banks of that river beside which he had been seized and dragged from his retreat, the last of the Stuart Kings was stricken from his throne, and his dynasty stricken from history! Does not the blood of the innocent cry to Heaven for vengeance?

The charges against Dr. Plunkett were, that he maintained treasonable correspondence with France and Rome, and the Irish on the continent; that he had organized an insurrection in Louth, Monaghan, Cavan, and Armagh; that he made preparations for the landing of a French force at Carlingford; and that he had held several meetings to raise men and money for these purposes.

From the accession of King James till his final flight from Ireland, in July, 1690, there elapsed an interval of five years and five months; a period fraught with consequences of the highest interest to this history. The new king was, on his accession, in his fifty-second year; he had served as Duke of York with credit, both by land and sea, was an avowed Catholic, and married to a Catholic princess, the beautiful and unfortunate Mary of Modena.

Within a month from the proclamation of the

King, Ormond quitted the government for the last time, leaving Primate Boyle and Lord Granard as Justices. In January, 1686, Lord Clarendon, son of the historian, assumed the government, in which he continued till the 16th of March, 1687. The day following the national anniversary, Colonel Richard Talbot, Earl of Tyrconnell, a Catholic, and the former agent for the Catholics, was installed as Lord Deputy.

On the 5th of November, the anniversary of the gunpowder plot, William of Orange landed at Torbay; on the 25th of December, James, deserted by his nobles, his army, and even his own unnatural children, arrived, a fugitive and a suppliant at the Court of France.

James at last determined to make an effort to regain his throne; and by this act rendered the attempt of his son-in-law simply a rebellion. Had the King declined the contest, had he violated the rules of government so grossly as no longer to merit the confidence of his people, or had there been no lawful heir to the throne, William's attempt might have been legitimate; under the circumstances, it was simply a successful rebellion. The King landed at Kinsale, on the 12th of March, 1689, attended by some Irish troops and French officers. He met Tyrconnell in Cork, created him a duke, and then proceeded to Bandon, where he received the submission of the people.

The great event of James' visit to Ireland was

the battle of the Boyne, which took place June 30, 1689. The Jacobite army was posted on the declivity of the Hill of Dunore. The centre was at the small hamlet of Oldbridge. Entrenchments were hastily thrown up to defend the fords, and James took up his position at a ruined church on the top of the Hill of Dunore. The Williamite army approached from the north, their brave leader directing every movement, and inspiring his men with courage and confidence. He obtained a favourable position, and was completely screened from view until he appeared on the brow of the hill, where his forces debouched slowly and steadily into the ravines below. After planting his batteries on the heights, he kept up an incessant fire on the Irish lines during the afternoon of the 30th. But James' officers were on the alert, even if their King was indifferent. William was recognized as he approached near their lines to reconnoitre. Guns were brought up to bear on him quietly and stealthily; "six shots were fired at him, one whereof fell and struck off the top of the Duke of Wurtemberg's pistol and the whiskers of his horse; another tore the King's coat on his shoulder."

William, like a wise general as he was, took care that the news of his accident should not dispirit his men. He showed himself everywhere, rode through the camp, was as agreeable as it was in his nature to be; and thus made capital of what might have been a cause of disaster. In the meantime James did all that was possible to secure a defeat. At one moment he decided to retreat, at the next he would risk a battle ; then he sent off his baggage and six of his field-pieces to Dublin, for his own special proctection ; and while thus so remarkably careful of himself, he could not be persuaded to allow the most necessary precaution to be taken for the safety of his army. Hence the real marvel to posterity is, not that the battle of the Boyne should have been lost by the Irish, but that they should ever have attempted to fight at all. Perhaps nothing but that inherent loyalty of the Irish, which neither treachery nor pusillanimity could destroy, and that vivid remembrance of the cruel wrongs always inflicted by Protestants when in power, prevented them from rushing over *en masse* to William's side of the Boyne. Perhaps, in the history of nations, there never was so brave a resistance made for love of royal right and religious freedom, as that of the Irish officers and men who fought on the Jacobite side that fatal day.

The first attack of William's men was made at Slane. This was precisely what the Jacobite officers had anticipated, and what James had obstinately refused to see. When it was too late, he allowed Lauzan to defend the ford, but even Sir Nial O'Neill's galantry was unavailing. The enemy had the advance, and Portland's artillery and infantry crossed at Slane. William now felt certain of victory, if, indeed, he had ever doubted it. It was low water at ten o'clock; the fords at Oldbridge were passable; a tremendous battery was opened on the Irish lines; they had not a single gun to reply, and yet they waited steadily for the attack. The Dutch Blue Guards dashed into the stream ten a-breast, commanded by the Count de Solmes; the Londonderry and Enniskillen Dragoons followed, supported by the French Huguenots. The English infantry came next, under the command of Sir John Hanmer and the Count Nassau. William crossed at the fifth ford, where the water was deepest, with the cavalry of his left wing. It was a grand and terrible sight. The men in the water fought for William and Protestantism; the men on land fought for their King and their faith. The men were equally gallant. Of the leaders I shall say nothing, least I should be tempted to say too much. James had followed Lauzan's forces towards Slane. Tryconnell's valour could not save the day for Ireland against fearful odds. Sarsfield's horse had accompanied the King. The Huguenots were so warmly received by the Irish at the fords that they recoiled, and their commander, Caillemont, was mortally wounded. Schomberg forgot his age, and the afront he had received from William in the morning; and the man of eighty-two dashed into the river with the impetuosity of eighteen. He was killed immediately, and so was Dr. Walker, who had headed the Ulster Protestants. William may have regretted the brave old General, but he certainly did not regret the Protestant divine.

He had no fancy for churchmen meddling in secular affairs, and a rough "What brought him there?" was all the reply vouchsafed to the news of his demise. The tide now began to flow, and the battle raged with increased fury. The valour displayed by the Irish was a marvel even to their enemies. Hamilton was wounded and taken prisoner—William headed the Enniskilleners, who were put to flight soon after by the Irish Horse, at Platten, and were only rallied again by himself. When the enemy had crossed the ford at Oldbridge, James ordered Lauzan to march in a parallel with Douglas and young Schomberg to Duleek. Tryconnell followed. The French infantry covered the retreat in admirable order, with the Irish cavalry. When the defile of Duleek had been passed, the royalist forces again presented a front to the enemy William's horse halted. The retreat was again resumed; and at the deep defile of Naul the last stand was made. The shades of a summer evening closed over the belligerent camps. The Williamites returned to Duleek; and eternal shadows clouded over the destinies of the unfortunate Stuarts—a race admired more from sympathy with their miseries, than from admiration of their virtues.

Thus ended the famous battle of the Boyne. England gained thereby a new governor and a national debt; Ireland, fresh oppression, and an intensification of religious and political animosity, unparalleled in the history of nations.

CHAPTER XVIII.

Flight of King James—William of Orange at the Siege of Limerick—Violation of the Treaty of Limerick—The Penal Laws—The Whiteboys—Grattan demands Irish Independence.

AS soon as the battle was over James took to flight. He reached Dublin late in the evening, and had the bad taste and cowardice to insult Lady Tyrconnell by telling her how fleetly her countrymen had run from the field of battle. With truth and spirit she very properly retorted that his Majesty had set them the example. James embarked for France at Kinsale, and left the command in Ireland to Tyrconnell. William marched to Dublin and was received there by the Protestants in great triumph. The siege of Limerick is the next national event of great importance. The French officers determined to leave the country, and Lauzan, their commander, ordered all his troops off to Galway. But the brave defenders of Limerick were not discouraged, and refused to yield.

William laid siege to the gallant city on the 17th of August, 1691. William sent for more artillery to Waterford; and it was found that two of the guns which Sarsfield had attempted to destroy were still available.

The trenches were opened on the 17th of August. On the 20th the garrison made a vigorous sortie, and retarded the enemy's progress; but on the 24th the batteries were completed, and a murderous fire of red-hot shot and shells was poured into the devoted city. The trenches were carried within a few feet of the palisades, on the 27th; and a breach having been made in the wall near St. John's Gate, William ordered the assault to commence. The storming party were supported by ten thousand men. For three hours a deadly struggle was maintained. The result seemed doubtful, so determined was the bravery evinced on each side. Boisseleau, the Governor, had not been unprepared, although he was taken by surprise, and had opened a murderous cross-fire on the assailants when first they attempted the storm. The conflict lasted for nearly three hours. The Brandenburg regiment had gained the Black Battery, when the Irish sprung a mine, and men, faggots, and stones were blown up in a moment. A council of war was held; William, whose temper was not the most amiable at any time, was unusually morose. He had lost 2,000 men between the killed and the wounded, and he had not taken the city, which a French General had pronounced attainable with "roasted apples." On Sunday, the 31st of

August, the seige was raised. William returned to England, where his presence was imperatively demanded. The military command was confided to the Count de Solmes, who was afterwards succeeded by de Ginkell; the civil government was entrusted to Lord Sidney, Sir Charles Porter, and Mr. Coningsby.

The famous battle of Aughrim occurred immediately after the gallant defence and fall of Athlone. St. Ruth removed his troops to Ballinasloe, and subsequently to Aughrim. He chose his ground well, and was fully prepared to meet the Williamites, who came up on Sunday, July 11th, while the Irish army was hearing Mass. The most probable estimate of the Irish force appears to be 15,000 horse and foot; and of the English, 20,000. Ginkell opened fire on the enemy as soon as his guns were planted. Some trifling skirmishes followed. A council of war was held, and the deliberation lasted until half-past four in the evening, at which time a general engagement was decided on. A cannonade had been kept up on both sides, in which the English had immensely the advantage, St. Ruth's excellently-chosen position being almost useless for want of sufficient artillery. At half-past six Ginkell ordered an advance on the Irish right centre, having previously ascertained that the bog was passable. The defenders, after discharging their fire, gradually drew the Williamites after them by an almost imperceptible retreat, until they had them face to face with their main line. Then the Irish cavalry charged with irresistible valour, and the English were thrown into total disorder. St. Ruth, proud of the success of his strategies and the valour of his men, exclaimed, " Le jour est a nous, mes enfans." But St. Ruth's weak point was his left wing, and this was at once perceived and taken advantage of by the Dutch General. Some of his infantry made good their passage across the morass, which St. Ruth had supposed impassable ; and the men, who commanded this position from a ruined castle, found that the balls with which they had been served did not suit their fire-arms, so that they were unable to defend the passage. St. Ruth at once perceived his error. He hastened to support them with a brigade of horse ; but even as he exclaimed, " They are beaten ; let us beat them to the purpose," a cannon-ball carried off his head, and all was lost. Another death, which occurred almost immediately after, completed the misfortunes of the Irish. The infantry had been attended and encouraged by Dr. Aloysius Stafford, chaplain to the forces; but when " death interrupted his glorious career," they were panic-struck ; and three hours after the death of the General and the priest, there was not a man of the Irish army left upon the field. But the real cause of the failure was the fatal misunderstanding which existed between the leaders. Sarsfield, who was thoroughly able to have taken St. Ruth's position, and to have retrieved the fortunes of the day, had been placed in the rear by the jealousy of the latter, and kept in entire ignorance of the plan of battle. He was now obliged to withdraw without striking a single blow. The cavalry retreated along the highroad to Loughrea; the infantry fled to a bog, where numbers were massacred, unarmed and in cold blood.

The loss on both sides was immense, and can never be exactly estimated. Harris says that "had not St. Ruth been taken off, it would have been hard to say what the consequences of this day would have been." Many of the dead remained unburied, and their bones were left to bleach in the storms of winter and the sun of summer. There was one exception to the general neglect. An Irish officer, who had been slain, was followed by his faithful dog. The poor animal lay beside his master's body day and night; and though he fed upon other corpses with the rest of the dogs, he would not permit them to touch the treasured remains. He continued his watch until January, when he flew at a soldier, who, he feared, was about to remove the bones, which were all that remained to him of the being by whom he had been caressed and fed. The soldier, in his fright, unslung his piece and fired, and the faithful wolf-dog laid down and died by his charge.

Ginkell laid siege to Galway a week after the battle of Aughrim. The inhabitants relied principally upon the arrival of Balldearg O'Donnell for their defence; but, as he did not appear in time, they capitulated on favourable terms, and the Dutch General marched to Limerick.

Tyrconnell had died there on the 14th of August, and on the 25th de Ginkell invested the devoted city on three sides. An English fleet assailed it from the river. But the valour of the brave Limerick men was more than a match for all, and on the 3rd of October the famous Treaty of Limerick was signed by the English. Whether they ever intended to keep it or not is another question.

The civil articles of Limerick were thirteen in number. Art. I. guaranteed to Catholics remaining in the kingdom, "such privileges in the exercise of their religion as are consistent with the law of Ireland, or as they enjoyed in the reign of King Charles II.;" this article further provided, that "their Majesties, as soon as their affairs will permit them to summon a parliament in this kingdom, will endeavour to procure the said Roman Catholics such further security in that particular as may preserve them from *any disturbance* on account of their said religion." Art. II. guaranteed pardon and protection to all who had served King James, on taking the oath of allegiance prescribed in Art. IX., as follows:—

"I, A. B., do solemnly promise and swear that I will be faithful, and bear true allegiance, to their Majesties, King William and Queen Mary; so help me, God."

Arts. III., IV., V., and VI. extended the provisions of Arts. I. and II. to merchants and other classes of men. Art. VII. permits "every nobleman and gentleman compromised in the said articles" to carry side-arms, and keep a gun in their houses." Art. VIII. gives the right of removing goods and chattels without search. Art. IX. is as follows:

"The oath to be administered to such Roman Catholics as submit to their Majesties' government *shall be the oath aforesaid, and no other.*"

Art. X. guarantees that "no person or persons who shall at any time hereafter break these articles, or any of them, shall thereby make or cause any other person or persons to *forfeit or lose the benefit of them.*" Arts. XI. and XII. relate to the ratification of the articles "within eight months or sooner." Art. XIII. refers to the debts of "Colonel John Brown, commissary to the Irish army, to several Protestants," and arranges for their satisfaction.

These articles were signed, before Limerick, at the well-known "Treaty Stone," on the Clare side of the Shannon, by Lord Scravenmore, Generals Mackay, Talmash, and De Ginkell, and the Lords-Justices Porter and Coningsby, for King William, and by Sarsfield, Earl of Lucan, Viscount Galmoy, Sir Toby Butler, and Colonels Purcell, Cusack, Dillon, and Brown, for the Irish. On the 24th of February following, royal letters patent confirmatory of the treaty were issued from Westminster, in the name of the king and queen, whereby they declared, that "we do for us, our heirs and successors, as far as in us lies, ratify and confirm the same and every clause, matter, and thing therein contained."

In a few short months every article in this treaty was violated. A "No Popery" cry was raised, and the Catholics were persecuted with unceasing cruelty. This persecution was formally legalized in the year 1695. Additions were made to the old penal laws enhancing their severity tenfold. It would be impossible here to give full details of these atrocious enactments. I must, therefore, again refer the reader to my larger history, or to the "Student's History of Ireland," where an exact account of these nefarious laws will be found.

In the reign of Queen Anne additional laws were made, and there was an attempt to "plant" some German Protestants in different parts of Ireland.

In 1723, when the quarrels between the Whigs and Tories were at their height, Dr. Swift's talent and influence did much for Ireland; and his letters accomplished what the Irish Parliament was powerless to effect. But the sufferings of the Catholics still continued, and were not a little increased by the cruel rapacity of the landlords. The immediate cause of the landlord grievance, and of what are called agrarian outrages, was the enclosing of certain commons from which the tenants were enabled to draw some slight profit, and thus to meet the exhorbitant rents demanded of them. But the landlords unhappily, like the Egyptian oppressors of the Jews, still demanded the rent, but refused the people the only chance they had of paying it. Immediately after the accession of George III., the Levellers and the Whiteboys commenced their rude method of obtaining revenge, if they could not obtain justice. A good deal has been said in condemnation of their outrages, but it seems to be forgotten in some quarters that there were "agrarian outrages" on the landlord side as well, or rather that the agrarian outrages commenced with the landlords.

On the 17th April, 1780, Grattan made his famous demand for Irish independence. The Volunteer Corps was formed in 1779, and in 1782 the delegates met in Dublin, and demanded civil rights and the removal of commercial restraints. They also passed a resolution most creditable to their good feeling, expressing their pleasure at the relaxation of the penal laws. Their unanimity of action had its effect, and on the 27th May, 1782, the Duke of Portland announced the unconditional concessions which had been made to Ireland by the English Parliament.

CHAPTER XIX.

Causes which led to the great Rebellion of '98—Cruelties of the Orangemen—Spies and Informers—Lord E. Fitzgerald—The Rising commences—Massacres at Wexford—Treatment of the Rebellion—Efforts made to procure the Union—The Last Night of the Irish Parliament.

 CATHOLIC meeting, held in Dublin, May 11, 1791, was really the origin of the United Irishmen. Catholics and Protestants began to work together harmoniously, for the first time, for the common good of their common country. Had they continued to do so, or should they ever thus unite again, no foreign power could resist their demands. The leading Catholics were—Keogh, M'Cormic, Sweetman, Byrne, &c. The leading Protestants were—Wolfe Tone, Butler, Napper Tandy, Neilson, &c. In May, 1794, the government attempted to put down this movement by arresting some of the leaders. It would have been incomparably more prudent to have removed some of the causes of discontent, for the movement at once resolved itself into the far more dangerous form of a secret society.

In May, 1799, the new organization lost the services of Wolfe Tone, who was compromised, by a strange incident, to a very serious extent. The incident was the arrest and trial of the Rev. William Jackson, an Anglican clergyman, who had imbibed the opinions of Price and Priestly, and had been sent to Ireland by the French Republic on a secret embassy. Betrayed by a friend and countryman named Cockayne, the unhappy Jackson took poison in prison, and expired in the dock. Tone had been seen with Jackson, and through the influence of his friends, was alone protected from arrest. He was compelled, however, to quit the country, in order to preserve his personal liberty. He proceeded with his family to Belfast, where, before taking shipping for America, he renewed with his first associates their vows and projects, on the summit of "the Cave Hill," which looks down upon the rich valley of the Laggan, and the noble town and port at its outlet. Before quitting Dublin, he had solemnly promised Emmett and Russell, in the first instance, as he did his Belfast friends in the second, that he would make the United States his *route* to France, where he would negociate a formidable national alliance, for "the United Irishmen."

In the year in which Tone left the country, Lord Edward Fitzgerald, brother of the Duke of Lienster, and formerly a major in the British Army, joined the society; in the next year—near its close—Thomas Addis Emmett, who had long been in the confidence of the promoters, joined; as did, about the same time, Arthur O'Connor, nephew of Lord Longueville, and ex-member for Philipstown, and Dr. William James McNevin, a Connaught Catholic, educated in Austria, then practising his profession with eminent success in Dublin. These were felt to be important accessions, and all four were called upon to act on "the Executive Directory," from time to time, during 1796 and 1797.

The coercive legislation carried through Parliament, session after session—the Orange persecutions in Armagh and elsewhere—the domiciliary visits—the military outrages in town and country—the free quarters, whipping, and tortures—the total suppression of the public press—the bitter disappointment of Lord Fitzwilliam's recall—the annual failure of Ponsonby's motion for reform—finally, the despairing secession of Grattan and his friends from Parliament—had all tended to expand the system, which six years before was confined to a few dozen enthusiasts of Belfast and Dublin, into the dimensions of a national confederacy. By the close of this year 500,000 men had taken the test, in every part of the country, and nearly 300,000 were reported as armed, either with firelocks or pikes. Of this total 110,000 alone were returned for Ulster, about 60,000 for Leinster, and the remainder from Connaught and Munster. Of this movement Lord Edward Fitzgerald was chosen Commander-in-Chief, but the funds at his disposal were miserably small, and he placed his chief reliance on assistance from France. Every effort was made to obtain this assistance; but the 20th of May, 1798—within three days of the outbreak in Dublin, Wexford and

Kildare—Buonaparte sailed with the *élite* of all that expedition for Alexandria, and "the Army of England" became in reality, "the Army of Egypt."

It is said that Buonaparte bitterly regretted his choice in his exile, and saw, when it was too late, how different his future might have been.

The rising was fixed to take place on the 23rd day of May—and the signal was to be the simultaneous stoppage of the mail coaches, which started nightly from the Dublin post-office to every quarter of the kingdom. But the counter-plot anticipated the plot. Lord Edward, betrayed by a person called Higgins, proprietor of the *Freeman's Journal*, was taken on the 19th of May, after a desperate struggle with Majors Swan and Sirr, and Captain Ryan, in his hiding-place in Thomas-street; the brothers Sheares were arrested in their own house on the morning of the 21st, while Surgeon Lawless escaped from the city, and finally from the country, to France. Thus for the second time was the insurrection left without a head; but the organization had proceeded too far to be any longer restrained, and the Castle, moreover, to use the expression of Lord Castlereagh, "took means to make it explode."

The first intelligence of the rebellion was received in Dublin, on the morning of the 24th of May. At Rathfarnham, within three miles of the city, 500 insurgents attacked Lord Ely's yeomanry corps with some success, till Lord Roden's dragoons, hastily despatched from the city, compelled them to retreat, with the loss of some prisoners and two men killed, whom Mr. Beresford saw the next day, literally "*cut to pieces*—a horrid sight!" At Dunboyne, the insurgents piked an escort of the Royal Fencibles (Scotch) passing through their village, and carried off their baggage. At Naas, a large popular force attacked the garrison, consisting of regulars, Ancient Britons (Welsh) part of a regiment of dragoons, and the Armagh Militia; the attack was renewed three times with great bravery, but, finally, discipline, as it always will, prevailed over mere numbers, and the assailants were repulsed with the loss of 140 of their comrades. At Prosperous, where they cut off to a man a strong garrison, composed of North Cork Militia, under Captain Swayne, the rising was more successful.

But the principal, and, indeed, the only really important rising took place in Wexford, then one of the most populous and prosperous parts of Ireland; and there can be but little doubt, that the people were mainly incited to it by the diabolical cruelties which were practised on them.

On Whit-Sunday, the 27th of May, the yeomen burned the Catholic Chapel of Boulavogue. Father John Murphy, the parish priest, who had hitherto tried to suppress the insurrection, placed himself at the head of the insurgents. The men now rose in numbers, and marched to Enniscorthy, which they took after some fighting. Vinegar Hill, a lofty eminence overlooking the town, was chosen for their camp. Some of the leading Protestant gentlemen of the county had either favoured or joined the movement; and several of them had been arrested on suspicion, and were imprisoned at Wexford. The garrison of this place, however, fled in a panic, caused by some successes of the Irish troops, and probably from a very clear idea of the kind of retaliation they might expect for their cruelties. Mr. Harvey, one of the prisoners mentioned above, was now released, and headed the insurgents; but a powerful body of troops, under General Loftus, was sent into the district, and eventually obtained possession of New Ross, which the Irish had taken with great bravery, but which they had not been able to hold for want of proper military discipline and command. They owed their defeat to insubordination and drunkenness. A number of prisoners had been left at Scullabogue House, near Carrickburne Hill. Some fugitives from the Irish camp came up in the afternoon, and pretended that Mr. Harvey had given orders for their execution, alleging as a reason, what, indeed, was true, that the royalists massacred indiscriminately. The guard resisted, but were overpowered by the mob, who were impatient to revenge, without justice, the cruelties which had been inflicted on them without justice. A hundred were burned in a barn, and thirty-seven were shot or piked. This massacre has been held up as a horrible example of Irish treachery and cruelty. It was horrible, no doubt, and cannot be defended or palliated; but, amid these contending horrors of civil war, the question still recurs—upon whom is the original guilt of causing them to be charged?

Father Murphy was killed in an attack on Carlow, and his death threw the balance strongly in favour of the Government troops, who eventually proved victorious. After the battle of Ross, the Wexford men chose the Rev. Philip Roche as their leader, in place of Mr. Bagenal Harvey, who had resigned the command. The insurgents were now guilty of following the example of their persecutors, if not with equal cruelty, at least with a barbarity which their leaders in vain reprobated. The prisoners whom they had taken were confined in the jail, and every effort was made to save them from the infuriated people. But one savage, named Dixon, would not be content without their blood; and while the army and their leaders were encamped on Vinegar Hill, he and some other villains as wicked as himself found their way into the jail, and marching the prisoners to the bridge, held a mock trial, and then piked thirty-five of their victims, and flung them into the water. At this moment a priest, who had heard of the bloody deed, hastened to the spot; and after in vain commanding them to desist, succeeded at last in making them kneel down, when he dictated a prayer, that God might show them the same mercy which they would show to the surviving prisoners. This had its effect; and the men who waited in terror to receive the doom they had so often and mercilessly inflicted on others, were marched back to prison.

The camp on Vinegar Hill was now beset on all sides by the royal troops. An attack was planned by General Lake, with 20,000 men and a large train of artillery. General Needham did not arrive in time to occupy the position appointed for him; and after an hour and a-half of hard fighting, the Irish gave way, principally from want of gunpowder. The soldiers now indulged in the most wanton deeds of cruelty. The hospital at Enniscorthy was set on fire, and the wounded men shot in their beds. At Wexford General Moore prevented his troops from committing such outrages; but when the rest of the army arrived, they acted as they had done at Enniscorthy. Courts-martial were held, in which the officers were not even sworn, and victims were consigned to execution with reckless atrocity. The bridge of Wexford, where a Catholic priest had saved so many Protestant lives, was now chosen for the scene of slaughter; and all this in spite of a promise of amnesty. The "rebellion" was at last subdued, and the unfortunate Irish were reduced to the greatest depth of misery; and this was the moment chosen by the English Government with more tact than justice, to effect a nominal union of the two countries. A cordial union there could scarcely be till men had forgotten the scenes of misery and cruelty so recently enacted. But Mr. Pitt had set his heart upon the Union, and Mr. Pitt had determined it should be carried; and he availed himself for this end of two all-powerful engines: force and fraud.

He secured the Orangemen by large promises to their leaders; he secured the Catholics by giving them to understand that Catholic Emancipation should be the first act of the united Parliament; and as people are generally willing to believe what they wish, the Orangemen and the Catholics, and the people generally, all believed, and all were duped. The great overture for a union was made by the then Viceroy, on the 22nd of January, 1799; and it was rejected by a majority of only one. But even this defeat was a triumph, for it showed the English Government what bribery and corruption could effect, and how nearly those means had accomplished the desired end. There were brave, true-hearted Irishmen in the house; there were men of wonderful powers of eloquence; Grattan was there, although in almost a dying state; Plunkett, Parnell, Ponsonby, Foster, and Egan were there also; but they were powerless where so many base and selfish motives were in action. The measure passed, as its promoters expected, and on the 1st of January, 1801, a new imperial standard was exhibited on London Tower, and on the Castles of Dublin and Edinburgh. It was formed of the three crosses of St. George, St. Patrick, and St. Andrew, and is popularly known as the Union Jack. The *fleur-de-lis* and the word "France" were omitted from royal prerogatives and titles; and a proclamation was issued appointing the words—*Dei Gratia, Britaniarum Rex, Fidei Defensor*. The *Dublin Gazette* of July, 1800, contained the significant announcement of the creation of sixteen new peerages. The same publication for the last week of the year contained a fresh list of twenty-six others. Forty-two creations in six months were rather an extensive stretch of prerogative; and we cannot be surprised if the majority of the nation had more respect for the great untitled, whose ancestry were known, and were quite above accepting the miserable bribe of a modern peerage.

THE END.

THE CATHOLIC PUBLICATION SOCIETY'S BOOKS.

Abridgment of the Christian Doctrine. By the Right Rev. Bishop Hay. 32mo, cloth, ... $0 25

An Amicable Discussion on the Church of England, and on the Reformation in General. Dedicated to the Clergy of every Protestant Communion, and reduced into the form of letters by the Right Rev. J. F. M. Trevern, D.D., Bishop of Strasbourg. Translated by the Rev. Wm. Richmond. 1 vol. 12mo, 580 pp., ... $2 00

An Illustrated History of Ireland, from the Earliest Period to the Present Time; with several first-class full-page Engravings of Historical Scenes, designed by Henry Doyle, and engraved by George Hanlon and George Pearson; together with upwards of 100 woodcuts, by eminent artists, illustrating Antiquities, Scenery, and Sites of Remarkable Events; and three large maps, one of Ireland and the others of Family Homes, Statistics, etc. 1 vol. 8vo, nearly 700 pp. New and enlarged edition. Extra cloth, $5 00; half calf, $7 00

Anima Divota; or, Devout Soul. Translated from the Italian of Very Rev. J. B. Pagani, Provincial of the Order of Charity in England. 24mo, cloth, ... $0 60

Anne Severin. By the Author of "A Sister's Story." 1 vol. 12mo, cloth, $1 50; cloth, gilt, ... $2 00

Apologia pro Vita Sua: Being a Reply to a Pamphlet entitled "What, then, does Dr. Newman Mean?" By John Henry Newman, D.D. New edition. 1 vol. 12mo, $2 00

A Sister's Story. By Mrs. Augustus Craven. Translated from the French by Emily Bowles. 1 vol. crown 8vo, pp. 558. Cloth, extra, $2 50; vellum cloth, gilt, . $3 00

Aspirations of Nature. By Rev. I. T. Hecker. 4th edition, revised, cloth, extra, ... $1 50

List of Books.

Beauties of Sir Thomas More. A Selection from his Works, as well in prose as in verse. A sequel to "Life and Times of More." By W. J. Walter. 18mo, cloth, . $1 25

Bona Mors. A Pious Association of the Devout Servants of our Lord Jesus Christ dying on the Cross in order to obtain a Good Death. 24mo, cloth, ... $0 25

Catechism of Council of Trent. 8vo, . . . $2 00

Catholic Christian Instructed. By the Right Rev. Dr. Challoner. 24mo, flexible cloth, $0 25; extra cloth, $0 40

The Same. 12mo, large type, flexible cloth, $0 40; extra cloth, ... $0 75

Catholic Manual; containing a Selection of Prayers and Devotional Exercises. 18mo, embossed, $1 00; roan, 2 plates, $1 50; roan, gilt edge, 4 plates, $1 75; turkey morocco, super extra, 8 plates, ... $3 00

Christian's Guide to Heaven. 32mo, cloth, $0 50; roan, 4 engravings, $0 60; roan, gilt edge, 4 engravings, $1 00; turkey, super extra, 6 engravings, . . . $2 25

Christine and Other Poems. By George H. Miles. Illustrated, ... $2 00

Compendious Abstract of the History of the Church of Christ. By Rev. Wm. Gahan. 12mo, . . . $1 00

Confidence in the Mercy of God. By the Right Rev. Joseph Languet. 18mo, cloth, ... $0 50

Cradle Lands: Egypt, Palestine, etc. By Lady Herbert. 1 vol. 12mo, vellum cloth, $2 00; cloth, gilt, $2 50; half calf, $4 00; full calf, red edges, ... $6 00

Daily Companion; containing a Selection of Prayers and Devotional Exercises for the Use of Children. Embellished with 36 very neat illustrative engravings. 32mo, cloth, $0 25; roan, ... $0 60

Defence of Catholic Principles. By the Rev. D. A. Gallitzin. 4th edition, 18mo, cloth, ... $0 60

Devout Communicant. By the Rev. P. Baker. New edition, 24mo, cloth, $0 60; roan, $1 25; roan, gilt edges, $1 75; turkey morocco, super extra, ... $3 00

Douay Bible. 12mo, suitable for Missionaries. Embellished, ... $1 50

Douay Testament. A beautiful pocket edition. 32mo, cloth, $0 45; roan, embossed, $0 60; roan, embossed, gilt edges, $1 00; tuck, gilt edges, $1 25; fine edition, roan, $1 00; fine edition, roan, gilt edge, $1 50; fine edition, turkey morocco, super extra $2 25

Douay Testament. 12mo, large type, embellished, . $0 75

Epistle of Jesus Christ to the Faithful Soul, . $1 00

Eugenie de Guerin, Journal of, ... $2 00

List of Books. 3

Eugenie de Guerin, Letters of, ... $2 00
Exposition of the Doctrine of the Catholic Church in Matters of Controversy. By the Right Rev. J. B. Bossuet. A new edition, with copious notes, by Rev. J. Fletcher, D.D. 18mo, $0 60; another edition, without notes, 32mo, cloth, ... $0 25
Father Rowland. A North American Tale. 18mo, cloth, $0 60
Following of Christ. In four books. By Thomas à Kempis, with Reflections at the conclusion of each Chapter. 18mo, cloth, $0 75; roan, plates, $1 50; roan, gilt edge, plates, $1 75; turkey morocco, super extra, ... $3 00
The Same. Pocket edition, without the Reflections, 32mo, cloth, $0 25; roan, $0 60; roan, gilt edge, $1 00; turkey morocco, super extra, ... $2 25
Garden of the Soul; or, A Manual of Spiritual Exercises and Instructions for Christians, who, living in the world, aspire to devotion. By Right Rev. Dr. Challoner. 24mo, arabesque, $0 50; roan, 2 plates, $0 75; roan, gilt edges, 4 plates, $1 00; turkey, super extra, 8 plates, ... $2 50
Genevieve: A Tale of Antiquity, showing the Wonderful Ways of Providence in the Protection of Innocence. From the German of Schmid. 18mo, cloth, ... $0 60
Glimpses of Pleasant Homes. By the Author of "The Life of Mother McCauley." Illustrated with four full-page illustrations. 1 vol. 12mo, cloth, extra, $1 50; cloth, gilt, $2 00
Gropings after Truth: A Life-Journey from New-England Congregationalism to the One Catholic Apostolic Church. By Joshua Huntington. 1 vol. vellum cloth, . . $0 75
Grounds of the Catholic Doctrine, contained in the Profession of Faith. Published by Pope Pius IV. 32mo, cloth, $0 20
Historical Catechism. By M. l'Abbe Fleury. Parts I. and II., revised by Right Rev. Bishop Cheverus. 18mo, paper cover, $0 12; complete, in four parts, 18mo, . $0 60
History of England, for the Use of Schools, to the end of the Reign of George IV. By W. F. Mylius. 12mo, . $1 00
History of the Church from its Establishment to the Reformation. By Rev. C. C. Pise. 5 vols. 8vo, $7 50; another edition, 5 vols. 12mo, cloth, ... $5 00
History of the Old and New Testaments. By J. Reeve. 8vo, half-bound, roan, ... $1 00
Hornihold. The Commandments and Sacraments Explained in Fifty-two Discourses. By the Right Rev. Dr. Hornihold, author of "Real Principles of Catholics." 12mo, cloth, $2 00
Home of the Lost Child. 18mo, cloth, . . . $0 60
Homilies on the Book of Tobias; or, A Familiar Explanation of the Practical Duties of Domestic Life. By Rev. T. Martyn. 12mo, cloth, ... $0 75

Hours of the Passion; or, Pathetic Reflections on the Sufferings and Death of our Blessed Redeemer. By St. Liguori. New edition, translated by Right Rev. W. Walsh, late Bishop of Halifax. 18mo, cloth, ... $0 60

Imitation of the Blessed Virgin. In four books. 18mo, cloth, ... $0 60

Impressions of Spain. By Lady Herbert. 1 vol. 12mo. 15 illustrations. Cloth, extra, $2 00; cloth, gilt, $2 50; half morocco, or calf, $4 00; full calf, . . . $6 00

In Heaven we know Our Own, ... $0 60

Interior Christian. In eight books, with a supplement; extracted from the writings of M. Bernier de Louvigny. 18mo, cloth, ... $0 60

Introduction to a Devout Life. From the French of St. Francis of Sales. 18mo, cloth, ... $0 75

Irish Odes and Other Poems. By Aubrey de Vere. 1 vol. 12mo, toned paper, $2 00; cloth, gilt, . . $2 50

Key of Paradise, opening the Gate to Eternal Salvation. 18mo, arabesque, $1 00; roan, 2 plates, $1 50; roan, gilt edge, 4 plates, $1 75; turkey morocco, super extra, 8 plates, ... $3 00

Lenten Monitor; or, Moral Reflections and Devout Aspirations on the Gospel. By Rev. P. Baker, O. S. F. 24mo, cloth, New edition, ... $0 60

Letters to a Prebendary. Being an Answer to "Reflections on Popery," by Rev. J. Sturgis, LL.D. By Right Rev. J. Milner, D.D. 24mo, cloth, ... $0 60

Letters to a Protestant Friend on the Holy Scriptures. By Rev. D. A. Gallitzin. 18mo, cloth, . . . $0 60

Life and Times of Sir Thomas More, Illustrated from his Own Writings. By W. J. Walter. With a portrait and autograph of More. 18mo, cloth, ... $0 25

Life of St. Catharine of Sienna, ... $1 75

Life of St. Vincent de Paul. 32mo, cloth, . . $0 45

Little Treatise on the Little Virtues. Written originally in Italian, by Father Roberti, of the Society of Jesus. To which are added, "A Letter on Fervor." by Father Vallois, S. J., and "Maxims," from an unpublished manuscript of Father Segneri, S. J.; also, "Devotions to the Sacred Heart of Jesus." 32mo, cloth, ... $0 45

Lives of the Fathers of the Desert, and of many Holy Men and Women who Dwelt in Solitude. Translated from the French. Embellished with 18 engravings. 18mo, cloth, $0 60

Louisa; or, The Virtuous Villager. A Catholic Tale. New edition. 18mo, cloth, ... $0 60

Love of our Lord Jesus Christ reduced to Practice. By St. Alphonsus Liguori. Translated by the Right Rev. W.

List of Books.

Walsh, late Bishop of Halifax. New edition, 8mo, cloth, ... $0 60

May Carols, and Hymns and Poems. By Aubrey de Vere. Blue and gold, ... $1 25

Memorial of a Christian Life. By Rev. Lewis de Granada. Revised edition. 18mo, cloth, ... $0 75

Memorials of those who Suffered for the Catholic Faith in Ireland during the Sixteenth, Seventeenth, and Eighteenth Centuries. Collected and edited by Myles O'Reilly, B.A., LL.D. 1 vol. crown 8vo, vellum cloth, $2 50; cloth, gilt, $3 00; half calf, ... $4 50

Month of Mary, containing a Series of Meditations, etc., in honor of the B. V. M. Arranged for each day of the month. 32mo, cloth, ... $0 40

Nellie Netterville; or, One of the Transplanted. A Tale of the Times of Cromwell in Ireland. 1 vol. 12mo, cloth, extra, $1 50; cloth, gilt, ... $2 00

Net for the Fishers of Men, ... $0 06

Nouet. Meditations on the Life and Passion of our Lord Jesus Christ for every Day in the Year. By Rev. J. Nouet, S. J. To which are added, "Meditations on the Sacred Heart of Jesus Christ," being those taken from a Nouvena in preparation for the Feast of the same. By Father C. Borgo, S. J. 1 vol. 12mo, 880 pp., . . . $2 50

Office of the Holy Week, according to the Roman Missal and Breviary, in Latin and English. 18mo, cloth, $0 75; roan, 1 plate, $1 50; roan, gilt edge, 2 plates, $2 00; turkey morocco, super extra, 4 plates, ... $3 50

O'Kane. Notes on the Rubrics of the Roman Ritual. 1 vol. 12mo, ... $4 00

Oratory of the Faithful Soul; or, Devotions to the Most Holy Sacrament and to our Blessed Lady. Translated from the works of Ven. Abbot Blosius. By Robert Aston Coffin. 18mo, cloth, ... $0 50

Packets of Scripture Illustrations. Containing 50 engravings of subjects from the Old and New Testaments, after original designs by Elster. Loose packages of 50, $0 75

Path to Paradise. A Selection of Prayers and Devotions for Catholics. 48mo, cloth, $0 20; roan, $0 40; roan, gilt edge, $0 60; turkey morocco, sup. extra, 4 engravings, $1 25

Pious Guide to Prayer and Devotion. Containing various Practices of Piety, calculated to Answer the Demands of the Devout Members of the Catholic Church. 18mo, arabesque, $1 00; roan, 2 plates, $1 50; roan, gilt edge, 4 plates, $1 75; turkey morocco, super extra, 8 plates, $3 00; various styles in velvet and turkey morocco, with clasps and ornaments, from $4 50 to $10 00. A new and beautiful edition, containing the same as the above large edition

24mo, arabesque, $0 60; roan, 2 plates, $1 00; roan, gilt edge, 4 plates, $1 50; turkey morocco, super extra, 2 plates, ... $2 50

Poor Man's Catechism; or, The Christian Doctrine Explained, with Short Admonitions. By John Mannock, O.S.B. 24mo, cloth, ... $0 50

Poor Man's Manual of Devotion; or, Devout Christian's Daily Companion. To which is added, "Daily Devotion; or, Profitable Manner of Hearing Mass." 24mo, arabesque, $0 50; roan, $0 80; roan, gilt edge, $1 50; turkey, super extra, ... $2 50

Poor Man's Controversy. By J. Mannock, Author of "Poor Man's Catechism." 18mo, cloth, . . . $0 50

Practical Discourses on the Perfections and Works of God, and the Divinity and Works of Jesus Christ. By the Rev. J. Reeve. 8vo, cloth, ... $2 00

Problems of the Age, with Studies in St. Augustine on Kindred Topics. By Rev. Augustine F. Hewit. 1 vol. 12mo, cloth, extra, ... $2 00

Questions of the Soul. By Rev. I. T. Hecker. New edition, $1 50; cloth, gilt, ... $2 00

Reason and Revelation. Lectures delivered in St. Ann's Church, New York, during Advent, 1867. By Rev. T. S. Preston. 1 vol. 12mo, ... $1 50

Sacred Heart of Jesus and the Sacred Heart of Mary. Translated from the Italian of Father Lanzi, Author of "History of Painting," etc., with an introduction by Rev. C. B. Meehan. 24mo, cloth, ... $0 60

St. Columba, Apostle of Caledonia. By the Count de Montalembert. 1 vol. 12mo. Toned paper, $1 25; cloth, gilt, ... $1 75

Sermons of the Paulist Fathers for the Years 1865 and 1866, ... $1 50

Sermons of the Paulist Fathers for the Year 1864. New edition, ... $1 50

Short Treatise on Prayer, adapted to all Classes of Christians. By St. Alphonsus Liguori. New edition, 24mo, cloth, ... $0 40

Spirit of St. Alphonsus de Liguori. A Selection from his shorter Spiritual Treatises. Translated by the Rev. J. Jones. 24mo, cloth, ... $0 60

Spiritual Combat. To which is added, "The Peace of the Soul and the Happiness of the Heart which Dies to Itself in Order to Live to God." 32mo, ... $0 40

Spiritual Consoler; or, Instructions to Enlighten Pious Souls in their Doubts, etc. By Father Quadrupani. 18mo, $0 3

List of Books. 7

Spiritual Director of Devout and Religious Souls. By St. Francis de Sales, ... $0 50

Stories on the Seven Virtues. By Agnes M. Stewart, Authoress of "Festival of the Rosary." 18mo, cloth, . $0 60

Symbolism; or, Exposition of the Doctrinal Differences between Catholics and Protestants, as evidenced by their Symbolical Writings. By John A. Moehler, D.D. Translated from the German, with a Memoir of the Author, preceded by an Historical Sketch of the State of Protestantism and Catholicism in Germany for the last Hundred Years, by J. B. Robertson, Esq., ... $4 00

Tales from the Diary of a Sister of Mercy. By C. M. Brame. 1 vol. 12mo, cloth, extra, $1 50; cloth, gilt, $2 00

The Clergy and the Pulpit, in their Relations to the People. By M. l'Abbe Isidore Mullois, Chaplain to Napoleon III. 1 vol. 12mo, extra cloth, ... $1 50

The Comedy of Convocation in the English Church. In Two Scenes. Edited by Archdeacon Chasuble, D.D., and dedicated to the Pan-Anglican Synod. 8vo pamphlet. Paper, $0 75; bound in cloth, ... $1 00

The Holy Communion: Its Philosophy, Theology, and Practice. By John Bernard Dalgairns, Priest of the Oratory of Saint Philip Neri. 1 vol. 12mo, . . . $2 00

The Illustrated Catholic Sunday-School Library. 1st Series. 12 vols. handsomely bound, and put up in a box. Cloth, extra, $6 00; cloth, gilt, ... $7 50

The Illustrated Catholic Sunday-School Library. 2d Series. 12 vols. handsomely bound in cloth, put up in a box. Cloth, extra, $6 00; cloth, gilt, ... $7 50

The Illustrated Catholic Sunday-School Library. 3d Series. 12 vols. in box. Cloth, extra, $6 00; gilt, . $7 50

The Inner Life of the Very Rev. Pere Lacordaire, of the Order of Preachers. Translated from the French of the Rev. Pere Chocarne, O. P. By a Father of the same Order; with Preface by Father Aylward, Prior Provincial of England. 1 vol. 12mo, toned paper, ... $3 00

The Life and Sermons of the Rev. Francis A. Baker, Priest of the Congregation of St. Paul. Edited by Rev. A. F. Hewit. 1 vol. crown 8vo, pp. 504. $2 50; half calf, $4 00

The Life of Father Ravignan, S. J. By Father Ponlevoy, S. J. 1 vol. crown 8vo, toned paper, . . $4 00

The People's Pictorial Lives of the Saints, Scriptural and Historical. Abridged, for the most part, from those of the late Rev. Alban Butler. These are got up expressly for Sunday-school presents. In packets of 12 each. One packet now ready, containing the lives of twelve different saints. Per packet, ... $0 25

List of Books.

The See of St. Peter. The Rock of the Church, the Source of Jurisdiction, and Centre of Unity. By Thomas William Allies, M.A. 1 vol. 16mo, ... $0 75

The Two Schools. A Moral Tale. By Mrs. Hughs. 12mo, cloth, ... $0 75

The Works of the Most Rev. John Hughes, D.D., First Archbishop of New York, containing Biography, Sermons, Letters, Lectures, Speeches, etc. Carefully compiled from the best sources, and edited by Lawrence Kehoe. This important work makes 2 large vols. of nearly 1,500 pp. 8vo. Cloth, $6 00; half calf, extra, ... $12 00

Think Well On't; or, The Great Truths of the Christian Religion for Every Day in the Month. By Right Rev. R. Challoner. 32mo, cloth, ... $0 25

Three Phases of Christian Love: The Mother, the Maiden, and the Religious. By Lady Herbert. 1 vol. 12mo, vellum cloth, $1 50; gilt, ... $2 00

Triumph of Religion; or, A Choice Selection of Edifying Narratives. 18mo, cloth, ... $0 60

True Piety; or, The Day Well Spent. A Manual of Fervent Prayers, Pious Reflections, and Solid Instructions for the Members of the Catholic Church. 18mo, arabesque, $1 00; roan, 2 plates, $1 50; roan, gilt edge, 4 plates, $1 75; turkey morocco, super extra, 8 plates, . . . $3 00

Visits to the Blessed Sacrament and to the Blessed Virgin for Every Day in the Month. By St. Alphonsus Liguori. 24mo, cloth. New edition, . . . $0 75

Way of Salvation. Meditations for Every Day in the Year. By St. Alphonsus Liguori. 24mo, cloth, . . . $0 75

Why Men do not Believe; or, The Principal Causes of Infidelity. Translated from the French of Mgr. Laforet. Cloth, ... $1 00

Any Book on this List sent by mail, post-paid, on receipt of the advertised price.

The Catholic Publication Society,

LAWRENCE KEHOE, General Agent,

126 NASSAU ST., NEW YORK.

This book is a preservation photocopy.
It is made in compliance with copyright law
and produced on acid-free archival
60# book weight paper
which meets the requirements of
ANSI/NISO Z39.48-1992 (permanence of paper)

Preservation photocopying and binding
by
Acme Bookbinding
Charlestown, Massachusetts

2003

www.ingramcontent.com/pod-product-compliance
Lightning Source LLC
Chambersburg PA
CBHW021209230426
43667CB00006B/626